VIC

ANEGONDI
Architectural Ethnography of a Royal Village

VIJAYANAGARA RESEARCH PROJECT MONOGRAPH SERIES

General Editors
JOHN M. FRITZ, University of Pennsylvania
GEORGE MICHELL, London
M.V. KRISHNAPPA, Karnataka Department of Archaeology and Museums

The General Editors of the Vijayanagara Research Project Monograph Series are most grateful to INTACH UK Trust and to its Chairman, Sri Martand Singh, for a grant given in support of this publication.

We acknowledge the continuing encouragement of the American Institute of Indian Studies, especially its President, Professor Frederick Asher, and Director-General, Dr. Pradeep Mehendiratta.

We also extend our thanks to Mr. Ramesh Jain and B.N. Varma of Manohar Publishers & Distributors for maintaining high standards while seeing this monograph through the press.

Jacket illustration: Graham Reed.

ANEGONDI

Architectural Ethnography of a Royal Village

NATALIE TOBERT

Illustrations by GRAHAM REED

MANOHAR
AMERICAN INSTITUTE OF INDIAN STUDIES
NEW DELHI
2000

ISBN 81-7304-280-2

First published 2000

Published by Ajay Kumar Jain
Manohar Publishers & Distributors
4753/23 Ansari Road, Daryaganj, New Delhi 110 002 for
American Institute of Indian Studies
D 31 Defence Colony, New Delhi 110 024

Typeset by AJ Software Publishing Co. Pvt. Ltd.
305 Durga Chambers, 1333 D.B. Gupta Road
Karol Bagh, New Delhi 110 005
and printed at Rajkamal Electric Press
B-35/9, G.T. Karnal Road,
Delhi 110 033

Contents

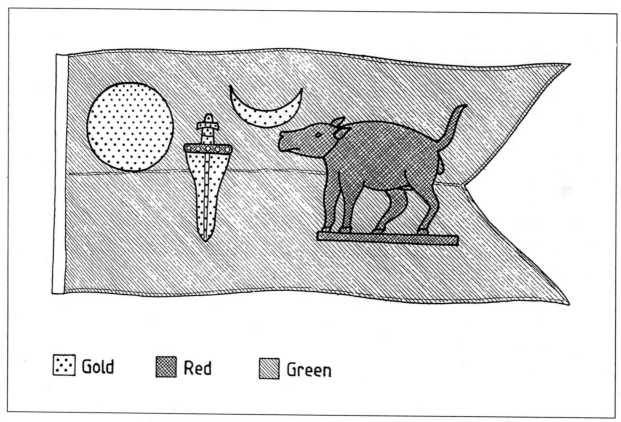

::: Gold　　■ Red　　▨ Green

Frontispiece. Flag of Vijayanagara kings, with sun, moon, dagger and male hog

Preface

ANEGONDI is located in the southern Indian state of Karnataka, on the banks of the Tungabhadra river at a point where it makes a turn northwards. Such a direction of flow is unusual and highly auspicious to Hindus, and so the river bank here is considered a holy spot and a place of prayer. Many pilgrims visit the area, and coracles convey them from place to place along the river. The village occupants are from all social and economic groups and include priests, royalty, businessmen, farm labourers and street sweepers. Many occupants are farmers, cultivating the fertile black cotton soil in the valleys and plains between the hills. To this day they benefit from the stone irrigation channels built by the kings of Vijayanagara in the fourteenth to sixteenth centuries. While the imposing ruins of this medieval capital lie to the south of the river, vestiges of the period can also be seen in Anegondi, sometimes combined with earlier, pre-Vijayanagara period elements.

Historical links with Vijayanagara also exist between Anegondi and Vijayanagara. The present-day ruler, Achyuta Deva Raya, claims descent from the kings of Vijayanagara: men from the Bedaru (warrior caste) claim that their forefathers were foot-soldiers of the emperor Krishna Deva Raya in the sixteenth century. Those descending from the ancient kings are given a certain status, and they do retain some ritual and religious privileges.

Anegondi means elephant pit: *ane* means elephant while *gundi* means pit. The elephant pit is identified as an area of water beyond the northern river-side steps of the village where it is deep enough for elephants to wash. Many sites nearby are mentioned in the *Ramayana* epic: Anegondi lies within the region of the monkey kingdom of Kishkindha, and the birthplace of Hanuman, the monkey hero, is identified with Anjaneya Parvata, a hill to the west of the village.

This monograph looks at how the inhabitants of Anegondi use and understand space in their own homes and within the village, visiting monuments and shrines for religious purposes. The work is multi-disciplinary, touching on the fields of ethnography, architecture and archaeology. It is intended to complement the work of Sugandha (1986) and the surveys of scholars currently working on the Vijayanagara Research Project, and to provide a stimulus for those wishing to conduct further research in the area. The main subject is the domestic housing and material culture found in the village of Anegondi. The volume is set out in two sections: Part One surveys the historical, social, religious and architectural context of Anegondi; Part Two consists of a catalogue of houses. These are followed by a set of appendices.

Chapter One introduces the village and describes the settlement layout, including the river, roads, market and burial grounds, as well as the village administration and the local governmental system. Ancient structures are examined briefly in the hope that this monograph will stimulate scholars to develop a greater interest in the history of Anegondi, and its relationship to the capital city of Vijayanagara just across the Tungabhadra.

Chapter Two presents brief details of caste, life cycle and economy, in order to provide an understanding of the people living in and around Anegondi. The castes which make up the village population are set out, and the many families with links to the royal lineage are presented. Occasional case studies are introduced to illustrate a particular marriage or death ceremony.

Chapter Three on worship illustrates how villagers use the ancient monuments of Vijayanagara for religious purposes and pilgrimage. Case studies of various festivities are presented. A listing is also given of some of the religious buildings in and around Anegondi. Religious customs are set out which relate to the devotion of deities like Vishnu, Siva and the Goddess, and to daily practice in the home. The myths and legends that abound in relation to the site are mentioned, in particular those about the goddess Pampa and the Kishkindha chapter in the *Ramayana.*

Chapter Four sets out the elements of house design and construction, and the way space is defined in vernacular dwellings. The survey was undertaken to illustrate a cross section of house types from all levels of society: those of extended and nuclear families, various castes, religions and economies. In each house where permission had been given to work, occupants were asked about the number of families living in the dwelling, their caste, occupation and kinship relations. Each dwelling was measured and photographed so that isometric drawings could be produced. The use of features and artefacts within a household was recorded. Social, historical and economic factors which affect the wide variation in house design, layout and construction are suggested in the final section.

The catalogue of house forms and room functions constitutes the main body of fieldwork undertaken at Anegondi. Over 50 houses have been described, varying from single-room dwellings to mansions occupied by descendants of the ruling lineage. A concordance of house types with the religion, cast and occupation of the inhabitants, a kinship chart for each house, a chronological summary, and a glossary of Indian terms are appended to the catalogue.

Acknowledgements

I was originally invited to India in 1987 by the directors of the Vijayanagara Research Project, Drs. John Fritz and George Michell. At Anegondi there are a number of large dwellings of palace proportions still occupied by several families. I had intended to carry out a brief project on domestic architecture, but I was unsure where to begin. Previously, I had carried out similar work in Africa, making an ethnographic survey of domestic architecture in a village in Sudan. I spent several years there and managed to do fieldwork by using rudimentary Arabic. However, when I arrived in India I had no knowledge of the languages. Most village occupants are from Karnataka or Andhra Pradesh, and speak either Kannada or Telugu; Hindi is rarely used. I spoke none of these languages and was, therefore, dependent on the goodwill of local assistants to introduce me to house owners and to come with me on visits.

My first trip to Anegondi was in 1987 to assess the feasibility of the project. On this occasion I was accompanied by a relative of Mr T.T. Guthi of the Aspiration Bookshop in Hampi bazaar. We took a circular coracle over the calm sparkling waters of the Tungabhadra. On the other side, we walked to the market place in Anegondi, and approached a group of men sitting around a shady tree. After my proposal was explained by my companion, one elderly man with pure white hair wearing a vibrant lime green scarf spoke to me. This was Tirumula Deva Raya, brother of Durbar Raja Sri Krishna Deva Raya. He suggested that I spoke to his brother's son Achyuta Deva Raya, and his own son Rama Deva Raya. These men and their families were my hosts throughout the years of my work in Anegondi, and without their support and the friendship of their female relatives I could not have begun the project.

Early on in my first visit, I was introduced to the family of James Babu Reddy, a pharmacist working in Anegondi for several years. All his family assisted me at some time with the survey, in particular his two teenage daughters came with me on house visits on many occasions. Since they were Protestants, they were considered outside the Hindu caste system, and could introduce me freely. There were problems with regard to making a survey of domestic architecture: to do the work I was intruding in people's personal living space, and I could only work at certain times of the day: in the mornings after meals had been prepared, and in the late afternoons.

Since 1987, I have visited Anegondi on several occasions, most recently in 1993, each time adding to the corpus of data. In this work I was assisted by Graham Reed who produced fine drawings from my preliminary sketches, and who joined me on later fieldwork trips. Graham also produced the final maps and architectural drawings with which this monograph is greatly enhanced. Many of the photographs are by Victoria Green and Jean-Pierre Ribière.

I am extremely grateful for the support given to this project by the British Academy, the Society for South Asian Studies, ICOMOS (International Council on Monuments and Sites), both in London, and INTACH (Indian National Trust for Art and Cultural Heritage) in New Delhi. Above all, I particularly want to thank the people of Anegondi who so generously permitted me into their homes, thereby facilitating the fieldwork on which this project is based.

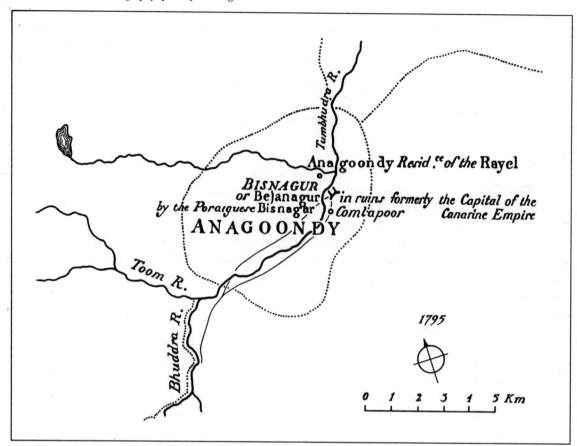

Figure 1. "Anagoondy Kingdom" from a map of India by William Faden, 1795

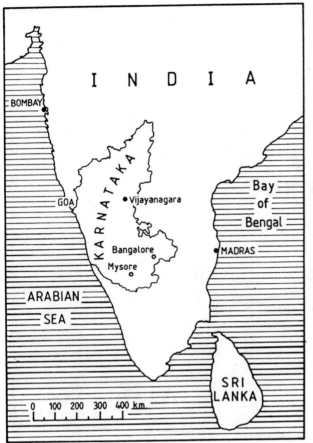

Figure 2. Karnataka state, south India

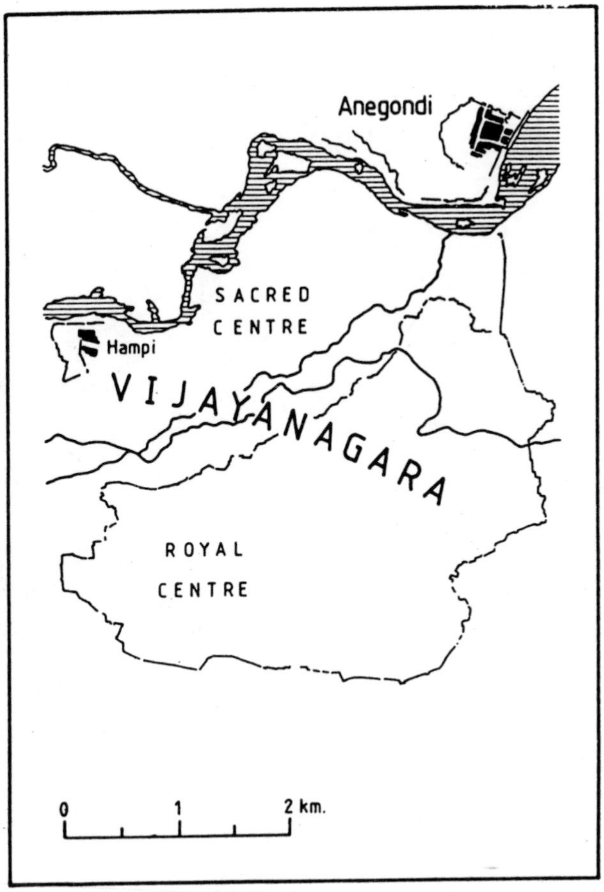

Figure 3. Vijayanagara and Anegondi

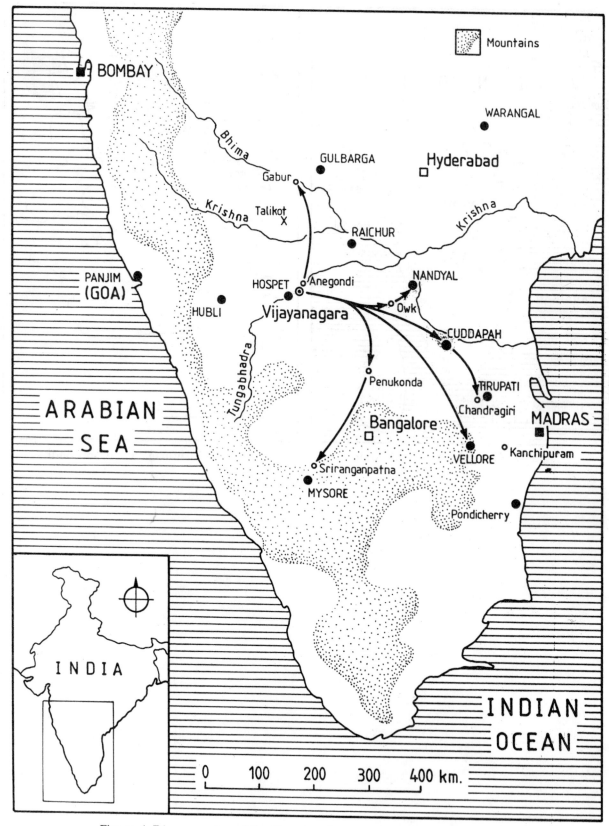

Figure 4. Diaspora of royal families after the sack of Vijayanagara in 1565

PART ONE

The Setting

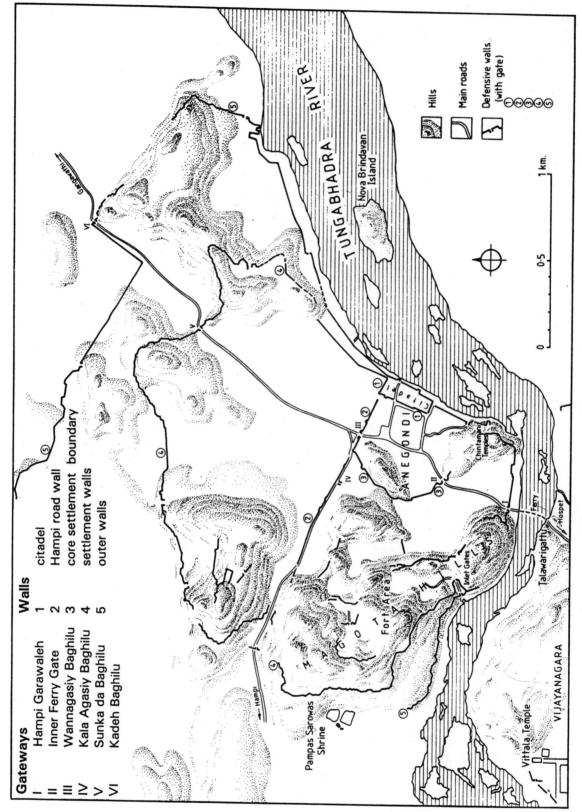

Gateways
I   Hampi Garawaleh
II   Inner Ferry Gate
III   Wannagasiy Baghilu
IV   Kala Agasiy Baghilu
V   Sunka da Baghilu
VI   Kadeh Baghilu

Walls
1   citadel
2   Hampi road wall
3   core settlement boundary
4   settlement walls
5   outer walls

Hills

Main roads

Defensive walls
(with gate)

Figure 5. Anegondi village and environs

CHAPTER 1

Settlement Patterns

Fortified Village (Figure 5)

At first glance, Anegondi looks like a typical southern Indian village, with a variety of small thatched houses and some large stone dwellings. It has a single tarmac road and a quiet market with several dozen stalls and a handful of tea-shops. However, this is no ordinary settlement. On entering the village, one can catch glimpses of ancient shrines, gateways and walls embedded into the houses; the surrounding hills are forti-fied with walls and gateways. Attacked several times throughout its long history, Anegondi was evidently an important administrative centre for the surrounding districts. In fact, its arch-itectural remains span a considerable period, from the twelfth and thirteenth centuries down to the present day. (For a summary of relevant political events see Appendix 3.) Sometimes, stone blocks and columns from different periods are assembled together to create composite structures. The chronological classification of these vestiges is a major task that has yet to be undertaken; it is not attempted here.

Anegondi is well protected by natural boundaries: the Tungabhadra to the south and east, and hills of huge granite boulders to the north and west. Further protection is provided by massive fortifications, the remains of which can be seen in and around the village. The settlement extends over an area of approximately 1 sq km; being bounded by the river and hills, the space available for buildings is limited. Many of the dwellings are contained within the Chariot Route, a wide road that runs around four sides of the square that constitutes the central core of Anegondi. (The four sides of the Chariot Route are here designated according to their cardinal directions.)

Anegondi is reached by road from the nearby towns of Gangavati and Hospet, and is served by the local bus several times a day. The main forms of transportation are bullock cart, motor bike, bus or taxi-van. However, the quickest route from Hospet is through the ancient site of Vijayanagara, from where one has to cross the Tungabhadra by coracle at the river crossing known as Talarighat. Villagers pay the coracle men in produce; relatives of the local raja pay nothing, while everyone else pays a few rupees. A coracle is also available from the east banks of the river for those who wish to visit the sacred island of Nava Brindavan.

Today there are a number of defensive gate-ways standing within and outside Anegondi, some partly dismantled to make way for the buses which serve the village. The fortified walls that surround the present settlement suggest that in the past Anegondi must have been a town of considerable importance, with a much larger population than its current 4,000 inhabitants (1990 figures). Walking around the village today, one is repeatedly surprised by the large numbers of ancient monuments, such as the temple built high on the ruined riverside citadel, the Ranganatha temple in the middle of the village, and the innumerable fine carvings and broken stone pieces that are to be discovered in the undergrowth.

As preserved today, Anegondi is the fortified nucleus of the old town which contains arch-itectural elements dating back to the time of Vijayanagara in the fourteenth, fifteenth and sixteenth centuries. Sugandha (1986: 62, 105) suggests that the village was the first seat of power in Vijayanagara times, antedating the city of Vijayanagara as the capital. Later, the fortunes of Anegondi declined to a nucleus around the square of principal roads which lead to the main Ranganatha temple.

To the east of the present village are the

1

bastions and gateways of a riverside citadel through which steps run down to the water's edge. From the northern end of the citadel, a wall runs in a westerly direction beneath the foundations of the road to Hampi. West of Anegondi are walls which encompass the rocky mass of Magota Hill which overlooks the village. They surround what must have been a major settlement. Some 2 km to the north and west of the centre, another series of walls runs along the tops of the granite hills, filling in the gaps between the boulders. The flat land between these walls is dotted with the remains of ancient house plinths, roof tiles, wells and pottery sherds. Enclosed within the southern part of Magota Hill are the remains of a fortress with associated buildings. A further series of walls surrounds Anegondi at a distance of some 4 to 5 km, beginning from the northern end of the citadel and running along the river banks. The flat land between the lower walls, though now mostly given over to agricultural use, also preserves the remains of building materials, ash deposits and pottery sherds (Sugandha 1986: 69).

The Present-Day Settlement (Figure 6)

The wide road which runs around the central square block of dwellings is referred to in the text as the Chariot Route because processions are held here during religious celebrations and funerals. The actual temple chariot, parked opposite the Ranganatha temple near to the market, is used to carry deities along this route. The Gagan Mahal, a screened pavilion previously housing local administrative offices, was built originally so that viewers could look directly along the route from the Ranganatha temple. To the north, the road is tarmac and leads to the Gangavati and Hampi roads; to the south, it becomes a smaller path and passes through fields to the ferry crossing leading to Talarighat. One subsidiary path proceeds in a south-easterly direction towards the Chintamani temple complex overlooking the Tungabhadra. Other paths run off the route that follows the ancient citadel wall on the eastern bank of the river.

The tarmac roadways are avoided by the raja's female relatives when walking across Anegondi; they follow the more secluded pathways that pass between the houses and through the ruined palace and deserted palm groves. Other modest

women also use back pathways so as not to be seen on the main roads. Women of lower caste do, however, walk along main roads.

There is a ribbon development of larger stone houses along the main routes through Anegondi. Smaller dwellings of thatch and daub occur in clusters to the south of the Ranganatha temple, to the north of the market place, and in the intervening spaces between the roads, river and hills. No area is inhabited by one caste to the exclusion of others. The priest at the Ranganatha temple says that the central area of Anegondi used to be occupied by Brahmana and Kshatriya castes alone. Today, however, the central area has a mixed occupancy: within the central square there is a range of all types of dwellings, many now in ruins. Many old stones lie around in the streets and there is much partial building. There are rough paths between the houses, and people take responsibility for the area immediately in front of their thresholds, but do not lift rough stones left from decades of destruction.

The market square
(Figures 7 to 9, Plates 22 and 23)

The market is established in the main square in front of the Ranganatha temple. It houses a number of shops, and is used by buses for turning around, and for public displays on occasions such as Republic Day (26th January). The shops include grocers, fruit and vegetable sellers, tea houses, a bike shop, barber, tobacconist and refreshment stand. Between the market and the gate to the Gangavati road, one can find blacksmiths, a carpenter, and a number of public buildings, including the pharmacy, bank and High School. Itinerant craftsmen, especially potters and tinsmiths, regularly set up shop in the market place; bullocks are brought here when the cattle shodding team come to Anegondi.

Burial grounds (Figures 10 and 11, Plate 15)

At Anegondi the cremation grounds are situated to the north-east of the town. There, each caste has a distinct area for its own cremation and burial, as castes never mix at death. Brahmanas and Kshatriyas are cremated so that their spirits do not remain on earth. Lower castes and children under 13 years of age, who have not yet

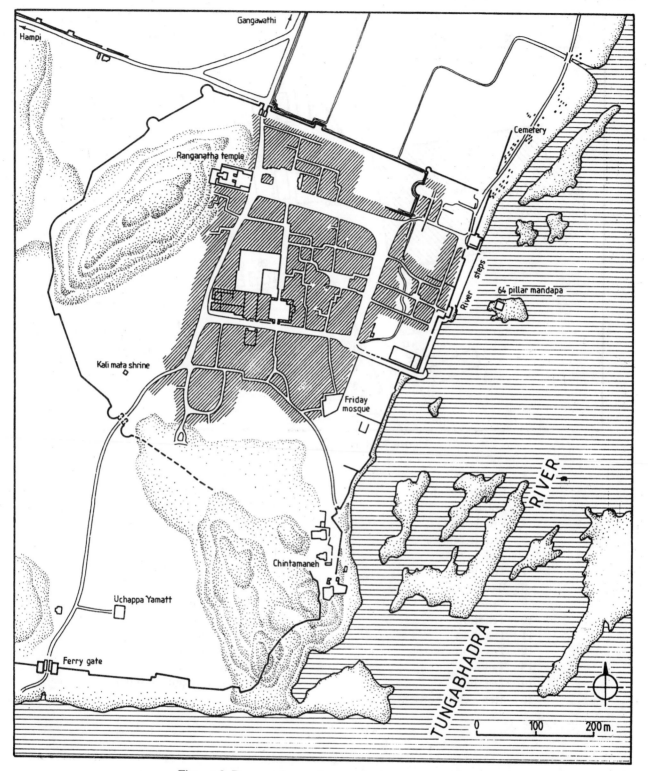

Figure 6. Present-day settlement in Anegondi, 1990

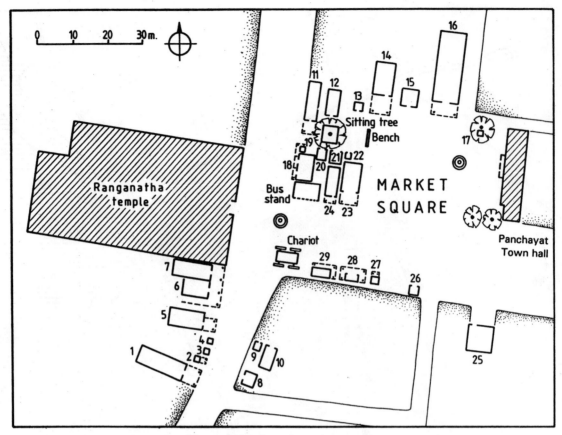

Figure 7. Market place, Anegondi

1	Tea shop	16	Flour mill
2	Grocer's shop	17	Basket maker's store
3	Tobacconist	18	Bicycle hire and repair
4	Unknown	19	Grocer's kiosk
5	Bicycle repairs	20	Bicycle repair
6	Tailor	21	Tea shop
7	Tea shop	22	Seating for tea shop
8	Barber	23	Tea shop
9	Grocer's kiosk	24	Grocer's shop
10	Tea shop	25	Grocer's shop
11	Tea shop	26	Grocer's kiosk
12	Tea shop	27	Grocer's kiosk
13	Tailor	28	Tea shop
14	Tea shop	29	Fruit and vegetable seller
15	Men's club house		

worn the 'threads of responsibility', are buried. Saints and holy-men are also buried so that beneficial vibrations might emanate from their final resting place. Christians are buried in a coffin. Muslims are buried on the Gangavati road, near to the village of Kadeh Baghilu.

The cemeteries at Anegondi are on common land, and are situated on grounds where the Tungabhadra flows to the north. Wealthy people buy land for burial, and the Lingayat community has demarcated its own territory. Disputes arise, for as the village grows, one community will not let another bury within its territory even though it is supposedly common land. Cremation usually takes place in one area of these grounds, though some hold funeral pyres of their relatives in a field or in some favourite place.

North-east of Anegondi lies Awaduth Matha, a building that marks the site of cremations and burials for Hindus. A standing trident, an ashy stone receptacle, a pair of wooden screens and some firewood are seen inside. Beside the Matha, a series of *brindavans*, or remembrance altars, are associated with the Banajiga caste. To the rear are the Lingayat graves and, beyond, the graves and tombstones of other castes. The Banajiga area is like a quiet garden with flowering trees. In it are many *brindavans* carved from single blocks of stone or cement, and even tin; *tulsi* (basil) bushes are planted on top.

Samadhis are traditional places of trance and meditation. The ancient royal *samadhi* area by the Tungabhadra consists of a series of stone platforms in a field. This area lies near a stream with a banana plantation to the north, at the foothills of a granite hill, known as Tara Parvata. The old *samadhis* (said to be those of women) lie almost opposite Nava Brindavan Island. It is interesting to note that in Vijayanagara times, Anegondi was known as the burial place of kings (Sewell 1991, p. 295). A more recent royal site, reserved for those of direct decent from the Anegondi kings, is situated on Magota Hill (see below). Nowadays it has become the fashion to cremate people in their own favourite fields: Harihara Deva Raya, Tirumala Deva Raya's youngest son, was cremated in the fields next to the Chintamani temple complex. Raja Venkata Deva Raya, younger brother of Raja Krishna Deva Raya, and father of Achyuta Deva Raya, was cremated near to his farm house, a few kilometres from the main entrance gate to Gangavati.

A new *samadhi* (remembrance stone) was constructed in 1991 just below Anjaneya Parvata beside an unkept shrine. A venerated man had lived there who had adopted a Lingayat youth and brought him up as his own son. A year after this man died, a *samadhi* was built. Immediately upon completion, while the cement was still wet, a prayer was made with coconuts, flowers and incense sticks. All the family and relatives came and ate a shared meal of coloured rice served on banana leaves. The *samadhi* can be seen from the top of Anjaneya Parvata. Another site of ancient *samadhis* is that at Nava Brindavan, a sacred island in the Tungabhadra which attracts pilgrims from afar at auspicious times of the year (see Chapter 3).

Administration (Figures 12 and 13, Plates 18 and 19; see chart p. 12)

Until 1994 the Panchayat Government Administrative offices of Anegondi were situated in the market square. The Panchayat has decentralised powers: villagers elect members of the village (*mandal*) and district (*zilla*) administrations. One member of the district Panchayat is responsible for several village Panchayats. The Panchayat at Anegondi has 14 or 15 members, one for every 500 inhabitants. It was originally a council of five members of the community who arbitrated on matters and disputes affecting the village. The *taluk* is the sub-division of a district, each in charge of Tahsildars, or revenue collection officers.

The Panchayat deals with development, agriculture, livestock, education, and water supply for the villages around Anegondi. There are two members who deal with house tax collection, and one with office duties. There are 26 staff in all, including 13 street sweepers, 6 of whom work in Anegondi. People wanting to settle on the land come to the Panchayat for authorisation, and the shop owners come to obtain a trading licence or pay their professional tax. Outsiders approach the Secretary after finding an empty plot of land and request permission to occupy it.

The Grama Panchayat system of village administration came into being in 1956. On 15th July 1967, Krishna Deva Raya donated the present building to the Panchayat for use as their administrative headquarters. Known once

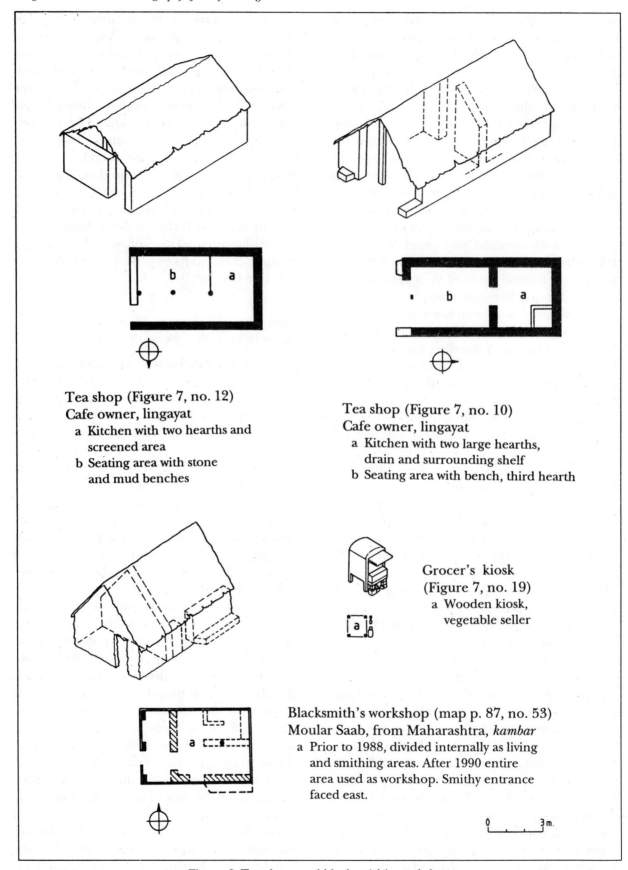

Tea shop (Figure 7, no. 12)
Cafe owner, lingayat
  a Kitchen with two hearths and
    screened area
  b Seating area with stone
    and mud benches

Tea shop (Figure 7, no. 10)
Cafe owner, lingayat
  a Kitchen with two large hearths,
    drain and surrounding shelf
  b Seating area with bench, third hearth

Grocer's kiosk
(Figure 7, no. 19)
  a Wooden kiosk,
    vegetable seller

Blacksmith's workshop (map p. 87, no. 53)
Moular Saab, from Maharashtra, *kambar*
  a Prior to 1988, divided internally as living
    and smithing areas. After 1990 entire
    area used as workshop. Smithy entrance
    faced east.

0   3 m.

Figure 8. Tea-shops and blacksmith's workshop

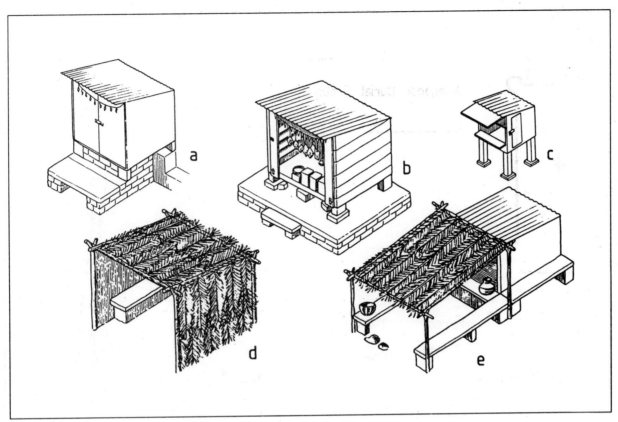

Figure 9. Stalls and shops in the market place

a Grocer's kiosk (Figure 7, no. 26)
b Grocer's kiosk (Figure 7, no. 27)
c Tobacconist (Figure 7, no. 3)
d Tea shop (Figure 7, no. 21)
e Tea shop (Figure 7, no. 28)

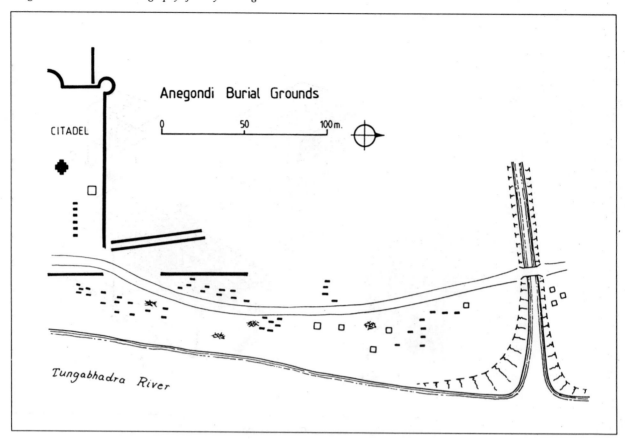

Figure 10. Burial grounds

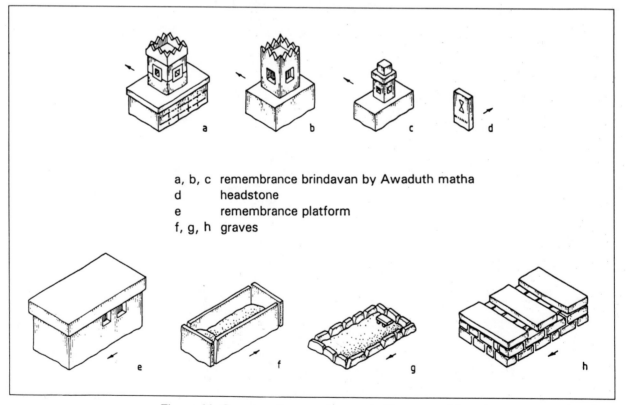

a, b, c remembrance brindavan by Awaduth matha
d   headstone
e   remembrance platform
f, g, h graves

Figure 11. Cemetery features (arrows indicates north)

as the Gagan Mahal, or Sky Palace, this courtly building was intended for the royal women to look out over the market square while remaining hidden from view (*purdah*). It was once believed that there was a spirit in Gagan Mahal, and so no one used the building until a man set up an office there.

Under the Mandal Panchayat system Anegondi became the administrative headquarters for 19 villages in the area. It deals with development matters concerning housing, animals, water, crops and education. The Zilla Parishad is the controlling body for each district. The Tahsildar, the *taluk* magistrate for each group of Mandal, resides at Gangavati. The Assistant Commissioner for each group of *taluks* is at Koppal, which is the new divisional headquarters. Prior to 1947 when the area came under the Nizam's authority, a Muslim head administrator, and a man called Kodandaramappa (personal assistant to Krishna Deva Raya) were in charge of Anegondi.

Government census

According to figures obtained from the Secretary of the Administrative Offices (Mandal Panchayat) at Anegondi in 1990, there were 398 houses of stone construction, 259 huts, and 173 open plots. There are 68 government supported Janata houses (belonging to the Scheduled Castes), a total of 54 temples and shrines, 10 old monuments, and 12 government buildings and offices. The 12 buildings include: the High School (111 students), the Middle School (625 students), the Harihara Deva Raya Youth Club, Wanita Yuwathi Mandal, Post Office, Farmers' Cooperative Society, Church, Animal Husbandry Centre, SCST Group Houses for Government Workers, Aurobindo Ashram Pondicherry Branch, and the Community Centre for Scheduled Castes which was government constructed for their meetings and marriages. The Women's Institute is accommodated in the Lotus Mahal, a Vijayanagara period courtly structure provided with a decorated doorway and interior ceiling.

Building work in the 1990s

Much building work was begun in Anegondi during the early 1990s. As there was no free land around the village, it was all used for wet-land farming, and so the government had to knock down old buildings in order to make way for development. The Mandal Panchayat allocated grants for building work from the State Government. These were sanctioned to each Panchayat, whose members divided it among their own projects. The Mandal Pradhan (head of local government) defined the projects, and the Secretary submited ideas and applied to get them sanctioned. Some of the changes that were observed between the author's visits are set out below.

The magistrate's residence (House no. 51) was demolished, and new offices for the Panchayat have been built on that site. The north wall was knocked away and a new building constructed there, now adjoining the Women's Institute. The steps of the Lotus Mahal had been knocked down completely, and the gateway moved. The original building had been given by the raja's family for common use.

The small dwellings at the back of the Panchayat were removed (House nos. 1, 2 and 3). The owners were paid off and given a new plot of land to the north-east of the village. The area was razed, so there was no trace of the previous decade's occupation. The Madhva Brahmanas coming from Karnataka, Andhra Pradesh and Tamil Nadu wanted a base in Anegondi when they came to make prayers on the sacred river bank sites. A residence, or *matha*, was to be erected behind the Panchayat to accommodate Brahmanas during the full-moon ceremonies in November and December, and at other auspicious times of the year, when they came to bathe in the sacred waters of the Tungabhadra.

During the period of fieldwork, a government library was built on the western Chariot Route. It has one room where books and magazines can be borrowed. A new ten-bed hospital has been built in the grounds of the health centre, together with an onsite doctor's residence. The pharmacy still stands at the same place with the chemist and dressing room. Behind it is an office for the midwife, and some public conveniences.

Water control (Plate 24)

Anegondi is bordered on its east and south by the Tungabhadra. Today the village is prosperous

Figure 12. Panchayat (administrative offices 1990) building known as the Gagan Mahal

Lotus Mahal
ANEGONDI

Figure 13. The Women's Institute building known as the Lotus Mahal

CHART OF THE ADMINISTRATIVE STRUCTURE

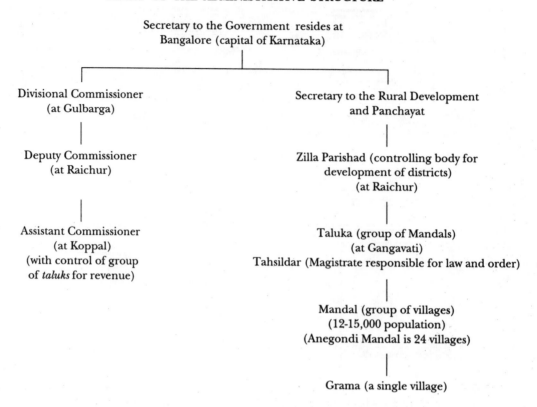

Secretary to the Government resides at
Bangalore (capital of Karnataka)

Divisional Commissioner
(at Gulbarga)

Deputy Commissioner
(at Raichur)

Assistant Commissioner
(at Koppal)
(with control of group
of *taluks* for revenue)

Secretary to the Rural Development
and Panchayat

Zilla Parishad (controlling body for
development of districts)
(at Raichur)

Taluka (group of Mandals)
(at Gangavati)
Tahsildar (Magistrate responsible for law and order)

Mandal (group of villages)
(12-15,000 population)
(Anegondi Mandal is 24 villages)

Grama (a single village)

and attracts a work-force from surrounding areas. One of the reasons is because the control of water is maintained by both the administrative authorities and by individual landowners. Channels built in the sixteenth century by the kings of Vijayanagara still irrigate an area of no less than 800 hectares today. There is a high water table: granite hills can be dammed in the narrow valleys to form small lakes (on Magota Hill, two lakes were dammed by the military). Sugandha (1986: 238) observes that had Vijayanagara been totally dependent on river water for all its needs, it would have been left vulnerable in times of strife. However, the town planners relied on canals, tanks and wells to attain self sufficiency in water management. Sugandha also noted the presence of two jetties, two bridges, an aqueduct, three dams, a sluice gate and 15 tanks.

The new system of pumping water was installed in mid 1985, but before that wells were the major source of drinking water: 42 wells were built inside the larger homes and three wells were public. The stone hills west of the village were also used to collect water, and one was constructed to act as a lake. There are two small dams on Magota Hill which Sugandha (1986:

241) suggests were originally for the use of the nearby barracks, as well as two larger dams in the valley. Anegondi is further served by drains which run on both sides of the Chariot Route; one drain flows to the stream in the field and out through the enclosure. The drains and road were relaid in the 1940s by a local administrator, while the taps and the pumps have been there since the 1960s and 1970s. Sugandha (1986: 249) gives a more detailed account of the structures in the village which relate to the control of water.

Riverside Citadel (Figures 14, 15 and 16, Plates 6 to 11)

Along the river banks to the east of the village are the remains of a series of massive stone walls, gateways and *ghats*. Behind the river front steps is a line of defensive walls and gateways.

The structures along the eastern side of the village are the remains of a riverside citadel or fort. The citadel exists with parallel walls and a bastion running some 100 m from the river front. The citadel walls were first suspected when a round bastion was found within the innermost enclosure walls of Anegondi's

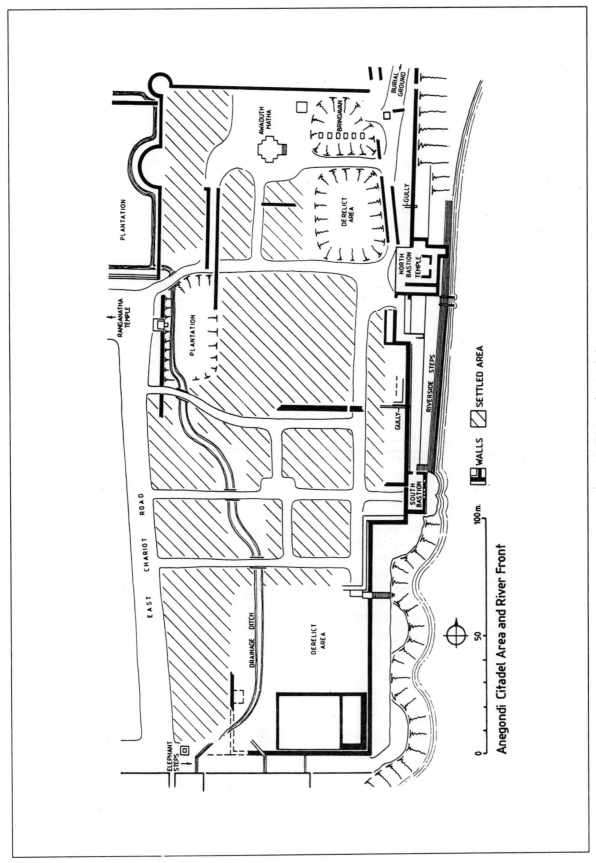

Figure 14. Riverside citadel

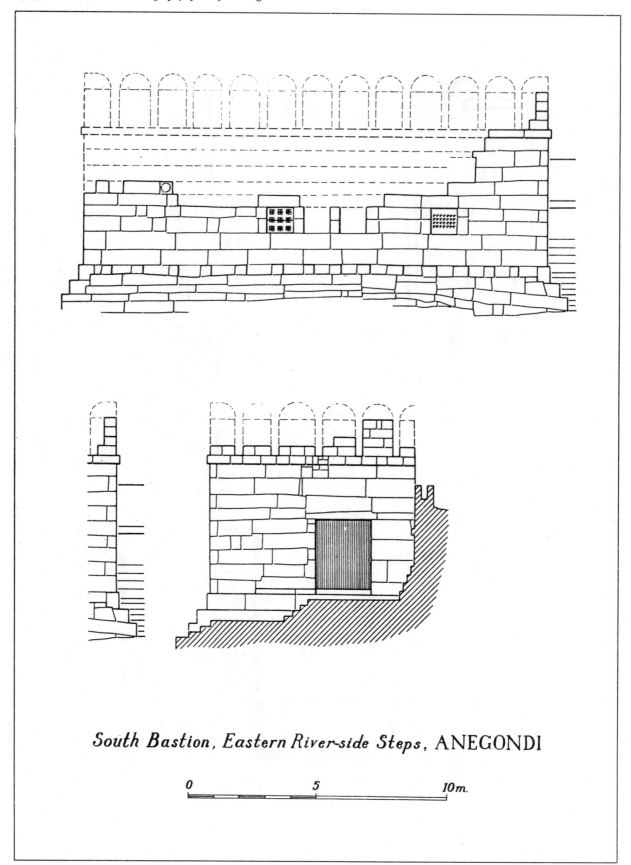

South Bastion, Eastern River-side Steps, ANEGONDI

0   5   10m.

Figure 15. Riverside citadel, south bastion

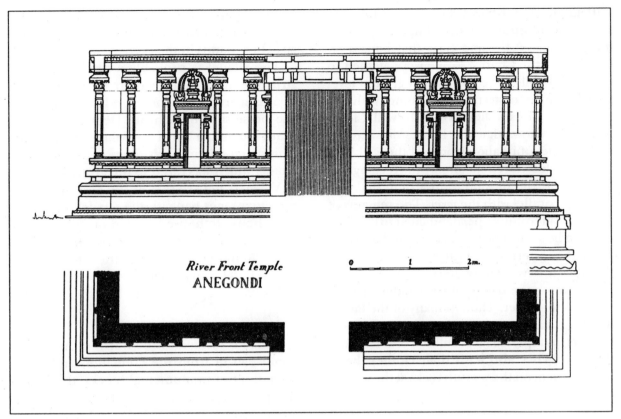

Figure 16. Riverfront temple

settlement (Sugandha 1986: 318). While the author and illustrator of this volume were checking the walls, it became clear that houses on one side of the Chariot Route were aligned to the citadel walls. The wall runs at ground level parallel to the eastern Cariot Route, with the backs of the houses aligned with the wall. Closer inspection shows that the houses are actually built on the foundation stones of the wall.

The enclosed area encompasses a rectangular zone, some 100 m wide, with an internal wall running parallel with the river. The remains of massive walls running perpendicular to the river can also be seen. The main access to the river is along the eastern wall of the citadel, notably by the church. Beyond the eastern edge is a stepped *ghat* running the length of the citadel, leading down to the water. Though many of the larger dwellings have wells and there is no shortage of water pumps, villagers still fetch water from the river. They also wash their clothes there, beating them on the smooth rocks at the water's edge.

The citadel served to protect not only its past occupants, but also their access to the waterfront steps. The southernmost gate to these *ghats* is constructed of large stone blocks with mortar infill. The upper levels are made up of smaller blocks, with small rocks in the spaces. This gateway is of fine tooled stone with blocks measuring about 200 by 75 cm. The lower courses are of larger blocks, rough cut and flat; some still display their cutting marks.

Within the enclosed area of the citadel are the remains of a temple with three black stone, rounded pillars. These are set low into the ground in a field which may have been a temple tank in the past, beside a modern Hanuman shrine which can be entered from beyond the wall. One Vijayanagara riverfront temple is used as a haystack.

On the corner of the walls by the Elephant Steps are the remains of walls (corresponding to the Big Structure in Sugandha: 1986: 109). The north corner has been used as a graveyard, and walls run here and there with deep hollows. Near the top, backing onto a house that lies on the eastern Chariot Route, is a stone plinth with mouldings. The granite blocks, which have weathered pink, appear to be of considerable age. There are two door jambs or thresholds, but these are difficult to see since the area is covered with heavy vegetation. A large stone structure stands in the corner.

The citadel is probably a pre-Vijayanagara structure that continued to be used during Vijayanagara times, and even later. Letters in the possession of Achyuta Deva Raya record that Tipu Sultan burnt the palace of Anegondi. This statement probably refers to the riverfront citadel which was razed to the ground.

Villagers believe that in the past there were secret passages beneath the citadel, which ran from house to house, and led outside the city. A concealed doorway on the riverfront is supposed to have been used by the king's women to reach the Tungabhadra.

Old bridge

A bridge is located to the north of Anegondi, about 250 m from the cremation and burial area. Built of monumental blocks, this carries the path over the rushing waters of a small stream which joins the Tungabhadra. It is possible that the path may not have been an original thoroughfare, but that the bridge was intended to carry the curtain wall over the river from the citadel. From the old cemetery nearby, the wall runs north into the hills, passing across two stream culverts. At the river front, the blocks are rectangular, but after the river front area the blocks become less well finished. A deep stone well immediately inside the eastern fortress wall, near to the Awaduth Matha, is no longer in use; a tall fruiting mango tree now grows out of it. A similarly dilapidated shrine is situated to the far north-east of the settlement.

Sirakal Mandapa

This 64-columned structure, standing on an island opposite the citadel, is popularly believed to have been built by Krishna Deva Raya (of Vijayanagara times). People say that it was his favourite picnic spot, and that he was cremated here together with his wives. A carved stone block near the riverfront entrance depicts a royal figure, identified by villagers as that of Krishna Deva Raya, together with his two wives who hold *sati* lemons. Women wash their clothes on the rocks nearby.

Elephant Steps

Immediately south of the citadel walls, beyond the end of the enclosure walls and flanked by the thick walls of a neighbouring palm garden and field, are some wide worn steps, originally with protective walls on both sides. The path is just off the alignment of the southern Chariot Route. There is a further set of steps at right angles which leads up to the city wall and continues south. In between the regular steps the pathway is paved, though this ends at a platform which projects from the city wall towards the Tungabhadra. No visible gateways are associated with this path, though a finely carved lintel lies on the ground nearby. Local people claim that this path down to the river was used by the royal elephants of Vijayanagara, where they were washed and watered by their grooms. They say that the name Anegondi derives from this place, for here the river runs deep, and the steps are wide enough to allow elephants to pass through to the water's edge.

Gateways

Among the stone gateways in and around Anegondi are several standing structures still in use. One in a state of collapse lies near some fields in an area that was previously settled. Remains of other gates can be seen at ground level, and there are more protecting the eastern riverbank. While carts drawn by bullocks are long and narrow, and can pass through the old gates, motorised traffic demands wider roads, and this has resulted in the demolition of several old gates.

Hampi Garawaleh (Outer Ferry Gate)
(Figures 5.I and 17)

This gateway leads to the river crossing at Talarighat and, beyond, to the Vitthala temple complex, the Vijayanagara ruins, and the Virupaksha temple at Hampi. Known also as the Agasi Baghilu or Entrance Gate, First Gate or Boatmen's Gate, this largest of all entrances to Anegondi from the Tungabhadra would have been the main gateway during Vijayanagara times. The gateway consists of double plinths, each supported by six rows of three columns, with the gap between the outer columns filled

in. The gateway is roofed, with the remains of a wall on the upper level rising over the south face only. Local people suggest that steps to the upper level once existed behind the east bastion. They say the water level can rise at least 2 or 3 m to reach the steps at the Hampi Garawaleh. The columned area of the gateway is built in the same style as the Wannagasi Baghilu. Large dressed blocks form the small bastions, whereas roughly hewn large blocks make up the curtain wall, and the large bastion has rough blocks with fitted joints. Facing the river to the south of this gateway, are square bastions forming part of the wall around Anegondi.

On the south side of the river (the same side as Talarighat) is a roofed structure built on a huge boulder. It is a multi-columned structure that faces the Hampi Garawaleh, even though the actual river crossing does not face the gate. This structure is probably a waiting area or traveller's rest-house. It is now surrounded by vegetation and is close by a banana plantation.

Inner Ferry Gate (Figure 5.II)

Visible at ground level are the remains of the Inner Ferry Gate which was built to the south of the town. This simple construction is situated between two semicircular bastions. Part of the plinth is visible projecting from the bastions above the surface of the present road. It is likely that each plinth once supported four pairs of columns. The wall built beside this gate appears to be later. On the path between this gate and the village there is a hero stone depicting a king riding a horse. The villagers say that in the past on celebration days the king used to ride around the village on horseback, make prayers at each of the five shrines containing a *lingam*, and complete the trip in 15 minutes.

Wannagasi Baghilu (Figures 5.III and 18)

This is the gateway through which buses enter from Gangavati. It is variously known as Second Gate, Golden Gate, Gate to Treasure, or Gate to God. It consists of two rectangular plinths with four pairs of columns either side of a central passageway. The internal row columns is finely carved and decorated, while the outer columns are plain and crudely cut. Gaps between the north facing columns on the eastern side may

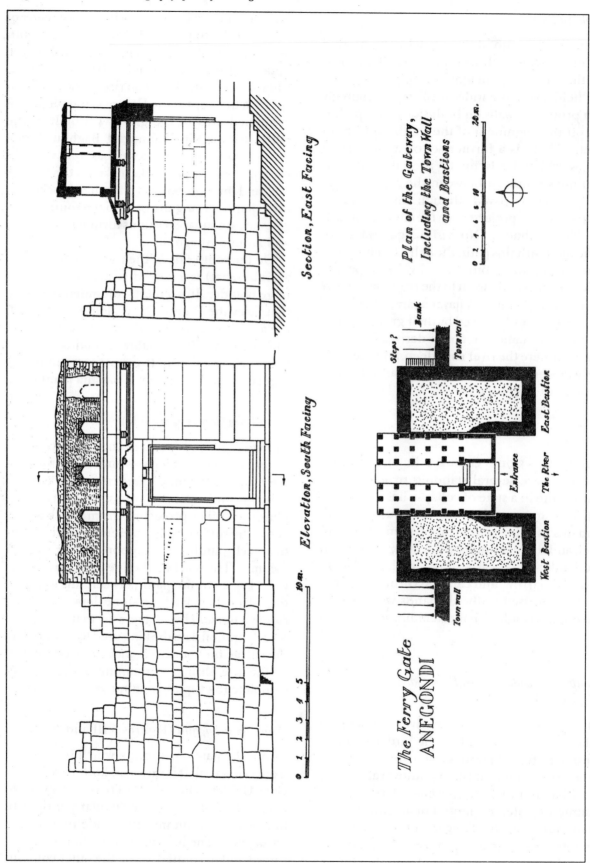

Figure 17. Hampi Garawaleh

have been filled in for security. A diamond pattern ceiling exists between the four central highly decorated pillars. Square bastions abut the gate plinths towards the outer corners on each side. A Koranic school is built up against the east bastion of the gateway. An aqueduct running through the gate, draining into the river next to the citadel, may have been used to fill the Ranganatha temple's old tank with water from the hillside dams. Additions to this gateway include finely carved door jambs at the northern entrance. On a rectangular slab on the first floor is a single rounded stone crenellation, the only example at Anegondi. Flowing towards the gate on the eastern side of the road is an irrigation stream. This turns east by the bastion along a sugar cane field to the north of the wall, and proceeds towards the Tungabhadra.

The remains of square bastions can be seen on the present-day Hampi road. This runs along the top of the old wall well above the fields at either side. Square bastions match the ones on the remaining wall east of the Wannagasi Baghilu, which also has square bastions. Vegetation has been cleared away to the north, exposing stone structures extending into the fields from the road edge. Between the town wall and Magota Hill are three bastions (with three others possible), each measuring about 8 by 8 m, some 90 m apart. Stones on the lower courses are long and rectangular, whereas those of the upper courses are squared. The walls and bastions remain to a height of up to 4 m. Round bastions seen by the High School on the town wall may be a later construction.

Kala Agasi Baghilu (Figures 5.IV and 19)

Meaning stone (*kala*) entrance (*agasi*) gate (*baghilu*), this imposing isolated structure is located to the west of the Wannagasi Baghilu. It is built past the last bastion on the Hampi-Hospet road, facing north beside a banana plantation. The gateway is of the same construction as the Wannagasi Baghilu, except that the north end has internal rebates for doors. It has the same type of columns and ceiling construction with a carved lotus, though this has now fallen to the ground. There are six beautifully decorated columns and a pair of finely finished doorway jambs standing some

5 m high. On the front lintel is a carving of an elephant. The frame has rough side panels on the front columns, indicating that a wall may have been built up against it. A huge stone slab lies on the ground beside the gateway, and at that point there may have been a bastion at some time in the past. The road width nearby the isolated gateway is some 8 m.

Sunka da Baghilu (Figure 5.V)

This gateway, now in total ruins, is built on the Gangavati road, some 3 km north of Wannagasi Baghilu, past fields of sugar cane and bananas. It marks the site where a toll was extracted from travellers; for this reason it is known as the Taxes or Toll gate. The road running northwards from Anegondi towards the Sunka da Baghilu passes several shrines and stone carvings of deities, including one of a seven-hooded cobra, painted silver. The gate was mostly destroyed when road widening took place to allow buses to pass through. Even so, the two flanking bastions are still visible, the western example is almost complete and rises to a height of 5 m. No evidence remains of the plinths or pillars. Curtain walls extend either side of the bastions and over the boulders, running up the nearby hillsides, thereby protecting the entrance to the narrow valley and its fields. Local people remember this gateway as having been an imposing structure.

Kadeh Baghilu (Figure 5.VI)

The outermost gate of Anegondi, known accordingly as the Last Gate, is situated in the environs of the village of Kadeh Baghilu which is named after it. Kadeh Baghilu lies about 500 m north of Sunka da Baghilu, at a point where the rocks from the hillside descend to the road. On its western side is a Muslim cemetery with a white open mosque and numerous gravestones. While evidence of the gateway has all but disappeared, a fortification wall on the east runs to the nearby hillside. A similar wall on the west runs for about 40 m before turning south and running parallel to the road, enclosing a narrow passage of land until it reaches the Sunka da Baghilu. The gateways appear to have been built first, with walls added later in times of war.

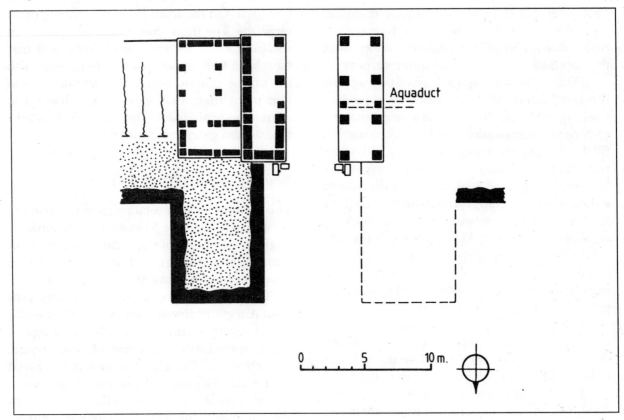

Figure 18. Wannagasi Baghilu

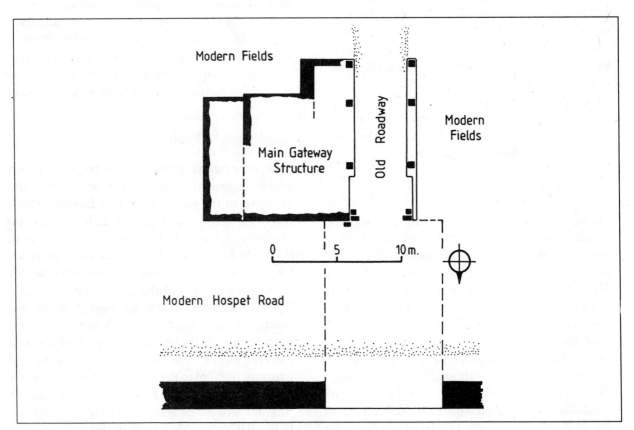

Figure 19. Kala Agasi Baghilu

Magota Hill Fort (Figure 20, Plates 12 and 13)

Magota Hill lies west of Anegondi; indeed, the most western village dwellings and the Ranganatha temple are built right up against its rocky foothills, and the shrine of Pampa Sarovar is situated on its western flank. Magota Hill is also known as Sukaduka Parvata, though Magota means upper fort. Mounds, pits and ash, together with areas covered in pottery, are seen between Hampi Garawaleh and Magota Hill. There is an old settlement area at the foot of the hills bounded by ditches and walls (Settlement H in Sugandha 1986: 68). To the south of this area is a path to the structures described below. The gateways mentioned in the previous section and the thoroughfares which pass through them are still used today by the inhabitants of Anegondi as they go about their daily activities. However, high up above the southern fort of Magota Hill there is another group of gateways which is seldom used today, except by the occasional farmer who cultivates pockets of land in between the boulders.

Military gateways (Figure 21)

An enclosed river inlet lies to the south-west of Anegondi on the Tungabhadra, not far from the Vitthala temple complex. One gateway stands beside the river, another on top of the ridge. Two other gateways, now in ruins and mostly unused, lead up from the path between the eucalyptus groves west of the Inner Ferry Gate. In the past this was an alternative river crossing for those living in the fortified area on top of Magota Hill, whereas today the only river crossing is by Talarighat. The bottom gateway at the river bank is of crudely cut stone, with flat slab-like steps on each side. The gateway is flanked by bastions, with low walls extending to the nearby inlet.

The ridge-top gateway is perched high on one ridge at the top of a valley which is completely fortified by curtain walls. A stepped path descending from the ridge-top gate to the bottom gate is defined by boulders. Towards the end of the path is a series of broken rocks, all approximately the same size (8 to 13 cm), laid to a width of about 2 m. The entire area, now overgrown with thorn bushes and high cactus

plants, might have been a military entrance.

The ridge-top gateway opens onto an enclosed flat plain and appears to have functioned as a reception and/or market area for the troops. From this entrance plain are two gaps in the rocks. The gap to the south leads to a second flat plain, also surrounded by rocks, where the remains of pottery can be seen. This might have been an enclosed village area made up of daub and thatch dwellings. The gap to the east is narrow and gives onto a shallow valley high in the hills used as a pathway to the barracks or stores (identified by Sugandha as the Long Mandapa; 1986: 116).

To the east of the ridge-top gateway, crossing the shallow valley, lie the ruins of a third gateway positioned at a gap in the boulders. This leads to a high flat plain, and onto a forth gateway (very ruined) at the very highest ridge overlooking Anegondi. From here, a path descends to the base of the steep hill, through the eucalyptus grove, across the fields, through an enclosed path between two palm groves, and into Anegondi itself.

Buildings inside the fort (Plate 14)

At the top of Magota Hill, beyond the fortress walls, is a quiet place of reflection. Here are situated the *samadhis* of the ancestors of Achyuta Deva Raya, including those of Krishna Deva Raya, Rani Lal Kumari and Sri Ranga Deva Raya. The fort is of stone, the interior walls being covered with a layer of concrete, finished with a smoothly polished, eggshell plaster surface, with red outlines. The arches are pointed. In one flat area of the fort are the remains of several small square structures. Small dips and hillocks suggest a fairly intense occupation in the past. Beside one of the granaries is a deep grindstone.

Beyond the fort and the ancestral *samadhi* is a stone bath-house that is almost completely masked by vegetation. This is built up against granite boulders, those at the back almost reaching the roof. The bath-house measures some 20 by 35 m, and there is a main entrance facing east towards the fort gateway. The entrance to the structure opens into a small reception area, from which a doorway with pointed arches leads into a central court with a sunken floor

Figure 20. Gateways and structures on Magota Hill

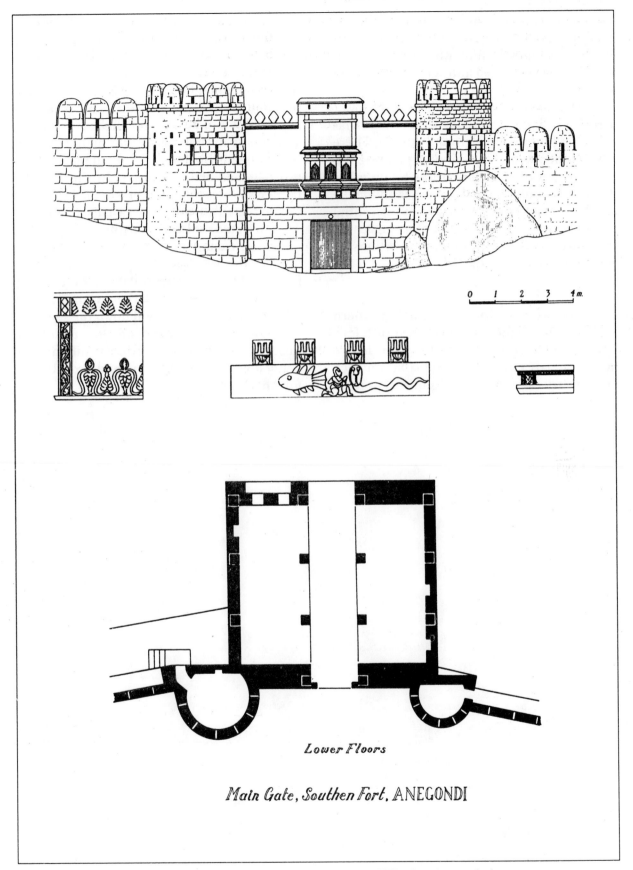

Figure 21. Main gate, southern fort, Magota Hill, elevation and plan

(2 m deep), surrounded by rooms. The walls are finely plastered, with a rough layer to cover the blocks, topped with a finer white layer (1 mm). Vertical gaps in the wall indicate the position of wooden pillars, now lost.

The bath-house has a drain hole in the lower part of the basin. The floor beside the bath is 75 cms higher than the ground outside. There are no windows, and the standing wall height is 4 m to the roof of angled bricks set on edge, now mostly collapsed. Thorn bushes invade the building, and a large tree occupies the central court. There is the suggestion of an enclosure wall surrounding the building, portions of which can be seen 10 m to the east.

North fort

Across the Hampi road, up towards northern Magota Hill, are the remains of the north fort. The summit was fortified with a small enclosure including two circular structures and a rectangular structure. A series of stone steps leads up to the summit of Jingar Betar hill, next to the Gavi Ranganatha shrine. Deep crevices between huge boulders are blocked by rocks. South of the fort area are the remains of rectangular buildings some 5 m across, surrounded by pottery remains. The structures are built of large stones for the lower courses, and smaller irregular stones for higher courses. Below the fortified area is a small plateau with two dammed areas of water. In the 1990s, a farmer, his wife and mother were living on the isolated plateau within a cave-type dwelling. They irrigated the fields from the dams, growing tomatoes, cucumber, caster oil and marigold flowers, the last used for prayer rituals. The farmer said that he had lived there for five years, and that he served the market in Anegondi by taking baskets of fresh food down the steep hill and hawking his produce from door to door. In this way, the ancient dams in the hills are still being used to water the land and provide food for Anegondi.

CHAPTER 2

People

Social Groups

Anegondi lies near the border of Andhra Pradesh and Karnataka and the inhabitants speak the Dravidian languages of Telugu and Kannada. Hindi is also used by some families who have taken brides from northern India states. According to the 1981 Population Census, Anegondi and Kadeh Baghilu village had a total of 3,258 inhabitants. Among these were 819 members of the Scheduled Castes. The majority of the villagers are Hindu, though there are about 600 Muslims, and 8 to 10 Christian families. Anegondi is unusual since it attracts migrants from outlying areas; many newcomers prosper due to the fertility of the soil and availability of irrigation. Many inhabitants are landowners having smaller or larger pockets of land, and there is plenty of work for the tenant farmer and labourer. Due to immigration to this prosperous region the residents are from numerous different castes.

The Hindu population of Anegondi divides itself into four principal caste groups, or *varnas*: Brahmanas (priests), Kshatriyas (warriors), Vaishyas (traders) and Shudras (workers). While caste identity may be derived from occupation in past times, caste today has little to do with a person's profession or standard of living. However, *gotra*, or eligible marriage partners, are almost always chosen from within the same caste. Outside marriages are still rare, though they may occur among the educated with wider social horizons. There were only two examples of outside marriage spoken about in Anegondi at the time of this project.

People's surnames in Anegondi often incorporate caste designations, especially Raju and Reddy. Kshatriya families are called after their town of origin, the name of which is used as a surname or family name. For example,

Nandial, Awk, Kadapathy are all towns in Andhra Pradesh; in Anegondi, they refer to particular families. Kadapathy and Kotehkany mean 'guards of the fort'. Other kshatriyas have the initials 'D.P.'; these refer to Delaway, or 'military commander'. Gabur is a town from which the ferrymen once came. Devaraya (god-king) was a common suffix for the names of the emperors of Vijayanagara, a tradition continued by the royal figures of Anegondi.

Villagers also indicate their caste affiliation during ritual prayers at a temple, especially in the manner in which they take the blessed coconut milk: those belonging to the Brahmana and Kshatriya groups receive the holy water by cupping their hands in a different way from those of the Vaishya and Shudra groups.

Brahmanas

In 1990 there were about eight resident Brahmana families in Anegondi, and another eight or so had come into the village to fill specific posts (suitable to their caste). After Independence in 1947, the old Brahmana families who were head priests of the temples all migrated, so that today in order to fill certain jobs within Anegondi, Brahmanas have to be recruited from elsewhere. They are employed within the Panchayat (local government), teaching professions, in a managerial capacity, or as clerical staff.

The manager of the Hyderabad Bank and his clerks are all Brahmanas as is the Panchayat Secretary (who lives within the temple walls). The post master was a temple priest before taking up the job in the post office (which lies within the temple walls). He has since retired, and another Brahmana has taken his place. His son is the main priest (*pujari*) for the Ranganatha and Ram Mandir temples. The present priest

a   Mace head
b,c Shaft details

Figure 22. Silver mace of the later Anegondi kings

lives inside the temple together with his parents and brother. Those responsible for the maintenance of the temple also live within the outer courtyard (but not the inner walls).

Kshatriyas

A large proportion of the Kshatriya families of Anegondi are descendants of Durbar Raja Sri Ranga Deva Raya, and are thus related. Among those families not related are the blacksmiths who have migrated from the north; they are descendants of the Maratha army. This is unusual since blacksmiths normally belong to the Shudra group. One other Kshatriya family at Anegondi comes from Andhra Pradesh, and the household head maintains the Sri Aurobindo library and shrine at Anegondi.

As already explained, most Kshatriya families are related to Achyuta Deva Raya, who claims a link with the kings of Vijayanagara. Proof of Achyuta Deva Raya's royal status is demonstrated by the mace, silver seals and other artefacts in his possession (Figures 22 to 24, Plates 62 to 66). He is invited to preside over religious ceremonies and to chair organisations; he is also a company director. Though the present kingship is not recognised by the modern political system, his exaulted social position is acknowledged by the inhabitants of Anegondi, and for this reason, local government officials have occasion to consult him. For example, when help was needed for a charitable project, such as the reconsecration of the Badavi Lingam at Hampi, government officials approached him and requested that he ask each village household to put aside a quantity of rice for charity.

It is not uncommon for members of the raja's family to become elected to political office because they come from 'known and respected' families. The present raja's father's brother, Tirumala Deva Raya, has been a politician, a member of the Legislative Assembly, and a leader of the local government headquarters at Anegondi and the four or five outlying villages. Evidence of his past political office can be determined by the modifications made to his dwelling (House no. 50). In 1987 this man's second son, Harihara Deva Raya, was requested to stand for office by the townspeople. A popular man, he was elected unopposed, but died in tragic circumstances several months later and

was mourned by all in Anegondi. The raja's brother, Sri Ranga Deva Raya, also holds office in the town of Gangavati: he was elected three times to the Legislative Assembly.

Kshatriyas at Anegondi are mostly members of the same family, but *rajaru* (royalty) are the direct descendants of a royal line or are adopted. To be adopted one must already be close to the royal line. The adoption of a son has always been an acceptable means of transferring power or wealth, both among the rulers and the ruled. An adopted son takes the new name, which in the case of the rajas of Anegondi includes the title of 'Deva Raya'. For example, Pampapati Raju was adopted to be ruler by his elder sister, and was accordingly renamed Sri Ranga Deva Raya. Achyuta Deva Raya was already of direct descent when adopted by his father's brother's wife, and so his name was not altered.

The 'Deva Raya' suffix used by the kings of Vijayanagara is maintained to this day by the *rajaru*; that is, those in direct line to 'the throne'. The name Deva Raya may be used by the raja himself, his brothers, and his brother's sons; his sister's sons may not use it, and their names end in Raju.

In the past, many among the royal families of Anegondi, have married but have had no issue, and have been obliged to adopt an heir. When Krishna Deva Raya died in 1872, his first wife Rani Kuppamma ruled. After obtaining permission from her eldest two brothers, she adopted her youngest brother Sri Ranga Deva Raya as heir. A ruler can only adopt a person who is 20 years younger, and only a male. The eldest females in a family do not count, though wives can be rulers, or single daughters with no brothers. When Sri Ranga Deva Raya died in 1918 his son was only eight years old, so Rani Kuppamma ruled again until he came of age. Sri Krishna Deva Raya had no issue. When he died in 1966 his wife Rani Lal Kumari became queen.

Achyuta Deva Raya was 'star blessed' at his birth in 1936. His father was the youngest of five siblings: two sisters and three brothers. The eldest brother, Sri Krishna Deva Raya, had held the kingship but had died without issue, and the second eldest brother had married late. The sons of the two elder sisters could not inherit the kingship, so Achyuta Deva Raya, the first born of the youngest brother, was adopted by Rani Lal Kumari. Achyuta Deva Raya married first and he

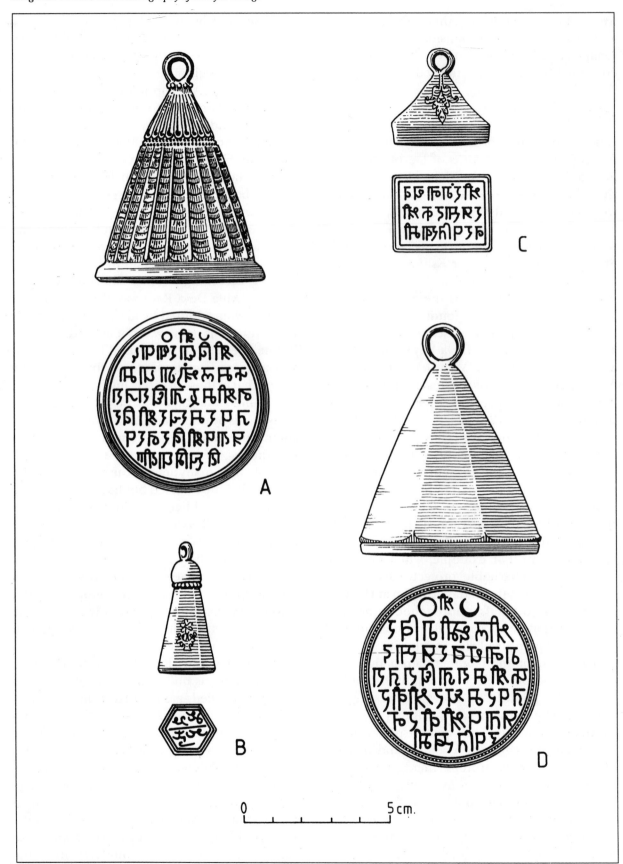

Figure 23. Royal seals of silver

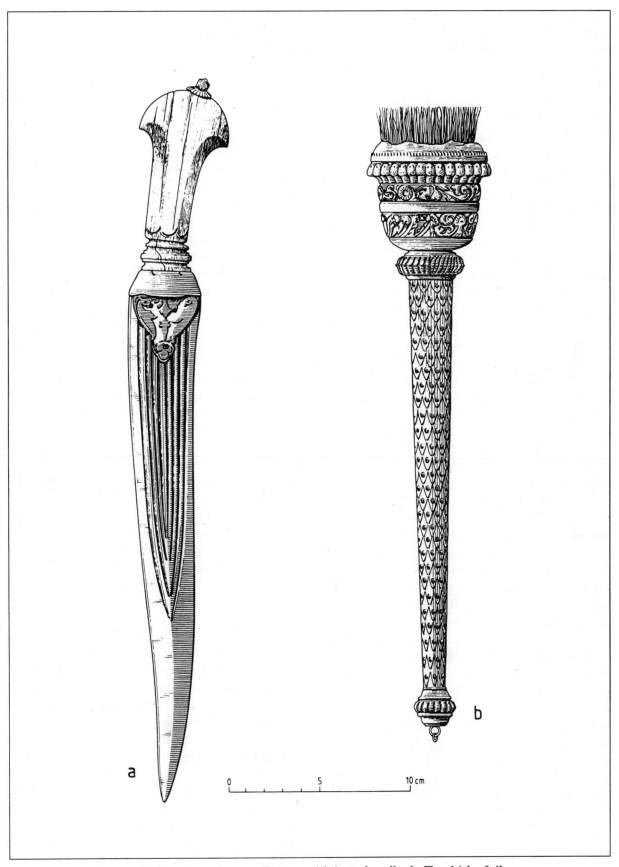

Figure 24. Royal artefacts: a. Dagger with ivory handle; b. Fly-whisk of silver

was then treated with full royal ceremony. He lived with Rani Lal Kumari when he married, and it was understood that he would be adopted as ruler. He took up politics in the 1990s because he was told by his guru at Kanchipuram that it was his mission to serve the people and make them aware of the current situation in India. The people of Anegondi are very respectful to Achyuta Deva Raya and his wife, always lowering their *lungis* so that their legs are covered, sometimes touching the feet of the royal couple on approach, and even walking out of a room backwards so as to continuously face the couple on exiting. Achyuta Deva Raya's wife is Rani Lal Kumari's brother's daughter, Chandrakanta. A silver throne presented to the Virupaksha temple by Achyuta Deva Raya is said to have once belonged to the last kings of Vijayanagara.

Even today Achyuta Deva Raya and his 'cousin-brother' Rama Deva Raya are informally expected to act as arbitrators of disputes and upholders of customary law, or *dharma*. Though at present Achyuta Deva Raya does not reside in Anegondi, his father's brother's son remains there and is constantly on call not only from Anegondi, but also from villages further afield, to assist in sorting out disputes. He is believed to be the last step in the process, since minor problems are usually sorted out using a council of elders. He is unofficially responsible for providing an arbitration service. It is said that in the past people went to the priest's house for help with spiritual problems, and to the palace for help with practical problems such as local quarrels, land disputes and financial difficulties.

The *rajarus* (royalty) usually marry outside Anegondi to distant or not so distant families in Andhra Pradesh or Madhya Pradesh, whereas those who are not *rajaru* are likely to marry within other Kshatriya families at Anegondi or to close relatives in Andhra Pradesh. Both communities are closely tied, and most of the Kshatriyas in Anegondi speak Telugu, the language of Andhra Pradesh. Brides from Madhya Pradesh speak only Hindi, and have to learn both Kannada and Telugu when they come to Anegondi.

Vaishyas

These business men, traders, small shop owners and grocers are known as Komataru, a term local to Karnataka. The name Setty is often used in their surnames.

Shudras

This group constitutes the bulk of the working peoples at Anegondi, and includes the Bedaru, Katguruh, Madagiru, Kurabaru and Vaddaru groups. The Bedarus (known also as Bhoi or Valmiki) were foot-soldiers in the armies of the ancient kings, and originally came from the Bellary area. At Anegondi, they live close to the river banks. The Madagirus were fishermen and vegetable-colour dyers in the past, though these days they are mostly farmers. The settlements of this large community are concentrated near to the banks of the rivers and to the east of the palace (House no. 50) at Anegondi. There are two categories of Vaddarus: priests and masons. The stone masons come from Andhra Pradesh and Tamil Nadu: the former are reputed to be good engineers, skilled at cutting blocks from the boulders; the latter are sculptors expert in carving rock. The Kurabarus were originally shepherds, of tribal origin, though now they are farmers. The Golarus are cow herders of tribal origin, but they too are now mostly farmers. Other Shudra groups at Anegondi include the Kambararus (potters), Badagarus (carpenters), Kumbararus (blacksmiths), Akkasaligarus (goldsmiths), Nekararus (weavers), Edigas (toddy-tappers), Chaparus (cobblers), Simpigarus (tailors) and Madigarus (sweepers and animal-skinners).

Other groups

Some Hindu groups are considered beneath the four *varnas*, especially the Schedule Castes, Harijans, or 'untouchables'. Other groups at Anegondi are considered outside the caste system, notably the Lingayats and Chetabanajigerus (though the latter are also sometimes thought of as a sub-group of the Lingayats). The Lingayats accept converts from all castes. Some people consider the Lingayats at the top of the Shudra caste; others say they belong to the Vaishyas. The originator of the Lingayats, Basaveshvara, was a saintly philosopher who advocated social reform, particularly the abolition of the caste system. Even so, the Lingayats include several sub-castes who intermarry and eat together. The Jangamas are the priestly leaders to the Lingayats, offering social and spiritual guidance to all.

The Chetabanajigerus (known also as Banajigas) were originally bangle-traders from Andhra Pradesh; more recently they were feudal lords who ruled villages in the Anegondi area. They are said to have enjoyed the confidence of the kings: they officiated and administered for them, as some still do today.

At Anegondi there are close ties between Kshatriyas and Banajigas. A number of marriages have taken place between a Kshatriya man and a Banajiga woman, but the children always take the (lower) caste of the mother. The Banajigas are divided into high and low castes according to wealth. While the entire community would be invited to a wedding celebration, only the immediate family would attend the actual ceremony. Both high and low caste Banajigas eat together but do not intermarry. The higher caste Banajigas are generally called Nayidu, and do not normally serve others, except Kshatriyas and *rajarus*. In the past, the sons of Nayidus would have looked after the king's sons. The Nayidus enjoy a particular status in Anegondi, known as Telugu Banajiga or Setty Banajiga. In past times they were advisors and ministers of the kings.

Muslims and Christians

It is estimated that there are some 600 Muslims in Anegondi, settled throughout the village, though with a greater proportion of households in the vicinity of the Friday Mosque. Only eight to ten Christian families live in the village at present. One is Protestant, and comes from Adoni, with the household head responsible for the pharmacy in Anegondi. The Catholic families reside near to the church to the east of the village.

Occupation

Farming (Figures 25 to 27)

Anegondi lies in a fertile wetlands area. The majority of the inhabitants focus their lives around the activities of agriculture and animal husbandry. Fields are cultivated for several kilometres north and west of Anegondi, both inside and outside of the fortifications. During Vijayanagara times, local rulers donated lands to temples, which enhanced their standing and religious merit. Temples authorities at this time improved reservoirs and irrigation canals so as to stimulate agricultural activity in the area. In 1990, a net area of 564 hectares was used for crops and plantations, of which 282 hectares were irrigated. Government officials are responsible for the repair and maintenance of irrigation channels, which are closed for one month annually for maintenance. The construction of the Tungabhadra dam in the 1950s has benefited a large number of people, and the region is now prosperous both for large and small farmers. However, as it is the general custom for brothers to divide their father's estates, this means that the inheritance of land and housing is increasingly fragmented. Portions of land are sold off for cash until families are left destitute.

Originally the land to the north and west of Anegondi had been forest, with no roads and no water, and there had been no buyers for it. Between 1947 and 1950, entrepreneurs had opened up this area, and gradually a village was established called Rampur. There were two categories of immigrant to Rampur: project labourers and land buyers. In the past there were ten houses, but by 1990 there were hundreds. The labourers made roads and cut irrigation channels, while the land buyers cut down the forest and sowed crops. The 1960s and 1970s witnessed the arrival of the government land ceiling: excess land was taken away from the large landowners and redistributed to the poor. Some people bought land from the temples and made their fields in disused temple tanks which had been filled in.

Achyuta Deva Raya's family have land on the northern side of the Tungabhadra, south of Anjaneya Parvata. The farm is at Madhuban, where local people believe the legend that Rama and Sita were seen dancing. (Actually, Madhuban in the *Ramayana* epic is a sweet garden in which the monkeys revelled and frolicked in joy after having discovered Sita.) Other farms owned by relatives and fed by the old Vijayanagara channels, have been left wild with many varieties of trees allowed to grow giving shelter to wild birds. Restoration work began in 1991 in a palm garden owned by Rama Deva Raya, between the

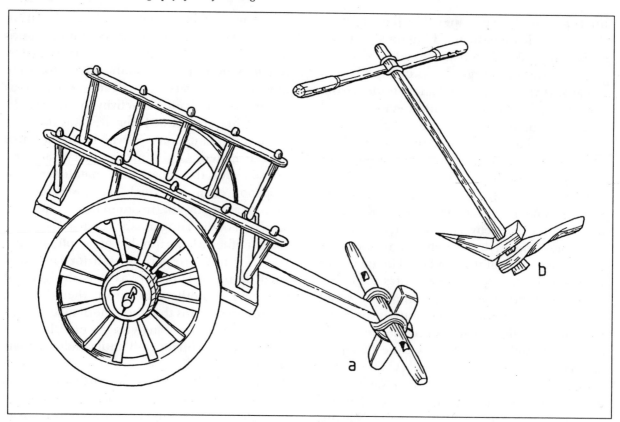

Figure 25. a. Bullock cart; b. Plough

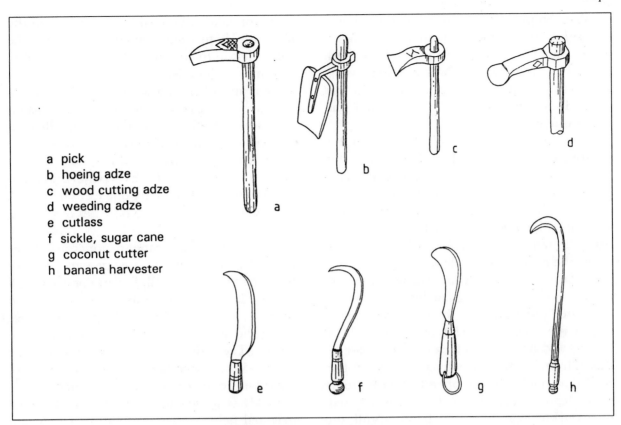

a pick
b hoeing adze
c wood cutting adze
d weeding adze
e cutlass
f sickle, sugar cane
g coconut cutter
h banana harvester

Figure 26. Farm implements

Elephant Steps and Chintamani. This had been left dry for three or four years after his brother's death. Banana suckers were planted amongst the palms, and the area was irrigated using an electric pump. The irrigation channel was desilted, and the stone well by the wall was reconstructed and redug.

The well has two sockets in the wall and a square gap below, and is built into part of the wall bordering a palm garden. It employs a pulley system for drawing water from a square stone well dug outside the city walls into the silt fields of the low river. The well slightly protrudes from the wall, though its top surface extends above the current wall height. Two horizontal stone beams stick out from each side pierced at the ends with rectangular holes. A square columned pulley fits into the protruding pegs, and a large bucket, about 50 cm across, made of a steel band at the top and leather at the base, is drawn from the well by bullocks pulling in the field. The bucket has an open leather bottom, with a leather cord attached which is released once the bucket has reached the stone gully on top. The water then rushes out into irrigation channels dug in the field of coconut palms.

Crops

Fields are ploughed and prepared in July when the monsoon proper starts, and sowing begins in August and September. The new rains which come in March and April are very light, and lower the temperature, though the monsoon proper begins in July. The cold season is between November and January when night temperatures drop as low as 10 degrees. Summer generally lasts from mid February to the end of May, with temperatures up to 40 degrees. The monsoon months occur between June and September when there is high humidity, skies are cloudy, and winds are westerly and south-westerly. In the dry lands (*marubhumi pradesha*) crops grown in alternate fields are sorghum, split peas, and sunflowers. In the wet lands (*niravari pradesha*) people grow tomatoes, cucumber, and egg plant.

Sugar cane is harvested in January when homes are closed up as every one is labouring in the fields. The cane is cut with sickles and taken to local, brown sugar (*jaggari*) factories where it is crushed, heated and made into demerara sugar.

The crop takes 12 months to mature, and the new crop is planted immediately. Either the root is left in for regrowth (two or three years running), or lengths of three segments of cane are cut and planted a week after the harvest. Usually once the sugar cane crop is over, bananas are harvested. They are bought by middle men who make a profit by selling at two or three times the price at auctions in town markets such as Hospet or Gangavati. Everywhere around Anegondi in early January one can see bullock carts loaded up with huge bunches of bananas for market.

Ground nuts are another major crop for they bring in good money on the open market after being harvested in April. Buyers come from all over India to purchase nuts for edible oils, and they take a commission on the price, but have to pay the market value at source, that is to the farmer. The ground nut crop is planted in the last week of December so it gets ten days of water before the canals close for repair.

Paddy is grown in small rectangular, well irrigated fields. Alternate fields of paddy and bananas are about 60 m wide. In late November, rice is harvested and the straw is brought by bullock cart from the farm to the houses for storage and to use as animal fodder. By early December the paddy has all been cut down. Before clearing a field, people come with the workforce before dawn and make prayers. No shoes are worn on the threshing area. After the initial release of grain, people do a secondary threshing, then the crop is dried, put into sacks, and taken to people's homes or to market. In the past people threshed paddy by collecting it in bundles and thrashing them on the ground. However, in the early 1990s, those with the means used a tractor and drove it round and round on a bed of straw. Others left their newly harvested crop on the road, so that vehicles would run over, thereby helping with the threshing. After the harvest, monkeys would cause havoc by ripping open bags of rice with their claws and eating the raw rice, spilling it everywhere. The new commercial crop of rice is fast ripening: taking one month in the nursery to germinate, then four months before harvesting. There used to be a belief that rice should receive the winter dew, but now the crop is harvested before the winter. Previously the crop had a longer season of around six months.

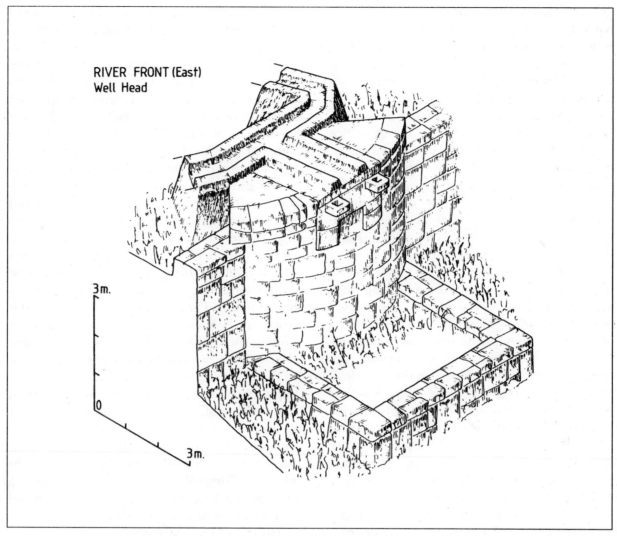

Figure 27. Stone well built into south-east riverside wall

Inhabitants of Anegondi are paid in rice to harvest the crop, whereas workers from surrounding villages are paid in cash. In 1990, labourers received one oval basket per week for 15 days of harvest work. A one-hectare field was priced at 300 rupees for a week's work or for 15 days. For a day's work a labourer could earn 10 kg of paddy. In late 1991, one sack of rice equalled three or four days pay; alternatively, day labourers in the field could earn 12 rupees. Wheat is harvested during December, and is also left drying on mats on the roadside; sometimes it is also placed on roads to be threshed by the car wheels. Too much rain later in the year can ruin a newly harvested crop.

Farms which border the Tungabhadra have many fruit trees including those bearing huge sop (durian) fruit. Coconut palms are planted in the boundaries between fields. There are also orchards of cashew-nut trees bearing red flowers: the fruit forms on the stem, and the seed containing the cashew nut hangs on the outside; it is only considered ripe when it drops to the ground. The fruit is so costly that only the rich can eat it. In 1990, cashew nuts were sold for 60 rupees a kilo, making it too expensive for local people. In the past, Krishna Deva Raya planted many varieties of mango tree. The fruit was stored on straw to ripen and everyone in the village shared the produce. Now the trees have all been cut down to make way for cash crops such as rice or groundnuts.

Animal husbandry

Animals are used for work or for the resources they provide. Wealthy people keep water-buffalo and cows close to their farms and have no animals in their homes, though poorer people often have neighbouring cow sheds. In some middle-income families one has to walk through the cattle shed which is the first room in their homes. Bullocks are used for drawing carts and ploughing. Cows are revered and never eaten.

At Anegondi there is a free-ranging stud bull, which belongs to the deities through the auspices of the Ranganatha temple; it is identified as Siva's mount Nandi. The bull is called *guwliy hohriy* (stud bull) or *devaru guwliy* (god's stud), and is owned by everyone and everyone looks after it. A particularly strong breed, it is allowed access to everyone's cows and fields. Such a majestic bull is given voluntarily by a member of the village, or by the government, for it would normally cost 10-50,000 rupees, and villagers would not be able to own one. It is of the Wangowl breed, named after a town in Andhra Pradesh. The practice of having a single stud bull is not unusual in southern India, and is used to increase the strength of the herd. People make prayers to the bull; for example, on the new moon day in January they dress it in fine cloths and embellish its horns. In Anegondi a water buffalo was also used for stud; however, it had a bad nature and trampled people's fields, and was eventually driven away to another village.

There are dry lands north of Anegondi, west of Gangavati. In this area herds of ponies can be seen, troups of up to 20 animals being used as pack animals. The owners are nomadic peoples from the Belgaum area who wander around finding the best fodder for their beasts. Large herds of sheep and goats, sometimes numbering in their hundreds, are also associated with dry lands. Christians, Muslims and Hindus of certain castes may eat sheep, goats and poultry; slaughter occurs once a week on Sunday. Sometimes the male of a species is sacrificed during certain festivals involving goddess worship. Fish is caught from the Tungabhadra by casting a net from a coracle. Black hogs keep the rubbish down and dogs are kept by many families.

Hordes of monkeys roam freely around the village, screeching and chattering in the early mornings. The black- and red-faced monkeys are said to be respectively the descendants of Vali and Sugriva. Bears are found to the south of Kamalapuram. Other wild animals in the hills include cheetahs, leopards, cranes and peacocks. People fear leopards and cheetahs and numerous dogs wear collars of nails. In the night when dogs and chimpanzees hear the panther or cheetah approach they begin to bark and chatter. Cheetahs were present in the village in 1990. One took a dog in Anegondi in January, and another took a dog near to Madhuban. Peacocks and cranes were seen at Magota Hill by the waterlily lake which had dried up in early February. An elephant is kept by the Virupaksha temple at Hampi. In the past, elephants were maintained by the royal family, and kept in the temple. A photograph taken on 10th April 1977 at the Car Festival, shows Achyuta Deva Raya and Tirumala Deva Raya atop a huge elephant.

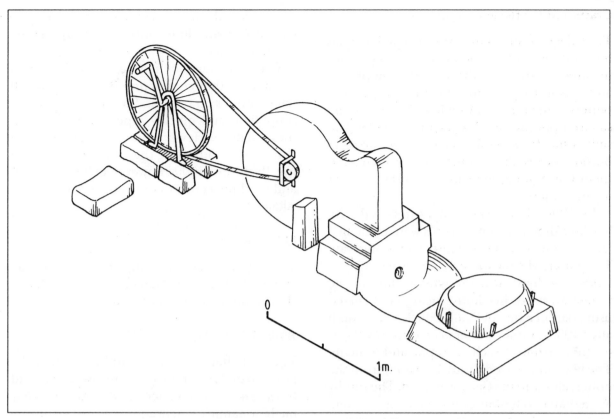

Figure 28a. Blacksmith's bellows

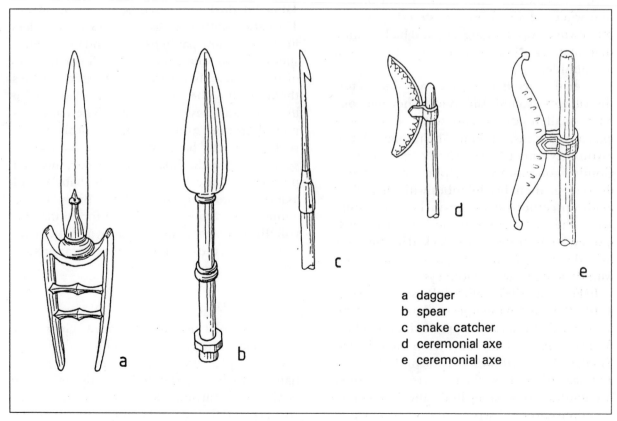

a dagger
b spear
c snake catcher
d ceremonial axe
e ceremonial axe

Figure 28b. Weapons

Crafts and Craftsmen (Figure 28)

The village of Anegondi is unusual in that it has few resident craftworkers: most people are involved in farming activities. Itinerant potters and tinsmiths pass through the village, and potters come for a day to sell their wares in the square opposite the Ranganatha temple. Tinsmiths stay for several days at a time, working outside the dwellings of those who commission them. Cart-pulling bullocks are shod by itinerant teams of men.

In 1990 there was one potter and one blacksmith in Anegondi. Tools were made in a factory, and bought in Hospet or Gangavati. The potter, who was a female, also worked in the fields. She lived near the gate leading to the Gangavati road, her house being constructed using part of a fine old wall. (She left Anegondi after 1990.) Other potters came from villages to the north-west such as Supur and Waligih. The blacksmith lived about 45 m away from the potter, closer to the Gangavati road. The smithy was a thatched building about 6 m long accommodating a hearth, some huge hammers and numerous tools. For bellows the blacksmith used an elaborate contraption like a bicycle, one wheel of which was plastered over. The other wheel was standing free and had a handle that rotated the first wheel, causing the charcoal to smoulder.

After the rice harvest, itinerant singers tour the villages around Anegondi. They may only have small holdings, and travel and sing in exchange for cash or flour. Their songs relate to mythology and history. They come from the Gondeli community at Bijapur. Dancing girls, dressed in their bright robes with their faces made up, come from villages in the surrounding area. They dance in order to beg for grain or money. Some bring cows bedecked in fine cloths in order to win extra sympathy; others travel with dancing bears or monkeys.

In February 1987, statue makers were working at the Ranganatha temple, fashioning life-size images of deities and their mounts for the chariot festival in April. They came from the village of Kinal, 65 km north-west of Anegondi. To make an image of this type, the men create a wooden framework with separate limbs and torsos which they then cover with a paste of sawdust and gum, a layer of cloth, and finally a paste of tamarind seed. When the form is complete the statues are coated with white lime, and then they are painted bright colours.

Only a few families in Kinal still make statues of this type, though they produce small toys and flat paintings on request. But their work is now simplified, and quickly reproduced. In 1991, they did make a few sculptures but only on paid commission, otherwise they could not afford to live. By the mid 1990s, however, exhibition areas and teaching centres were being set up in their village.

Life Cycle

This section gives a brief introduction to the life of people living in Anegondi through birth, childhood, marriage and death.

Birth and birthdays

The inhabitants of Anegondi believe that the position of the planets at the precise moment of birth determines character and future life. After birth, a naming celebration takes place in the third month of life; the first haircut is done in the third year. When a new baby has to cross the Tungabhadra for the first time, prayers are made. The baby's mother brings yellow and red powders in two small newspaper packets, and two incense sticks. The boatman puts the powder on the side of the coracle, lights the incense sticks, waves them around the powders, then places them into the sand beside the water. The coracle is moved around, and a coconut is broken on a rock beside the bank. Water from the river is splashed onto the boat with the oar, and red powder from the side is put on the baby's head as it is handed over onto the boat. Birthdays are a time of meditation and prayer for adults who visit the temples. If there has been a death in the family within the previous year, celebrations are muted.

Girl's maturity

At the time of a girl's first period, a celebration takes place. The girl is dressed up in a new sari, jewels are placed on her forehead and in her hair, and she is garlanded with flowers. Four lamps are lit around her and placed at four corners, and friends and family come and offer sweets.

Coming of age

Within the Brahmana community, the coming of age, or coming to the priesthood, is called *munji*. It is the ceremony of the initiation of the sacred threads (*yajnopavita*). In the past, this was done before a male was 12 years old, but nowadays it happens before marriage. If a man has no threads then he has no right to perform ceremonies and prayers. It is the custom for a man of the upper castes to wear threads around his shoulders. On marriage he is given three threads to indicate his responsibilities to his wife; on the birth of his first child he wears an additional thread.

Marriage

Marriage is patrilocal, and in the past girls were married or accepted for marriage at a very young age. If a girl became widowed she could not marry again, even if the marriage was not consummated. The choice was always given to the brother's sister's offspring for a man's first marriage. It is said that there is a closer tie if a brother and sister are exchanged by both households. It is rare for a future husband and wife to meet before marriage unless they are related. After the parents have selected a suitable marriage partner, photos of the couple are exchanged, their horoscopes are examined, and the parents may visit with a note. If the horoscopes are unsuitable, the match does not take place. Usually, a man has only one wife at a time, but if the couple is childless, he may take another wife. In the past it was considered incorrect for a family to have unmarried girls. If there were an excess of female offspring they would have been married to a man who already had a wife, so that they could bear children. The precise hour of marriage is determined by a priest, who advises on the correct time, to the minute, when the religious ceremony must begin and end.

When a woman born of a father with Deva Raya as a name ending marries a husband from a Raju father, she takes her husband's name and her children become Rajus. Those belonging to the Rajus are of the same caste (Kshatriya) as the Deva Rayas. Deva Raya is the name extension used by men who are in direct line of kingship, and those eligible to inherit this position. As a mark of respect, one never calls one's elders or betters by their given name. The king may be referred to as *anaya* (elder brother), *nayina* (father), *dhaniy* (master), *rayaru* (royal man) or *sarakah* (government). In a royal family, the elder brother's wife has the same status as a mother, and can speak and be spoken to by her husband's brothers, but the younger brothers' wives must remain in seclusion (*purdah*), and they must not speak to the elder brother. A husband and wife will not speak together in front of elders, except when necessary.

In Anegondi, a wedding of moneyed families is announced by a parade with brass band and drums marching around the town, followed by the men of the family delivering invitations. Wedding invitations are distributed to the sound of trumpets and drums: they are taken around the square chariot procession route in a clockwise direction, past the Ranganatha temple, then turning right.

Married women wear a necklace to indicate their marital status. This is composed of two gold pendants, one from the wife's family, the other from the husband's. The pendants are strung together with black beads, sometimes interspersed with gold. Rings on the toes of women also show that they are married. Kshatriya married women can wear silver toe-rings, although direct royalty wears gold. All women wear ear-rings no matter what their caste or circumstances. Wrist bangles represent life's revolving wheel of birth and death. On their marriage days, women wear red and green bangles: dark red for strength, green for fertility, though some will not wear the colour green when they are pregnant. However, as the day of childbirth draws near, the wearing of green bangles is recommended. Upon the death of a woman's husband, her glass bangles are removed and broken. A widowed woman does not wear jewellery and should even stop wearing the *bindi* (red dot on the forehead).

A Kshatriya marriage

During the author's stay in 1991, a marriage took place between descendants of Sri Ranga Deva Raya: Tirumala Deva Raya's daughter's girl married her father's sister's son. The rituals began five days prior to the final ceremony. A special prayer was carried out at the bride's home at the time of her dressing. After this her status changed to 'bride' and she could not leave her mother's home until the marriage ceremony when she became 'wife'. During these days gifts were given: saris for the bride, shawls for her husband, and clothes for the bride's brother. Each gift was taken into the prayer room to be blessed by the household deities, while devotional songs were sung. The married woman's necklace, consisting of two rows of tiny black beads, was given to the bride's sister. A similar item was given to the bride, but without the black beads since she was not yet married. The black and gold beads are only worn after marriage with a double gold pendant, the latter only used by Kshatriyas.

The wedding took place at Naren Pett, the family's farm house. On arrival at the gateway, the guests were sprayed with scented rose-water. That evening, visitors from Madhya Pradesh donned fine jackets and red turbans. They travelled from Anegondi by jeep and motor cycle, turbans flowing in the wind, with the people of the nearby villages staring at their northern outfits. The reception began at 7 p.m. on Thursday the 19th December, although the main prayers were scheduled after midnight, at 00.47 a.m. The bride's father was a doctor, and her mother was the grand-daughter of the last king of Anegondi, Sri Ranga Deva Raya. All the politicians and eminent people of the region had been invited.

High-status Kshatriya families practice long-distance endogamy and on this occasion close relatives came from Gujarat, Rajasthan, Delhi, Madhya Pradesh, Andhra Pradesh and Tamil Nadu. On marriage, a woman moves to her husband's family, often a long distance away, and has to learn the local language. Such a woman is often lonely, and long-distance marriages offer opportunities for brides to be reunited with their families. At this wedding, women came together who had been separated from their maternal relatives for years. They stayed in the house, where one room was set aside for the groom. Sparkling antiques that had been handed down through the generations were on view at the marriage night. Gold, pearls, emeralds and rubies were removed from the family safe to be worn on this one occasion.

A field nearby was taken over and decorated for feeding the more than 3,000 people on trestle tables and chairs. Near to the river bank an area had been set aside for massive cauldrons on hearths. Eating began at 7 p.m., and continued on through the night, with hundreds of people at a single sitting served by members of the Brahmana caste. All the farmers and inhabitants from the surrounding villages were invited to participate. The food was a mixture of Karnataka and Andhra dishes. The trees around the tables were glowing with coloured fairy lights Classical music was played over the loud speakers.

A dais was prepared and hung with garlands of orange and white flowers. After eating, the women changed into even finer sumptuous flowing silks and gold brocades. At about 11 p.m., the local band played live music with drums and a trumpet. The tempo of the gathering changed, excitement rose. Women sat on one side of the dais and men on the other. First the bridegroom came onto the dais and was blessed by the Brahmanas. There were so much photography and video film being taken around the dais that no one behind could see anything. This was a truly modern wedding.

Later, towards midnight, the bride was brought out of the house, totally shielded by a golden blanket held in place over her head by various female relatives. This blanket continued to be held in front of her until the auspicious hour was reached. At that time, all the men in the audience, well over 1,000 in number, came up and threw coloured rice as a blessing over the couple; then came the women who did the same. Presents and money were handed over as gifts. The giving of gifts eventually came to an end at about 2 a.m. The couple left for Hospet at around 3 a.m., well before sunrise, since it was not auspicious for them to travel on a Friday during daylight hours.

Pregnancy and birth

After a marriage in Anegondi, it is customary for the bride to move to her husband's household or village. For the first and sometimes for subsequent births, however, women return to their mother's households during the last months of pregnancy. The husbands' kin may, after five months of pregnancy, send gifts to their in-laws. At that time food is prepared for the entire family. The expectant woman spends her confinement at her parent's house, staying in a room without light. On the 11th day, a cloth is draped over the threshold and the woman is allowed out to participate in a coming-out ceremony attended by all her relatives.

Divorce

Divorces are said to be rare in Anegondi. If a couple have problems with their marriage, all the elders of the family gather to discuss their interests. After separation, some husbands agree to maintain their wives; if they refuse, she is obliged to return to her father.

Death

After a death has occurred at Anegondi, the body is laid out on the house verandah for viewing, and all the village including children should pass by. It is said that the burial or cremation should take place on the same day as the death. After the viewing, a funeral procession leaves from the deceased's house, and proceeds via the east Chariot Route to the cemetery by the coconut palms beyond Awaduth Matha. The procession is led by trumpets and drums, and the whole population of Anegondi turns out to pay its respects. During the cremation, guns are fired regularly for half an hour, first rifles and then smaller pistols. After the first shots comes a slow continuous drum beat. The procession with trumpets and drums then goes around the Chariot Route.

After the cremation, the ashes and bones are kept. It is believed that the soul stays on earth for three days, then there is a group prayer to let the soul rise to the place of ancestors. Some ashes are sprinkled in the Tungabhadra, itself a holy river, though some may be taken to the holy Ganga river. Close male relatives may make an offering of their hair: they are unwashed from the death till the 13th day, then they sacrifice their hair and beards. Other kin with special affection also offer their hair. A *brindavan* is built at the place of the ashes. If the deceased person was very popular, some people will mix the ashes with water and then drink this mixture.

Death of Rani Lal Kumari

Rani Lal Kumari, the last queen of Anegondi, passed away in 1984. (Details of her funeral were noted from a family video which was made on this occasion.) Rani Lal Kumari was laid to view on the verandah of House no. 44. Men sat on one side of her body, and women on the other. All the villagers came through the house and touched her feet. Leaders of the Christian and Muslim communities said their prayers over her, and Hindus read prayers. So many villagers attended that microphones were used to broadcast the prayers to those standing outside in the street.

The Rani was covered from head to foot with a mound of flowers, so that only her face showed. Two bands of sacred basil leaves were placed above the flowers on her chest, and rice was thrown over the body. She was brought down from the verandah and given a final bath by her adopted son who poured an earthen pot of water over her. Then she was wrapped in white cloth, placed onto a carrier, and taken out into the street. The pall-bearers were male relatives.

A band dressed in white caps and red coats led the mourners. The procession turned right out of the house, and proceeded past the houses in the villages, and in a clockwise direction around the central square of the Chariot Route. As they walked, women came out and laid coloured saris along the route, so that the pall-bearers trod a woven path. They walked up the Chariot Route past the chariot itself, past the Ranganatha temple, and out through the Gangavati gate. They walked up the Hospet road and climbed the rocks of Magota Hill, and all the while saris were still being laid before them. Achyuta Deva Raya, her adopted son and heir, walked ahead of the bearers, swathed in a white *lungi* and his threads, carrying an earthen water jar.

The procession passed through the fort gate and up to the royal *samadhis* where a pyre of wood had been prepared. Achyuta Deva Raya walked several times around the pyre, water spilling onto the earth from the earthen vessel that he carried. The flames were lit, and Achyuta Deva Raya was shaved of his beard and hair, which were then offered as a sacrifice to the deceased. Food was eaten off banana leaves.

The following day the ashes were collected, after which they were conveyed to the Ganga in northern India.

Self-immolation of widows (sati)

Near to Talarighat is a place with a large accumulation of calcium and ash. Local people say that this marks the spot where royal women whose husbands had been killed in war had immolated themselves with a blanket hiding their view of the flames. During Vijayanagara times only Kshatriya women committed *sati*: it was not done by the wives of Brahmanas. Women who underwent self immolation were given a very honourable status, but widows who did not do this led a very restricted life. It is believed that the two wives of Krishna Deva Raya committed *sati* when he died, the principal form of evidence being the carving of a royal figure with two wives holding *sati* lemons which has already been noted. The people of Anegondi consider that the 64-columned structure on a rock in the river indicates the cremation spot of Krishna Deva Raya himself, but there are no historical records to prove this.

CHAPTER 3

Worship

This chapter looks at mostly Hindu religious practices in Anegondi, and gives examples of prayers and festivals showing how the inhabitants use the shrines in the village and the surrounding area. The principal places of worship are noted, together with various mythical sites.

Other than Hindus, who comprise some 85 per cent of the population in the Anegondi region, there are also Muslims (15 per cent) and a handful of Christian families. Since the author was the guest of a Hindu family, many of the customs noted here pertain to Hinduism.

Local Practices

Home worship

Religion and daily life customs are intertwined for most people at Anegondi. Each morning before the sun rises, women sweep their houses and the area immediately in front of the entrance. They clear away debris to beyond the boundaries of their homes, and sprinkle the ground surfaces with water. Some women smear a coating of cow dung which purifies the ground and helps to keep flies away. Since most houses are not enclosed, this activity takes place on the verandah and in the street in front of the house. Elaborate designs (*rangoli*) are sprinkled on the surfaces with a white powder. A series of dots is laid out around which a pattern is interwoven. Drawings are also produced at sunset, though they tend to be more simple. Both types serve as a blessing to the sun.

In the past, drawings done in the morning on the thresholds of houses were geometrical diagrams which evoked divinities. From such drawings, *sadhus* who passed by could tell the devotional nature of the people within, and could choose which house to visit. Thresholds are often decorated with patterns: it is said that

the vibrations (*prana*) of *rangoli* designs could cause a ferocious man with evil intent to change his ways. *Rangoli* designs are also made to welcome the god Rama to the home, providing a means of identifying devotion to him. People used to mix rice powder with the colours as almsgiving for insects. The base powder is sold in Hospet market.

The white colour of *rangoli* designs is crystalline quartz, widely available in the hills around Anegondi. It is obtained by local peoples and crushed to a powder. The red is iron ore or haematite, crushed to a powder. It is now available ready-made, and is used to paint doorways and house walls. The green colour is more rare, even though it is obtained from the north of the village. *Rangoli* designs on concrete or black slab flooring employ a paste of rice powder; they are usually done at night so that the designs have time to dry before dawn. *Rangoli* designs are used for festivals, on prayer days and on new moon days. The mixture for temporary floor painting is a liquid paste of rice powder. The coloured powders are from cloth dyes mixed with water and allowed to dry. Some colours are those used for the Holi habba festival in April.

The harvest festival, known as Pongal or Sankranti, falls on the 13th or 14th January, the day when the sun passes into the Tropic of Capricorn on its journey northwards. The festival heralds the end of the cool season and the beginning of the hot season. On this day large elaborate drawings are done in front of the houses, some with a fine multi-coloured infill. Cow dung, shaped into five cones is placed in the centre of the design, embellished with flowers. Some people paint or whitewash their houses in celebration of Pongal; the extensive drawings on the floors look like newly patterned carpets.

Most Hindus in Anegondi have an area of

their home set aside for devotion. This takes the form of a prayer room, niche or shelf which contains images of the gods, and provides a focus for family devotions. These areas are generally near to or in the kitchen, since this is considered a consecrated space. Muslim and Christian homes in Anegondi also have prayer rooms or niches which are the focus of their religious rituals. People make sacrifices as part of prayer rituals in their homes and shrines. These are often vegetable (*harbowaiseh*), such as a coconut smashed open so that its milk anoints the shrine, or a pumpkin. For special celebrations, however, people of certain castes make blood or animal sacrifices (*korniwaiseh*). Only the male of any species is sacrificed, whether it be goat, sheep, chicken or bullock. Later, the sacrifice is cooked and eaten. At some shrines there are also sacrifices of fire and light (*yajna* and *homa*): the burning of clarified butter (*ghee*) and grain is believed to kill bacteria and purify the atmosphere. It is the custom that once the prayer rituals inside the house have been completed, prayer water from the copper pot is poured onto a sacred *tulsi* (basil) plant growing in a *brindavan* in the garden outside the house.

Almsgiving

Almsgiving is still a regular part of daily life in Anegondi: the ideal is to set aside each day a portion of new unused food, some of which may be given to a cow. Food taken from the prepared evening meal may be given to a dog, perhaps also to birds, and even to the household fire. Some men exploit people's sympathy by wandering around the village dressed in coloured cloths and blowing a horn, accompanied by a sacred cow decked with ribbons on its horns.

In the past, it was the duty of a *sadhu* to instruct a family in spiritual knowledge, in return for his daily meal. Although Achyuta Deva Raya and his close relatives acts as arbitrators, if people are not happy with their judgements then they turn to venerated *sadhus* or holy men known as *babas* who may suggest an alternative solution. Sites around Anegondi, such as Anjaneya Parvata, Pampa Sarovar and Durga matha, are all shrines with resident *sadhus*, who make prayers for any passing person. At Anjaneya Parvata in 1991,

there was an old blind man with long white hair sitting on a raised concrete platform, cared for by half a dozen younger *sadhus*. Pilgrims came from far and wide to pour out their troubles to him, hoping that he would provide some answer to their problems.

Worship of main deities

Different deities regularly receive worship in Anegondi. Many of the upper castes have Vishnu as their main deity, though they also worship Siva. The Setty caste worship Vishnu, while the Lingayats are devotees of Virabhadra. A shrine to this ferocious form of Siva stands outside Anegondi on the road to Gangavati. At present, there are no Jains in Anegondi, though in the past they came as traders from Rajasthan.

Vishnu is the presiding deity of Anegondi. His shrine is at the Ranganatha temple which lies on the western Chariot Route that runs from Talarighat to the Gangavati Gate, facing eastwards onto the main square. Saturdays are Vishnu's day. In Anegondi, Vishnu is worshipped by the Brahmanas, Kshatriyas and Banajigarus, all of whom offer *tulsi* leaves as part of their prayer rituals; worshippers of Siva prefer the leaf of the bilvapatra tree. Ayengar Brahmanas make a single vertical line in white on their forehead as a symbol of Vishnu, whereas other worshippers of this deity may employ three vertical lines. Madhva Brahmanas have three vertical lines on their forehead, the two outer white, and the central one red. Follower of Siva have three horizontal lines of ash on their forehead. These are made from burnt cow dung, a reminder that humans are as ash, and return to ash.

The family deity of Achyuta Deva Raya is Vishnu in the form of Venkateshvara, Lord of the Seven Hills, the god venerated at Tirumala in south-eastern Andhra Pradesh. As a rule, however, royalty does not have a preferred deity, and so the family worships both Siva and Vishnu, participating in public ceremonies of all the deities at Anegondi. The family prays at Hampi every Monday. After visiting the Virupaksha temple, they go on to the Badavi Lingam. Achyuta Deva Raya used to lead the chariot in the festival at Hampi that celebrates the marriage of Siva and Parvati, and which takes place on the full moon day in April. He and his family also join in the ritual ceremonies that take place at Nava Brindavan. In addition, they make pilgrimages to holy sites throughout southern India, travelling regularly to Kanchipuram to visit their guru.

Many of the lower castes worship Siva and the *shakti* goddess who attract a popular following. Local *shakti* deities often take natural forms, such as trees, rocks and uncut black stones. The deities of the Bedarus, Vaddarus and Madagirus include Uramma, Yellamma and Uligamma. Deities of the Madagirus also include the goddesses Uramaguli, Gunlameh and Thaiyamma, as well as the god Malemah. The shrines to these divinities are invariably mud built, open to the sky, and sometimes painted with designs. Inside, a natural stone is often worshipped as the god or goddess. Offerings include miniature ceramic lamps, torn pieces of saris, incense sticks and green bangles. The last, which are considered particularly appropriate for fertility, are placed at the shrines of goddesses.

Shudras worship Siva and participate in *shakti* worship, as do Harijans. According to higher caste people of Anegondi, the Yellamma goddess is worshipped by untouchables. They say that a *shakti* goddess such as Yellamma demands merriment, animal sacrifice, drinking of alcohol and meat eating. Large numbers of worshippers gather to participate in such celebrations. In the past, a girl is said to have been dedicated to the *shakti* goddess Irama on the full moon day in March-April.

Once images of deities are broken they can no longer be used for worship, even if only slightly chipped: they must be buried, thrown into a well or into a river. Recently, casual digging for sand along the river bank unearthed large fragments of broken black stone sculptures: a female torso with rounded breasts; a pair of feet. These were perhaps abandoned in times past.

Water is essential for life and for rituals of birth and death: it is a symbol of sacredness and a natural purifier. Before people cross the Tungabhadra they ask the boatman to bless them with water. He splashes them with the coracle oar while they kneel at the river's edge. After they bless the boat, everyone else embarks. Such prayers are also offered when a new baby crosses the river.

Snake prayer

Stones of the snake god, called *nagara deva kallu*, are found all over Anegondi. Once a year people make a prayer to such stones, anointing them with milk and turmeric. Nagara Chowti is the snake festival when people make prayers on the stones. At this time, people may make a pilgrimage to one of the more famous snake temples such as the Nataraja temple at Nagercoil in Tamil Nadu, or the Mannarassala temple at Haripad in Kerala.

Protestant services

The single Protestant family in Anegondi is visited every few weeks on a Sunday by a pastor who comes from a nearby village to hold a service in the family home. He reads a couple of passages from an English Bible, and then sings hymns in Kannada. Family members clap their hands and burn incense on the ground in the centre of the gathering, while sitting cross-legged around the pastor. The service ends with a coin being placed by every member on a leather bound Bible, and the recitation of the Lord's Prayer.

Prayers and Festivals

Villagers worship at ancient shrines in Anegondi, and make regular pilgrimages to sites within the Vijayanagara city area on the other side of the Tungabhadra. They also make special pilgrimages once every year or so to more distant sacred sites. Deities are treated as divine guests: they are bathed and clothed, and offered food and sacrifices, including those of fire, light, water, air and sound. Whomever the residing household deity, villagers worship other gods on their special days and at festival times. There is also a vibrant tradition of constructing new shrines outside the village, near to sacred stones, and beside lakes and trees. Such zones then become the focus for devotional prayer. Furthermore, in the last few years, neglected shrines have been refurbished and reconsecrated at the initiative of the villagers. On the occasion of Siva Ratri in 1989, for instance, it was decided to inaugurate prayers at the Badavi Lingam which had fallen into decline. Every household in Anegondi was asked to donate a handful of rice each time they prepared a meal. These offerings were collected every Saturday, taken to Hampi, and then given to the priest at the shrine so that prayers could be maintained.

The case studies below illustrate how the people of Anegondi use shrines (both ancient and modern) and landscape features around the village as part of their religious observances. Prayers associated with holy places are manifested in the form of processions, singing devotional songs, and image worship. Each caste has its own way of performing ceremonies. This is most obvious during Karttika, the 'lamp-lighting' month that follows the Diwali festival. Diwali occurs at the beginning of Karttika, and is symbolic for lighting up the darkness. People say they should be like a lamp, giving off light to others. At the end of the month, people come from all over the area to celebrate and offer devotional songs. Karttika is also a period of *shakti* worship; this takes place from Diwali until the second new moon.

Sacred moon festivities

In southern India, festivals like Diwali run from one new moon to the next. On the day of the full moon, people fast to some degree, either totally abstaining from food, or restricting themselves to a single meal during the day, and water-based drinks (avoiding tea or milk) and fruits. The author always visited Anegondi during the winter months and observed a number of festivities held at this time. At the time of the new moon in Karttika, these included processions from the Ranganatha temple; prayers to the water goddess held by the Madagirus, Koruberus and Vaddarus; prayers held by the Brahmanas at Nava Brinda-van; prayers anointing Hanuman at a shrine near the Pattabhirama temple; and the festival celebrating the engagement of Siva and Parvati at the Virupaksha temple in Hampi that occurred on a full moon night.

The total eclipse of the moon is an inauspicious, yet sacred occasion. People eat their last food in the afternoon, so that they are not digesting food during the eclipse. A bath is taken in cold water just before the eclipse, and a prayer is said during the eclipse itself. Once the eclipse has passed, people bathe again in river water and take food. They believe that stored water becomes contaminated, and so fresh water is collected. People from Gangavati come to Anegondi to ritually wash in the Tungabhadra before and after the eclipse. Brahmanas and those who hold orthodox religious views also participate in such rituals.

At the time of the new moon there are three days of prayer: during the new moon day of Karttika month, people wash and then bless their motorbikes, lorries and agricultural tools. Such useful and powerful items are considered to manifest the energy of *shakti*, and prayers ensure peace, or *shanti*, thereby maintaining the balance. For example, in order to bless a motorbike it is first washed, marks of Siva and red *kumkuma* dots are applied, prayers are said, flowers added, and smouldering incense sticks held over it. On the evening of the new moon in December, prayers are held in many temples and shrines. Walls are lit up with electric lights or with lamps using wicks and *ghee*. At the Hanuman temple by the Elephant Steps, men sing devotional songs to the accompaniment of the harmonium, drum and cymbals. Some shrines have songs blasted through the village on a loud speaker.

In the Harijan area of Anegondi, a small tree (*bunnih*) serving as a Yellamma shrine was the focus of devotional songs. A group of men sat with a harmonium, drums and brass castanets, singing throughout the new moon night. An audience of women and children was assembled in a shelter covered with banana leaves. The whole banana tree had been sacrificed for the occasion, and the trunks formed the edges of the frame. A single light bulb hung from the centre illuminating the players. Elsewhere, other shrines were decorated with sugarcane stems and leaves at the corners, with tied banana leaves in front, and hanging mango leaves at the entrance. The presence of banana trees cut and bound at the corners of a shrine is auspicious since it is the sacrifice of an entire tree for a deity. To cut the tree with a full bunch of bananas hanging off it is even more auspicious since it the sacrifice of the entire tree and its fruit before harvesting. Coconuts are also offered as a sacrifice, since once broken, they cannot be used for seed. Other fruits, such as apples or cherries, have seeds that can be thrown away and from them the plant can grow. Coconut is the most generous offering, since the seed is destroyed when the fruit is broken open.

*Festival of lights procession of the
Ranaganatha temple*

This procession is organised by the priests of the
Ranganatha temple to benefit the whole village.
At dusk, they head a procession of deities led by
a brass band and drums. A palanquin is brought
before the Ranganatha shrine, and decorated
with sugar cane and banana leaves. Three deities
are brought out from the inner shrine by the
priest, set upon a pillow on the palanquin, then
covered with garlands of flowers.

The procession begins with the lighting of
double rows of lamps on a wooden frame. The
brass band sets off, proceeded by men throwing
firecrackers into the streets. Next come those
carrying the lamp frame, and four men who
support the palanquin with temple priests
alongside. Few people actually follow the
procession, but many wait outside their houses
for it to pass. Women and young boys offer oil to
renew the lamps, taking back the flame and light
into their homes. Others bring coconuts and
bananas to be blessed. Even a new born baby
may be brought out to receive a blessing. Once
the procession has passed people return to their
homes.

The procession goes along the Chariot Route
in a clockwise direction, stopping only to receive
and to give benedictions. It only diverts from its
straight march to reach the house of Achyuta
Deva Raya and that of his father's brother,
Tirumala Deva Raya. Finally, the procession
returns to the Ranganatha temple, which by this
time is lit up with burning lamps of *ghee* wicks.
The procession enters the temple precinct,
proceeds to the rear of the shrine, and ends at
the front steps to the inner sanctuary, where it
stops.

New moon prayers at Nava Brindavan

The island of Nava Brindavan is a site of extreme
sanctity and antiquity: the earliest *samadhi* is
believed to predate Vijayanagara times.
Brahmana groups have been coming here in
buses, vans and cars since the mid 1970s, when
the new roads were built. The men are bare-
chested for prayer, wearing only a *dhoti* and their
sacred threads. They take their vows and walk in
a clockwise direction around the nine *brindavans*.
After prayers, mass feeding takes place. The

visiting pilgrims are mostly followers of
Madhavacharya and his successor Padma Nabha
Tirtha. The four princial sects are the Mantralaya
matha based near Guntakal in Andhra Pradesh,
the Sosale Vyasaraja *matha* from Mysore, the
Mulbagal Sri Padaraja based in Kola near to
Gulbarga, and the Uttaradi *matha* which has its
head office in Bangalore. The four sects have
the same philosophy, the same followers and
the same guru.

In 1990, one group fought the other three for
the right to first perform prayers before noon
on the auspicious day for the anniversary
celebrations of Padma Nabha Tirtha. In 1991,
the head of the households in Anegondi,
discussed the situation with the police, and
invoked Section 144 of the Police Act to stop
a congregation of more than four people on
the island. Until the quarrel was sorted out,
no prayers could be performed. On these new
moon days Brahmanas bathed in the river on
the Talarighat side, and police patrolled in pairs
in the market streets. Brahmanas performed
prayers at Chintamani, near to one of the
samadhis. According to the newspapers, the
following were required to ensure the peace
that year at Anegoni: two district reserve police
forces from Raichur, one state police group
from Gulbarga, one Commissioner of Police,
one District police, and the Koppal subdivision
reserve police. At the time, it was suggested that
the right to worship at that sacred site be drawn
by lots over a three year period.

New moon ceremony at the Hanuman shrine

On the third day of the new moon in December
1991, the following anointing ceremony took
place at a Hanuman shrine south of the
Tungabhadra, near the Electricity Board
workers' residences, east of Kamalapuram
village. The ceremony was attended by those of
the Kshatriya Rajaru caste. While the stone image
of Hanuman was ancient, the shrine was newly
constructed. The 1.5 m high Hanuman sculpture
was bathed with water and milk, and then covered
with offerings of sugar and banana. All the
foodstuffs were eventually removed, and the
sculpture washed once again with water. Bells
were rung, turmeric and white paste added, and
the image was garlanded with flowers, and

dressed in a white cloth around his waist. This prayer of anointing the deity is known as *abhisheka*.

New moon prayers at the Ishvara shrine

On the same day, prayers took place at the Ishvara shrine in Anegondi. At this Lingayat place of worship, the ceremony was held in the inner sanctuary where the priest washed the *lingam*. He was dressed in a red *dhoti* and threads, and bore the ash marks (*vibhuti*) on his forehead. He had prepared a frame of *pan* leaves, each one ending with a flower. Prayer marks of Siva were made on the *lingam*, which was then garlanded with flowers. Outside, men lit tiny lamps all around the shrine until it glowed with flickers of flames. Children arrived and offered coconuts, bananas and flowers to the priest. These were blessed and after smashing open the coconuts the priest kept the milk in a silver bowl. A tray with burning *ghee* was carried around on which children placed coins, waving their hands over the flames. A copper pot with coconut milk was on the same tray, and a spoonful was handed out to each person present who took a sip, rubbing the residue over their hair to anoint themselves. After blessings, the *prasada* (god's offering) was handed around. Everyone was given something wrapped in leaves, with bananas and coconuts. All the children were given a taste of the sweet paste.

Procession for Gangamma

For a fortnight after the new moon in December 1991, various groups made processions around Anegondi in praise of Gangamma, the goddess of water. The focus of their attention was the Gangamma shrine near the Ferry Gate opposite Talarighat. Each group gathered, then called in at the houses of the raja and his cousin to invite them to participate, before proceeding towards the river bank in a frenzy of drumming and singing. Each caste group took a pot of water from the river and offered it to the goddess. Among those who took part were people of the Kurabaru, Madagiru and Vaddaru castes.

The Kurabaru procession, led by musicians with cymbals and drums, made animal sacrifices beside the shrine. Two chickens and a goat were slaughtered. A pot of holy water taken from the Tungabhadra was used to bathe Gangamma and Lakshmi. A plate of flowers was also offered, as was a copper pot containing *pan* leaves and coconuts borne by a young girl with a burning lamp. One boy carried an image of Gangamma on his head, as well as a big copper pot. The pot was washed with tamarind, then used to collect water from the river which was carried to the shrine by the boy. Another group of Kurabarus was led by a number of elderly women wearing green saris. They started from a bangle shop where they purchased red and green bangles. Offerings of green bangles were made to promote fertility and prosperity, of persons and land, while red was bangles were presented for energy.

The Madagiru procession was celebrated by their entire village community. They too went down to the river front, collected a pot of water, and brought it back to the Gangamma shrine. The shrine was lit up and a banana leaf framework was erected at the front. All unmarried teenage girls wore a garland of flowers in their hair. There were between 20 and 30 of them, followed by older women in saris. The men walked first throwing firecrackers, beating drums, and cymbals.

The Vaddaru community invites people from other villages and towns to come to Anegondi for the Gangamma celebration which ensures prosperity and wards off evil.

Pilgrimage to Hampi

In 1991, the marriage ceremony of Siva and Parvati at the Hampi temple took place on the 23rd December. People came from all over the area to attend the prayers and celebration that continued throughout the night. Anegondi was seething with hundreds of pilgrims waiting to cross the river. Phalapuja, the prayer of flowers and fruit, marks the occasion of the engagement between Siva and Parvati. This takes place in the Kodandarama temple overlooking the south bank of the Tungabhadra, followed by the chariot procession at Hampi.

The bazaar street leading to the Virupaksha temple on this occasion was crowded with itinerant salesmen and women. Some set up their goods on cloth on the ground, others brought in their own stalls; some even hawked their wares from cross beams on long poles, from which goods swayed. They provided much competition for the local market traders. Bangle-sellers sat in front of banks of coloured glass. There were plastic toys, beads, bells and rattles, baskets, posters, coconuts, and an astrologer reading cards for their clients with the help of a parrot let out of a cage. Cows and dogs wandered among the crowds of people. Everyone stayed awake that night to witness the procession of deities.

At around 9 p.m., the procession started from the Virupaksha temple. Led by drummers and proceeded by two staffs of authority, the multi-garlanded Siva seated on his bull mount, Nandi, was hauled on his chariot along the bazaar street. The procession travelled along a path through the coconut plantations towards the Kodandarama temple. Just before a narrow pathway though the boulders beside the river, Siva was transferred to a palanquin in order to continue his journey. The steps by the Kodandarama temple were swarming with people, lit up by bright lights.

Siva Ratri at Hampi

On Siva Ratri which falls in February or March, all of the people of Anegondi go to Siva temples irrespective of the deities that they may worship on other occasions. The day before the festival, the villagers in Anegondi spring clean their homes: all the columns and cupboards are washed, and many whitewash their houses inside, renewing all. People wake at 5 a.m., and begin bathing, washing their hair. Many people fast, though some take fruit and snacks, and drink juice. Some have a white round grain or semolina, mixed with potatoes and spices and eaten off a banana leaf.

At 8 a.m., the women and girls of Anegondi set off for Hampi, carrying food and collecting banana leaves on the way. They crossed the Tungabhadra at Talarighat, and walked along the path in the rocks past the crowds of people bathing in the river near to the Kodandarama temple. Many of the group visited Sugriva's Cave, a natural opening between boulders not far from the bank. Threads of crystal in the sheet rock in front of the shrine are considered to be marks made by Sita's sari dragging on the stone when she was kidnapped by the demon king

Ravana. Near to here are numerous piles of stones made by those who desire a husband, house or child. The piles generally consist of four stones, a large one resting on three smaller ones. Various members of the group added to the piles.

At the Kodandarama temple, prayers were offered and the women rang the bell in front of the shrine. Some even prostrated themselves on the ground in front. Within the shrine are deities of silver, brass and gold, with eyes outlined in silver mosaic and red. Each woman received sacred water from the small spoon offered by the priest. Before departing, the women linked their hands together as if to look at the sun though their fingers, saying 'namaste'. From here, the group proceeded to Hampi, passing by beggars, holy men and lepers who lined a narrow path that led through the rocks, holding out their dishes for money or rice. The beggars were all dressed in orange cloth like *sadhus*.

At Hampi the women left their shoes outside the Virupaksha temple, and entered barefoot, washing their feet at the taps in the outer court. In 1991, there was a one-rupee entrance fee, but as relatives of the Anegondi raja, these women were admitted freely. The crowded inner shrine of the temple was hot and sticky, with priests sitting within the inner sanctuary. The women handed over their coconuts which the priests broke on a small square stone some 30 cm across. A bell was rung and then everyone in the group filed past the shrine, lighting a camphor flame, and taking holy water: first the right hand and then the left hand was passed over the flame. A golden mask of Siva was on display immediately beside the shrine. On show only on high festival days, it is protected by bars and a guard.

From here the group proceeded to the goddess shrine in the Virupaksha temple, where flowers were placed and incense lit. Outside, in the courtyard of the temple, there was an elephant. Members of the group offered coins which the animal passed to its keeper and then touched the head of the donor with its trunk. People believe that to receive an elephant's blessing is very auspicious. A sign of Siva and a red *kumkuma* spot marks the forehead of the animal.

On leaving the Virupaksha temple the women collected their footwear. The guardian who had looked after the shoes was grateful to receive a small piece of coconut as *prasad*. After leaving the Virupaksha temple, the women ascended Hemakuta hill, passed by the Ashram there, and walked along the road leading south towards Kamalapuram. Almost 1 km along the way they visited a shrine in the banana groves known as the Badavi Lingam. This square sanctuary accommodates a 2.5 m high, monolithic *lingam*, surrounded by a pool of water in which flowers were floating. The women brought coconuts to sacrifice, and threw a selection of flowers onto the *lingam* pedestal. At the edge of the water, coconuts were offered, and a bundle of bananas was placed. Incense sticks were lit and waved in a circle. Camphor was also lit and women passed their hands over the flames saying 'namaste'.

Throughout the day not one member of the group ate or drank anything; only after visiting the Badavi Lingam shrine could people break their fast. The group took shelter in one of the *mandapas* at the end of Hampi bazaar. There they enjoyed bananas peeled and broken into tiny pieces, as well as a special mixture of white grains including sorghum and millet.

Mythical Locations

The Anegondi area is linked with two main legends: one relates to the goddess Pampa, the other to the *Ramayana* epic. Sugandha (1986: 23) suggests that they resulted from two groups of people who colonised the area: the first were food gatherers and followed Pampa; the second were farmers who needed to placate the monkey spirits. The monkeys present on the site, who have such an important role to play in the *Ramayana* story, are a menace to farmers and their spirits have to be appeased in order to ensure a successful harvest.

Sites associated with the goddess Pampa

It is believed that the goddess Pampa performed penance to win the hand of Siva beside a lake near to the Tungabhada now known as Pampa Sarovar (see Figure 5). Local people believe that Pampa Sarovar is also associated with the origins of Vijayanagara, since it was here that Madhva Seva, the great sage, was bathing when he received the inspiration to build the city.

When visiting Pampa Sarovar, a group of women first remove their shoes before going into the shrine which is lit up with flames of camphor. On the wall, a curiously formed natural root is lit up in an orange glow. Stone carvings of the goddess have finely painted faces; they are clothed in silks and swathed in garlands of flowers. Offerings are regularly made here by visitors who arrive with a prayer basket filled with coconuts and flowers. The brightly painted stone image of Lakshmi inside the shrine is tended by a priest. The shrine is surrounded on all sides by containers of burning oil. The priest takes burning camphor on a spoon, and chants continuously, while others ring a bell to purify the atmosphere with sound. The offering is taken from the basket, the flowers placed beside the shrine, and the coconuts smashed on a square rock in front of the shrine so that the milk flows over the stone. Those who pray are given *tulsi* water and flowers, received in cupped hands; the coconut halves, now blessed, are returned.

Ramayana sites

Many sites in and around Anegondi are connected with the *Ramayana*. Indeed the whole area is famous throughout India, and coach-loads of pilgrims come to visit sites on both banks of the Tungabhadra. Many of these are related to Kishkindha, the monkey kingdom, where a number of key episodes in the legend take place. *Ramayana* brochures for sale in Hampi bazaar point out the relationship of the Tungabhadra landscape to the mythical Kishkindha. Among the *Ramayana* characters who are of particular significance for Anegondi and Hampi are Sugriva and Vali, rival claimants to the throne of Kishkindha, and the monkey general Hanuman. Today Hanuman is the most popular deity in and around Anegondi, and there are numerous shrines and boundary stones with carvings of him on large boulders. Anjaneya Parvata and Sugriva's Cave, two of the most popular sites, have already been mentioned. The small pond known as Sita Sarovar, is said to be where Sita bathed.

At the summit of the steep hill of Anjaneya Parvata is a shrine to Hanuman believed to mark the birthplace of Hanuman; a cave is hidden in the boulders below the shrine. Anjaneya Devi is Hanuman's mother, and a shrine dedicated to her is also found here. Ajaneya Devi is painted in bright colours and clothed in a sari; a diminutive image of Hanuman sits on her arm. Inside the shrine is a much larger stone image of Hanuman: in 1989 this was painted vivid orange, and clad in scarlet satin shorts lined with silver thread; the god wore a garland made of magnolia flower petals. Four or five holy men live within the shrine area. They revere an elderly blind man who reclines on a couch covered with a cotton sheet and a leopard skin. The holy men always feed the monkeys that run unafraid around the shrine.

The Chintamani complex is identified as the place where Rama came looking for his wife Sita after she had been abducted by Ravana. The monkey spirits that inhabited this land of Kishkindha helped him find his wife in Sri Lanka. Also the wife of Sugriva was kidnapped and held behind Chintamani. The sage who protected Sugriva and Hanuman resided on Matanga Hill that rises to the rear of the Kodandarama temple on the south bank of the Tungabhadra. A mound of ash near to Anegondi, but on the other bank, is said to be the cremated remains of Vali. The black- and red-faced monkeys that scamper over the area are popularly considered to be the descendants of Vali and Sugriva. The hills of rounded rocks which make up the site are even said to be the materials collected by the monkeys to build the bridge to Lanka.

Malyavanta Hill, near the road linking Anegondi with Kamalapuram on the south side of the Tungabhadra, is another significant *Ramayana* site. The temple built high on the ridge here is known as Kishkindha Kshetra Venkatapura. Within the temple enclosure is a natural cleft with a well used by the priests and several holy men who live here. Another similar cleft is seen outside the enclosure. The *Ramayana* connection is confirmed by the images of Rama together with his brother Lakshmana and his wife Sita sculptured onto a boulder inside the sanctuary. The spot is believed to be where Rama and Lakshmana waited while Hanuman searched for Sita. It was here that that Rama heard the news of his father's death, and needed water to make a prayer. Lakshmana drew his bow and fired an arrow; where the arrow landed, the rock miraculously split to reveal drinking water. Carvings on the outer walls of the complex depict all aquatic creatures, both natural and fantastic. The hill is also inhabited by screeching hordes of monkeys and flocks of noisy green parrots.

Religious Buildings (Figures 6 and 29)

According to the 1990 census, there is a total of 54 religious buildings in Anegondi. The places of worship listed here demonstrate the variety of religious architecture in and around Anegondi. Because of the turbulent history of the village, many of these temples and shrines date from different periods; indeed, several are built of blocks assembled from different periods. This list given here is not intended as an architectural survey, such as that given in Sugandha (1986: 133-237).

Ranganatha temple (Figures 29.A, 30 and 31, Plate 21)

This is the largest and most important temple still in worship at Anegondi. It houses Vishnu reclining on the serpent, the family god of the rajas of Anegondi. The priest says that many pilgrims from outside the village also come to pray here. The inner sanctuary of the temple, which is padlocked, accommodates the principal deities; images and palanquins used during festival processions are kept nearby.

The family of the resident priest maintains the inside of the temple, while the outer court is the responsibility of the Secretary of the Mandal Panchayat. The outer buildings beyond the arched gateway to the complex are rented out to Brahmana families. The palm trees in the garden to the east of the temple used to belong to the deities and were maintained by the priests; they were also used as flower gardens for the provision of prayer garlands. The enclosed banana plantation running beside the lower end of the northern Chariot Route used to be a sacred water tank.

Sri Ram Mandir (Figure 29.B)

This temple dedicated to Rama is used by all Hindus of Anegondi. The key is kept with the priest of the Ranganatha who is responsible for both temples. The temple houses images of Sita, Rama, Lakshmana and Hanuman, the last sitting on the coil of his tail.

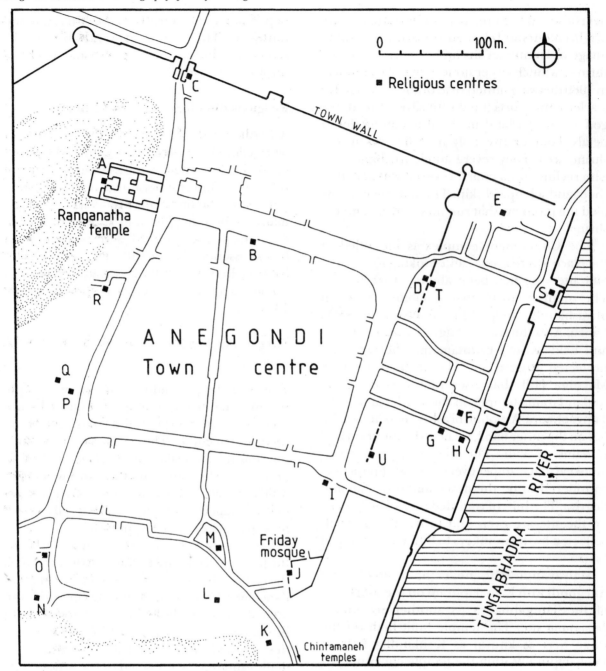

Figure 29. Places of worship and devotion

A	Ranganatha temple	H	Catholic church	O	Thaiyamma shrine
B	Sri Ram Mandir shrine	I	Hanuman shrine	P	Ganapati shrine
C	Koranic school	J	Friday Mosque (Jami Masjid)	Q	Jain temple
D	Hanuman shrine	K	Hanuman shrine	R	Ishvara shrine
E	Awaduth matha	L	Koranic school	S	ruined temple
F	Durgamma shrine	M	Lakshmi Venkateshvara	T	ruined temple
G	Koranic school	N	Malemah shrine	U	ruined temple

Brightly coloured murals depicting stories of the *Ramayana* were commissioned in 1989 by the priest, and painted according to his own designs. *Ramayana* scenes are also found sculpted onto several of the temple columns.

Hanuman shrines (Figure 29.D, I and K)

It is said that there should be four shrines to Hanuman in a village, one in each corner to provide protection for the inhabitants. Anegondi conforms to this model with Hanuman shrines at each of the four corners of the Chariot Route. People visit each of these Hanuman shrines once a week, usually on Saturday. The shrines are each distinguished by a flag-pillar that stands in front. One example faces west onto the Chariot Route; another lies on the road to the Chintamani complex.

Surya Bhagavan shrine

This is situated beyond the modern Hanuman shrine on the riverside eastern Chariot Route. The shrine has enclosed deities facing east, with an old sundial placed on the roof. In the banana cane field below are the remains of an older shrine (T), with polished green chlorite columns.

Awaduth matha (Figure 29.E)

This is no longer used for religious purposes, and is sometimes taken over by squatters.

Durgamma shrine (Figure 29.F)

This tree shrine, with a statue of Basavanna and several snake stones, is situated in the Janata area of the village, near to the Catholic church.

Lakshmi Venkateshvara shrine (Figure 29.M)

This temple is visited by followers of Vishnu.

Malemah shrine (Figures 29.N and 33, Plate 25)

The shrine to this god has a mud wall adorned with flower designs painted onto its inner surface. In 1990, offerings were seen of green bangles and shreds of saris and blouse pieces.

Thaiyamma and Gunlameh shrines (Figure 29.O)

Dedicated to the goddess Thaiyamma, this small shrine stands next to House no.5. Several sets of green bangles and incense sticks are seen here. Nearby is the shrine of the goddess Gunlameh. This simply consists of two stones used for devotional purposes set in the wall of one house. Ceramic votive offerings are placed onto the raised step.

Ganapati shrine (Figure 29.P)

This shrine to Ganesha has an entrance frame of slate, with carvings of elephants either side of Lakshmi. Various incarnations of Vishnu and a peacock are also depicted here.

Ishvara shrine (Figure 29.R)

Frequented by Lingayats, the shrine accommodates a *lingam*, together with carvings of Ganapati and Basaveshvara. It too lies on the western Chariot Route.

Ruined temples (Figures 16 and 29.S, T and U)

A number of disused shrines are found in and around the village. One example within the riverside citadel is often hidden under mounds of straw banked up against its walls. Another example stands in a sugar cane field below one of the Hanuman shrines. Its dark green, polished stone columns stand in a field which was once part of the old gardens of the Ranganatha temple. Yet a further example with the remains of pink granite blocks can be seen in the undergrowth, aligned with the west wall of the citadel.

Kali matha

This temple belonging to the Vaishya caste is seen in the gardens of House no. 46, near to the foothills of Magota Hill. The temple has fallen into disuse and is now overgrown, but may have been in use when the valley between the hills was settled.

The temple is built of roughly hewn blocks, and inside is a large, finely carved Nandi bull, as well as depictions of the goddess Kali and the god Virabhadra. A snake and fish are carved onto a beam. Over the entrance is a

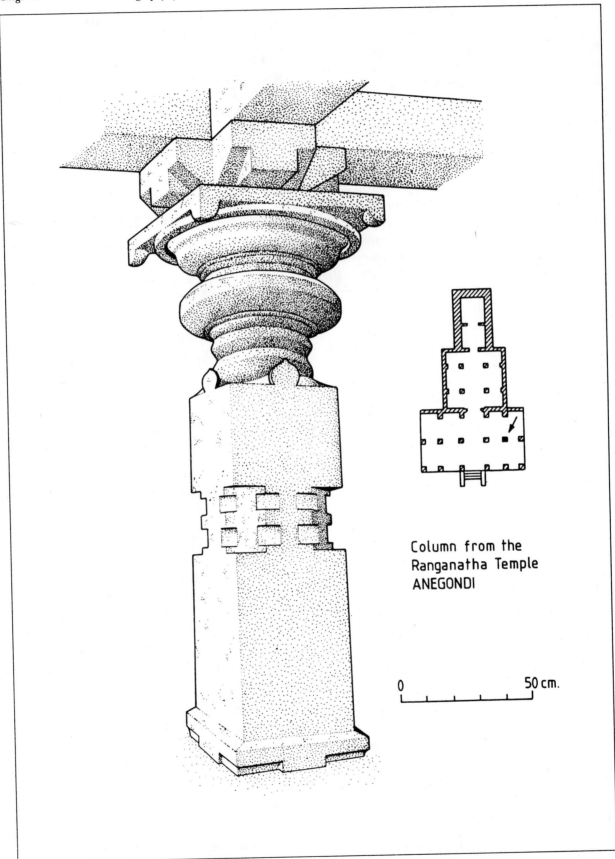

Column from the
Ranganatha Temple
ANEGONDI

0   50 cm.

Figure 30. Column from the Ranganatha temple, pre-Vijayanagara period

Figure 31. Column from the Ranganatha temple, Vijayanagara period

representation of Gajalakshmi, with armed guardians on the jambs beneath. In front of the temple is a well, now covered in vegetation. Here too stands a tall pillar next to which is a block onto which is sculptured a pair of feet.

Uchappaya matha

This ruined structure stands in the banana plantation beside the road leading to the Ferry Gate, but originally may have faced east onto a road (see Figure 6). The structure was once owned by Husain Pompana, who sold it to a resident of Kamalapuram in the 1960s. It may have been used earlier as a residence for accommodating visitors to the area. The *matha* is of interest for the fragments of paintings preserved on the ceiling beams (described and illustrated in Kramrisch, 1937: 105).

Gangamma shrine

Near to the Uchappaya *matha* is the shrine of Gangamma, the deity worshipped by those crossing the Tungabhadra. It is a small white-washed structure with columns carved with birds, ducks and geese.

Durga matha

The newly furbished shrine to the goddess Durga stands by a magnolia tree on the hillside beneath the Magota Hill fort.

Rama Linga Doniy

This small shrine built of bricks and mortar stands on the top of a low rise between Anegondi and Magota Hill. The shrine enjoys a fine view over the valleys on both sides and the lakes. Local people say it was originally a *samadhi*, for beneath the boulders onto which it is built ashes, pottery and human bones were found. The interior walls are smoothly plastered with an egg shell finish; the floor is of concrete.

Boulders to the rear of the building form a canoe-shaped hollow in which water collects during the monsoon, and green plants grow.

Nava Brindavan (Figure 5, Plate 16)

The holy island of Nava Brindavan lies off the eastern bank of the Tungabhadra river at Anegondi, and can be reached only by coracle. Some Brahmanas come every day to pray here. The central *samadhi* is called Padmatirth and is said to be of considerable antiquity. The other *brindavans* are known as Kavindra Tirth, Vagis, Virasarayi, Rama Tirth, Sujendra Tirth, Raghu Wari, Shrinivas and Govinda. One example, said to have been erected by Krishna Deva Raya of Vijayanagara, has a procession of elephants carved around the top frieze. The whole area is enclosed by a low stone wall topped with red brick.

It is the custom to walk around each *brindavan* seven or nine times, chanting all the while, but one must not touch the *samadhi*. Women kneel in front of each one and clasp their hands on a flat stone on the ground. Brahmanas first bathe in the river and then put on a clean *dhoti*.

The *mahal*, a two-storeyed building outside the *brindavan*, is built of stone blocks topped with a plaster balustrade, and has a concrete door frame and floor. This may have served as a shaded place for ritual meals after devotions have been completed. On such occasions, Brahmanas are traditionally served first, then Kshatriyas and others, each group sitting separately.

Chintamani complex (Plate 4)

This complex lies to the south of the village and faces east directly onto the Tungabhadra (see Figure 6). Its various sanctuaries were constructed during different periods, and some are still used today. A more detailed description is available in Sugandha (1986: 178).

Vyasaraja matha

The disused temple, distinguished by its dome-like brick superstructure, is now occupied by peoples who have settled within its walls. The rear wall which once enclosed a covered walkway now provides the spaces for five residences. One still uses the door that may have been the original entrance to the temple's antechamber; the sanctuary, however, is uninhabited.

Jain temple (Figure 29.Q)

This large but dilapidated Jain temple faces east onto the main Chariot Route. The altar stone is

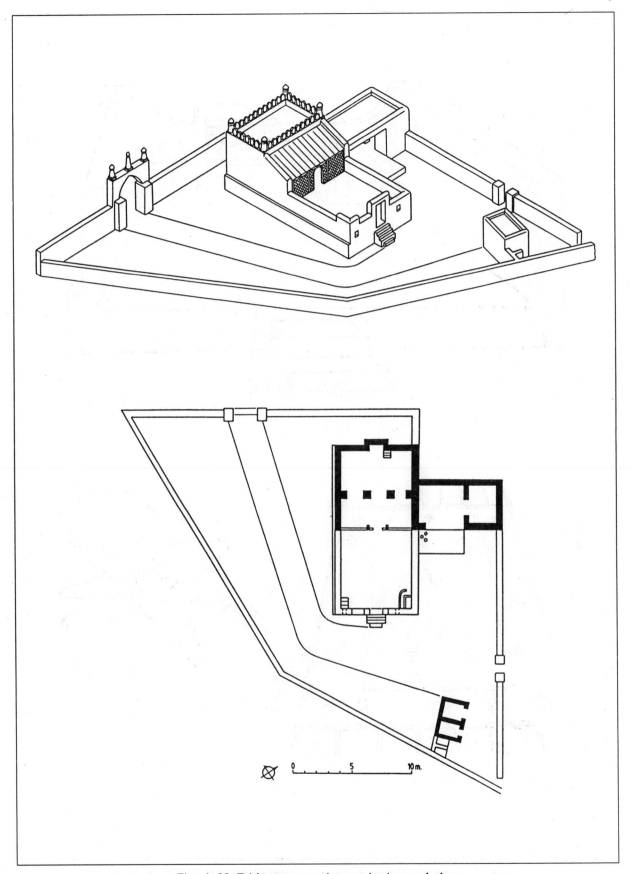

Figure 32. Friday mosque, isometric view and plan

Anegondi: *Architectural Ethnography of a Royal Village*

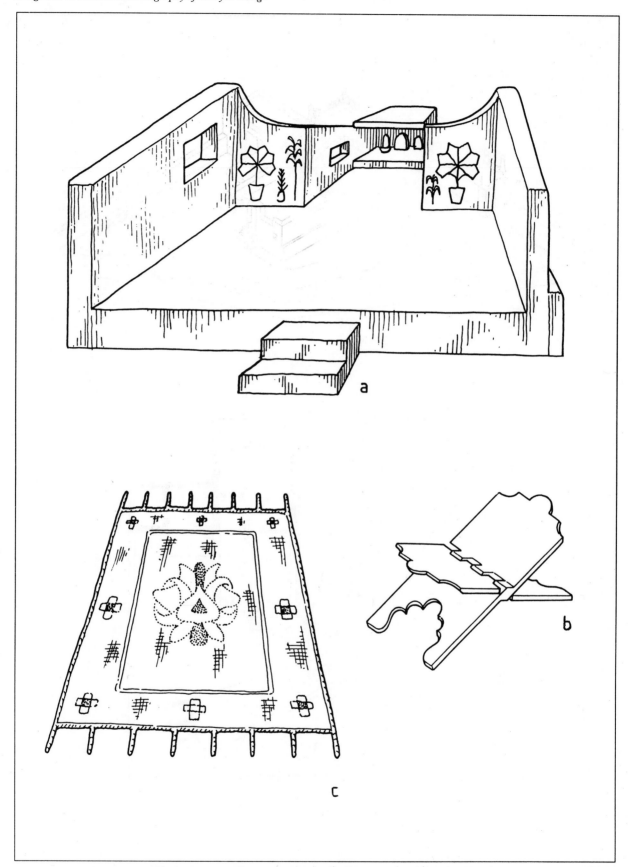

Figure 33. Prayer: a. Malemah shrine; b. Prayer book-stand; c. Prayer mat

58

carved in the form of a lamp, and in the main chamber is a long central drain for ablutions. The temple is constructed of well finished, granite blocks, and has a Sanskrit inscription on one wall dated to 1342. It has long been unused for religious purposes, and a migrant family lives and cooks within its front verandah, though they do not venture into the sanctuary at the rear.

Jami masjid (Figures 29. J and 32)

The Friday mosque in Anegondi occupies a prime location overlooking the river. Many Muslim families live in its immediate vicinity, and the surrounding gardens are well watered. The mosque is painted white and is kept clean, the grounds being regularly swept, and the flower beds and latrines well maintained. The complex is surrounded by a low wall with palm trees at the entrance. There is a painted wooden trellis next to the *mihrab*, also a loudspeaker to call the faithful to prayer. Below the mosque lie the palm groves where the wife and youngest son of Tirumala Deva Raya were cremated.

Koranic schools (Figure 29.C, G and L, Plate 20)

There are two Koranic schools at Anegondi: one is located within Wannagasi Baghilu; the other lies on the pathway leading to Chintamani. The latter is painted white and embellished all over with red dots.

Catholic church (Figure 29.H)

Used by members of the Janata class, this recently built church lies close to the river frontage. Many of the nearby residents are Catholic converts.

CHAPTER 4

Dwellings

Survey Notes

This chapter examines the way space is used in vernacular dwellings in Anegondi. A selection of house types is surveyed, using homes occupied by people from different social and economic groups. Among the types of houses examined are those which are fully designed before construction, as well as those built in an ad hoc manner. The survey assesses the factors which affect house design, choice of building materials and size of plot; they include variables such as wealth, caste, family size and kin relationships.

The chapter takes a brief look at building materials and construction, house design and renovation, followed by an overview of fixtures and fittings, and household artefacts. A catalogue of dwellings follows in Part Two of this monograph where a plan and isometric view of each house is provided. Rooms are labelled on the drawings and the function identified; additional notes describe the fixtures and fittings within. The accompanying text offers additional information about any changes to the structure noted during the period of fieldwork.

It is important to point out that the houses described here were not randomly chosen; the author was mostly dependent on introductions and invitations. A particular difficulty was faced with Brahmana families, many of which were sensitive to the author's visits. Only one Brahmana house (no. 18) is included here.

Construction (Figure 34)

Two main materials are used for wall construction at Anegondi: mud, with a ridge roof, and stone blocks with a flat roof. The different means of construction can, however, be used either on their own, or can be combined. Ridge-roof houses are mostly found along the periphery of the settlement, while stone dwellings are found within the central core. Both types are built on plinths.

Ridge-roof houses

Houses with ridge roofs generally have walls of stone, mud or wattle and daub. Woven screens are made up by the house builder, or can be bought directly from builders' yards in nearby towns such as Hospet or Gangavati. Ridge roofs are constructed of thatch (usually date or coconut palm); supporting poles can either be a palm trunk or a tall stone column notched at the top. The thatch is lashed together using rope of coconut fibre; cross members are of bamboo. Doors can be made of a vertical weave of bamboo strips. These houses may be built on a low plinth of irregular stones (around 10 cm high). Grindstones and depressions for pottery stands set into the ground are coated with cow dung. Floors and house walls may also be coated with a layer of cow dung since this acts as an insecticide by keeping away flies. In some houses, the flow of light is obstructed by a wall to allow privacy in the deepest rooms. Straw houses near Ranganatha temple and beneath Little Magota Hill have small ridge roofs; opening off narrow pathways, they give the appearance of a separate village. Cows are kept beside the dwellings.

If people find an empty plot in Anegondi, they approach the Government Secretary to request permission to occupy and settle the land. The government allocates free of charge a certain size of plot which measures 20 by 30 m, or 30 by 30 m. Inhabitants on the lowest incomes may apply for government grants to help with housing. They would be given a plot and some building materials, and would be able to hire people of the house-building Vaddaru caste for a few rupees a day.

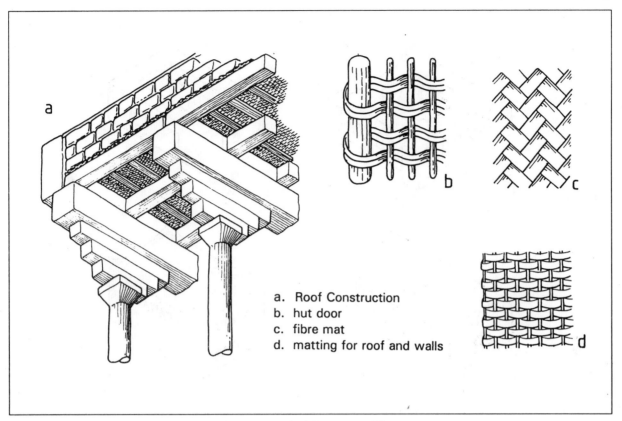

a. Roof Construction
b. hut door
c. fibre mat
d. matting for roof and walls

Figure 34. Building materials

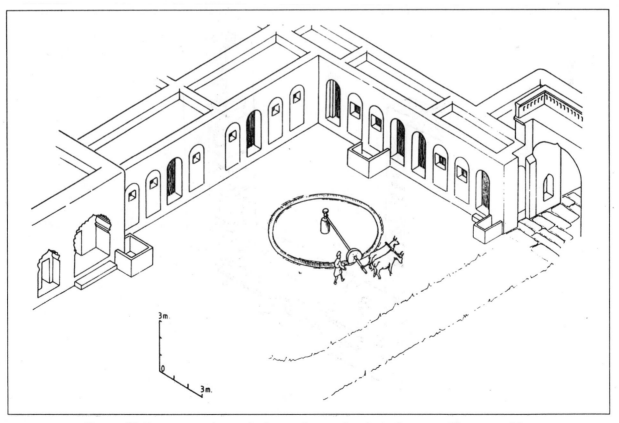

3 m.

3 m.

Figure 35. Reconstruction: grindstone for production of mortar, House no. 50

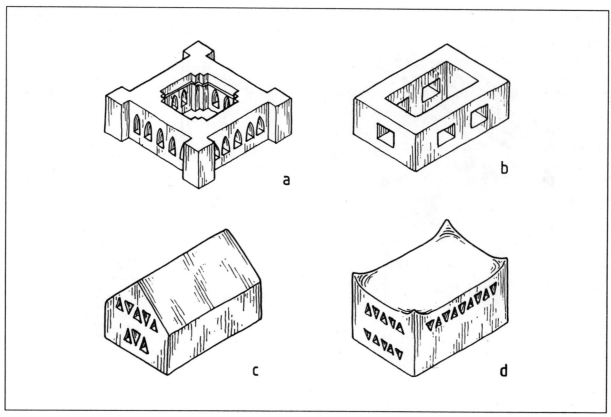

Figure 36. Roof features: a. and b. Skylights, House no. 44; c. Chimney, House no. 48;
d. Chimney, House no. 43

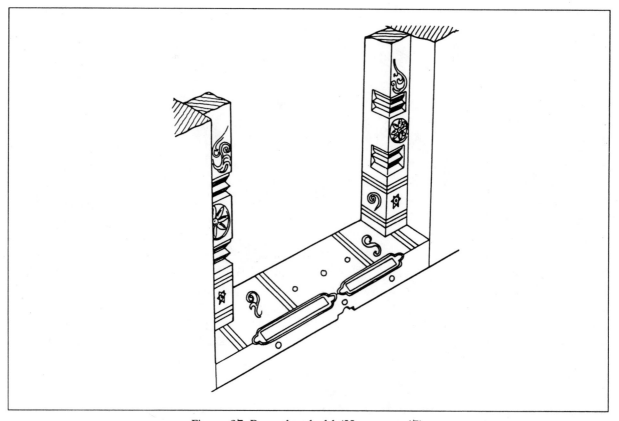

Figure 37. Door threshold (House no. 47)

Stone-block houses

The second group of houses are those within the core settlement at Anegondi. Built of regular stone blocks, they stand on a foundation constructed with two rows of blocks with stone infill, and mud coating. A string is held at each course so that the row can be kept straight. The upper layer is made of blocks added one at a time, with mud poured onto the base so that the block sits on top. Gaps are plastered over with mud. Later, a sand, earth and concrete mixture is added, dampened each day. Spaces for doors (about 50 cm) are left after several courses have been laid. The most frequently used building material is granite taken from surrounding rocky hills. Bare patches there are the evidence of extensive quarrying.

Many of the larger houses that line the Chariot Route are built onto stone plinths rising some 50 cm high. Most of the houses are single storey on a rectilinear plan. As with larger houses, the flow of light from the front to back is sometimes unobstructed, so that from the front entrance one can see right through to the prayer altar at the back. Most larger houses also have a prayer altar on the premises.

The roofs are supported on wooden columns of various designs. A typical example has wooden cross beams, across which lengths of stripped bamboo are placed. Over this framework is a layer of matting, generally either a herringbone or twill weave of palm fronds. Finally, small stone blocks cover the roof, over which a layer of mud is placed.

Mortar production (Figure 35)

House building requires large quantities of mortar and plaster. In House no. 50, the remains of an old circular grinder can be seen in the south-east corner of the garden. It is 3 m from the centre to the trough at the edge. Bullocks had been used to turn the huge stone that ground the mixture. All the ingredients were mixed in a stone trench at the circumference, which was about 30 cm wide and deep. The plaster was composed of lime (to repel insects), sand, sugar cane (*jaggari*) to bind the mixture, and betel-nut (*supari*) which also acted as an insecticide. For the final coating, egg white was added to give the wall a smooth silky finish.

It is customary for floors to be of rectangular granite slabs in larger houses, or of irregular slabs in smaller ones. Walls are usually whitewashed or covered in a layer of cow dung. Often the base of the walls is picked out with a painted red line. Concrete floors are embellished with incised patterns; large diamond shapes coated with a haematite slip and polished, are popular.

House Design

Architectural treatises, known as *shastras* and available in the local Kannada language, give directions on how a house should be designed and constructed. In practice, such suggestions are only followed by those who are aware of them and who can afford them. Occupants of dwellings who are experiencing family, health or wealth problems may from time to time seek the advice of a skilled specialist known as a *vastushilpi*.

In December 1991, the author met one such specialist, G.V.R. Raju from Bellary. He was originally a school teacher, but later worked only as a practitioner advising others on the design of their homes, offering suggestions for rectifying layouts that have caused unhappiness or unease. Such a practitioner can tell from a house plan that there is stress within and would advise that a room's position be altered, or a window or door opened or blocked up. A few examples of his advice are give here.

A house with an unsymmetrical ground plan or a place built in an ad hoc manner is said to promote disharmony among the occupants. A house built in the shadow of a hill is suitable for Kshatriyas since they are warriors, but not for those of other castes. If there are not windows on both sides of the front door, there may be eye trouble for the owner. There should be no pole in front of the door, since this will mean quarrels or financial troubles. Properties should be rectangular or square, with plans worked out according to the points of the compass. No dwelling should ever be built outside the alignments of the cardinal points. The threshold is the most important part of the house, the so-called 'lion doorway' over which everything enters and leaves. Traditionally, it should face east. The house should be in the south-west corner of a plot or compound, with the maximum open space always reserved for the east and north.

The roof should be flat, or may be raised at the south-west corner, and low to the north-east corner. A well should only be in the extreme north-east corner. The flow of water should be from the north-east corner. Doors should be to the north or east of the corners of a house. The door in the middle must open to the north or the east. There should only be an even number of doors; in a large house the number of doors should not add up to 10, 20, etc. It is auspicious for the doors to align since this allows light to flow unhindered through the dwelling. The kitchen or fireplace should be in the south-east corner, whereas the prayer room should be in the north-east corner. The bedroom should be in the south-west part of a house. Even if the dwelling consists only of a single room, the bed, hearth and prayer shelf should be correctly located. The store room should be situated in the north-west corner of a house. The west side of the house is suitable for a staircase ascending to the top of the roof.

In a house laid out as a square of nine rooms, the central space may be used variously. It may have a skylight and a water basin, though this is sometimes considered inauspicious. If there is a construction in the south-east corner, then bad things will happen to the occupants. However, it is not considered good if the west side of a plot is open, and construction should take place on that side. If the south-east corner of the house projects outwards, this too is bad. In one case, where the occupants built a master bedroom in the south-west corner, great success came to the owner. This plot is also considered suitable for an office.

Local people say that the residence of Achyuta Deva Raya (House no. 44) was designed in such a way that those who lived in it would never have offspring: the well was in the wrong place, and the covered area to the east should have been open. In fact, the last three generations of the royal family of Anegondi have died without issue, and have had to adopt an heir for the monarchy to continue. People believe that Achyuta Deva Raya has been blessed by offspring only because he now lives in Hospet and is thus not adversely affected by the unfavourable design of his Anegondi dwelling.

House Rituals

Moving-in ceremonies

The house moving-in ceremony takes place at an auspicious moment determined by learned men (*pujaris*) who select the precise time for going in through the front door. Such specialists are present to perform the ceremony. Prayers are offered to the deities of the family and the individual, as well as to Lakshmi, the goddess of prosperity. A copper pot (*kalasha*) filled with a coconut, betel leaves and other items is used in prayer to represent Lakshmi herself. The ceremony may last for up to two hours, during which time the coconut is broken and the flowers offered to the deities. This ceremony is considered so important that houseowners sometimes send out invitation cards for people to attend.

Certain rituals are required before a new house is considered habitable. These may be in the form of a ceremony to install a small flat metal image of a deity beneath the threshold of the entrance door. Known as *vastu puja vigraha*, such amulets can be purchased in shops in Hospet which sell general household goods. Taking the amulet, the priest sprinkles holy water on it and makes a blessing for a ceremony at a newly built house. Another type of amulet, a *thaiyata*, is a talisman which contains sacred texts. These are written by the *pujari* and used by the house occupants as protection against sickness or bad luck. After being informed about the specific problem, the priest defines the auspicious moment for preparing the amulet. A third type of amulet is buried in the foundation on construction of the front door (or lion's entrance). Known as *navadhanya* or *lowhas*, this is made of five metals, and is installed together with nine different grains (for example, black gram, green gram, channa, rice, sesame and wheat), each of which is said to represent one of the planets. People also offer grains to the priest when he makes prayers for departed souls. In the past, goldsmiths used to make amulets for houses: but now objects are machine made in blocks. It used to be a personal mission (*tapasya*) or penance to make artefacts, but now people only do it for money. Patrons have found it more difficult to commission such objects since craftsmen require enough time and the correct

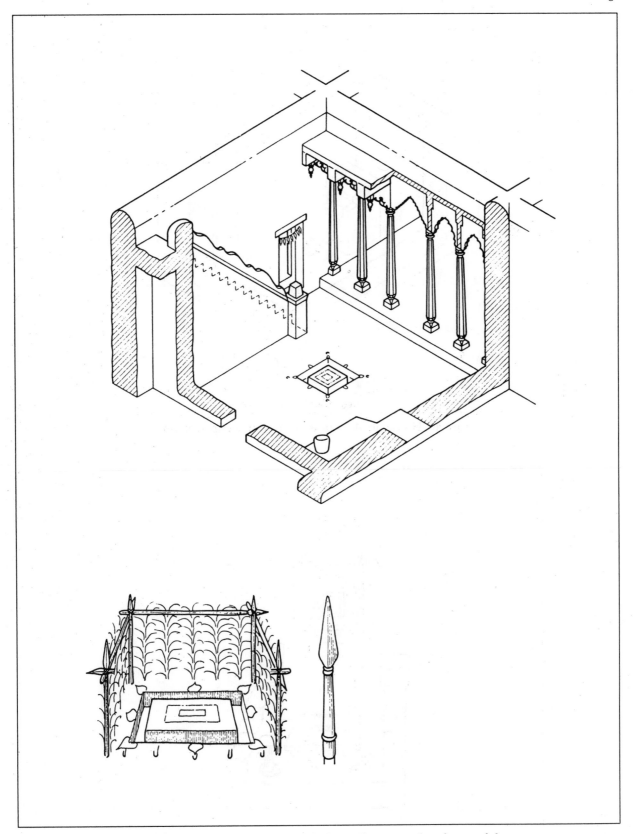

Figure 38 (above). House no. 46: Central courtyard and verandah
Figure 39 (below). House no. 46: Central basin with spears for post-birth coming-out ceremony

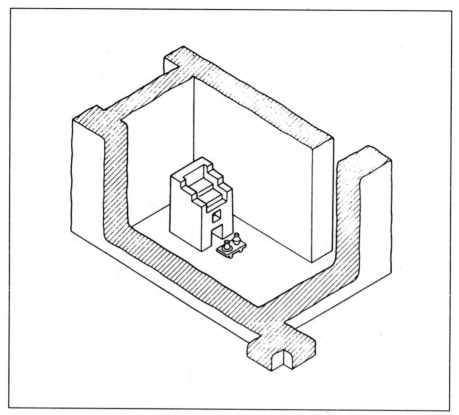

Figure 40. House no. 46: Prayer room with stepped stand

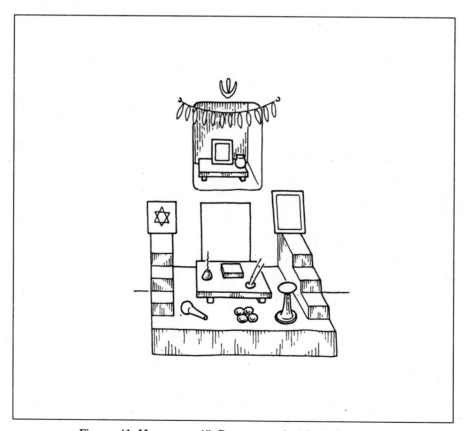

Figure 41. House no. 45: Prayer stand with niche above

metals, and the skills are fast disappearing. Today, craftsmen are not rigorous in their use of the five metals, and are using anodised aluminium which is not considered as efficacious.

In 1991 the author attended a ceremony to lay the foundation stone at the old magistrate's house (no. 51). A *vastushilpi* was consulted who recommended a time after 10.30 a.m. as the most suitable. The ceremony was held between the north and east corners of the site where a trench had been dug and where the local priest said some prayers. It was a small gathering attended by a local politician and several government officials, with a photographer recording the occasion. The ground was cleared with an adze. The priest of the Ranganatha temple performed prayers and made offerings of coconuts, bananas, *pan* leaves, dates, areca nuts, flowers and coloured rice. These items were set out on two dishes, together with red and yellow *kumkuma*; another copper dish contained burning camphor. One small stone block was placed on the ground, onto which coconuts were smashed, and over which milk was poured. Rice was thrown on the ground, flowers were placed here, a bell was rung, burning camphor flames were waved around, and incense sticks were lit. The men clapped, the blessed fruit was handed out, and then everyone left the site.

Renovations

Full house cleaning is done once a fortnight, on new moon or full moon days. Whitewashing is carried out for special occasions, as are the elaborate *rangoli* designs. It is said that rich people can have a tiled floor, but even the poorest person can have a fine floor decoration of ephemeral patterns. Saturdays are considered good for washing areas of the house and making *rangoli* drawings, especially if there is a forthcoming celebration such as a wedding.

House renovation takes place at particular times of year, depending on the pride of the family. Some people whitewash inside and outside their house at the time of the new moon, the Chariot festival, or a wedding. Some Hindus and Muslims place crossed branches containing prayer marks of red and white in the doorway. Muslims flick a mixture of flour or lime and water over the walls to purify their dwellings, particularly if a death or something inauspicious

has happened. Some people use cow's urine to wash the walls since it is known to kill bacteria. Cow dung is also used to smooth the floor surface of yards and courts. This task is generally performed by women every morning and evening, and after making *rangoli* designs as an offering to the sun.

During house construction, in many cases no mortar is used between the stone blocks so that it is possible for house occupiers to modify the layouts of their dwellings. They remove walls and add doors, but do not demolish the entire structure.

House Typology (see diagram p. 88)

Domestic dwellings in Anegondi have been classified into five main types; however, this statement immediately needs qualifying since these house types are not rigid. Though a dwelling may fit into one particular category when one first observes it, several months or years later, the occupants may modify it. The passage of time can affect the category a house is placed in. As the personal and financial circumstances of home owners change, they may make alterations. However, social and other practical factors mean that houses of one type do not automatically develop into those of another. Furthermore, there exists an intermediate group of dwellings which has little symmetry of design. Such houses are probably constructed at different times during the occupants' life, and are made up of a series of rooms or dwelling spaces that has accumulated in an ad hoc manner. Such houses have been fitted into one of the five main categories where appropriate. Dwellings of Types A and B are usually built of more ephemeral materials, and are constructed at the periphery of the settlement. Those of Types C, D and E are usually stone built, and are found within the core settlement of the village. They are more urban in character, more typical of a built-up environment.

Type A: House nos. 1 to 6

These individual single-cell dwellings are usually free standing, without any walls adjoining the adjacent property. They may have a ridge roof of thatch, with walls of wattle and daub, or of stone covered with mud. Interiors consist of a one-room space which is multi-functional and they have one door. The single-cell dwelling is for certain groups of people at Anegondi the first type of house built on marriage, or when they first move to an area.

Over time, such houses are often extended as wealth and circumstances permit. Interior doorways may be aligned to allow the passage of light through the house, or they may be set in a position to obstruct sight of the innermost room, thereby creating privacy. Although such houses retain a single entrance doorway, an extra two or three rooms may be added: for example, a sleeping platform built onto the front of the house may be extended, then roofed over, and finally walled in, with a doorway facing onto the street. Local government officials often regard this process as a form of encroachment onto streets and footpaths.

Type B: House nos. 7 to 13

This type consists of two or more adjoining single-cell, multi-functional spaces, each with its own door. They may stand freely within a common yard, or may share walls with an adjacent property. House nos. 11 and 12 have separate bathing areas for the families of two married brothers, each of which lives in a discrete, multi-functional room. Such dwellings are often the result of the growth of families who are able to take advantage of free land beside their homes as it becomes vacant, or as they obtain money to finance an extra plot. Some houses also incorporate cattle byres. Like Type A, such houses have a thatch ridge roof on walls of wattle and daub, or of stone covered with mud.

Type C: House nos. 14 to 24

This type consists of a flat-roofed dwelling with a single door, one room space wide, with walls of mortared masonry. Such houses usually share walls with an adjacent property, and may at first have been built as extended single-cell houses. Sometimes the rooms are partitioned, and the smaller dwellings are occupied by nuclear families. Though the plans of these houses appear to be similar to those in Type A, they are more the product of compact urban settlements. The dwellings may be extended with the addition

of two or three rooms, though the single entrance is generally retained. House nos. 14 and 15 are multi-purpose dwellings, and may have been store rooms or guard rooms attached to the adjoining House no. 50. Larger houses have skylights and arched fireplaces; House nos. 16 and 17 have steps up to the roof.

Although their situation is unusual, houses with concealed entrances (nos. 21 and 22) also fit into Type C, as single-cell extended dwellings. Likewise, House no. 23, which was enlarged during the period of the author's fieldwork, has little symmetry of layout or design. House no. 24 also fits into this category, although it somehow acquired a room from within the space of the adjoining property.

Type D: House nos. 25 to 37

Dwellings of this type are two rooms across, several rooms deep, and may have a passage or hallway. They may be enclosed in a walled garden. Some examples have little symmetry of design, as in House nos. 38 to 43.

Smaller dwellings in this group usually have a single entrance leading to two rows of two rooms wide (such as House no. 25). In the larger examples with two rows of five rooms (such as House no. 30), rooms are used for single functions, such as food preparation, bathing and sleeping, and there may be two entrances (House nos. 28, 30 and 31). House nos. 25, 26, 28, 31 and 37 have multiple rows of two rooms, while House nos. 27, 30, 32 and 33 have a passage or hallway running between the rooms. House nos. 34, 35 and 36 are enclosed within a walled garden. Some homes have polished concrete flooring decorated with geometric shapes in red.

House nos. 28 and 37 accommodate cattle within the property; occupants must walk through the water buffalo byre before reaching their living space. In these case, the cattle byre is part of the occupants' living space. Features and artefacts indicating that cattle shared accommodation inside houses in past times can be seen in a number of other dwellings.

Intermediate type dwellings: House nos. 38 to 43

Among the larger dwellings, there are some with little or no symmetry of design, either

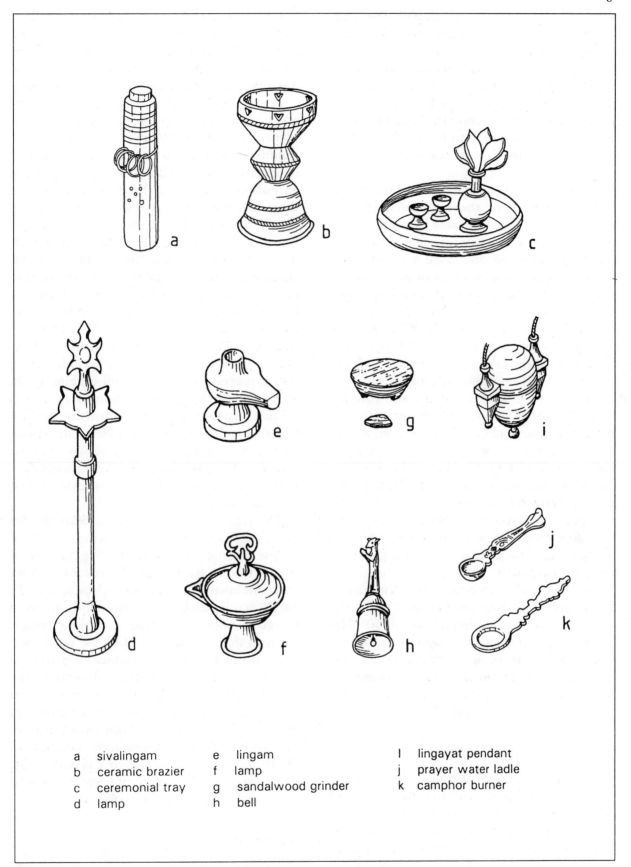

a	sivalingam	e	lingam	l	lingayat pendant
b	ceramic brazier	f	lamp	j	prayer water ladle
c	ceremonial tray	g	sandalwood grinder	k	camphor burner
d	lamp	h	bell		

Figure 42. Artefacts of prayer

within the house or the overall plot. They may have been built up in an ad hoc manner. Some houses consist of up to four rooms added to a property when space becomes available, or as wealth or circumstances permit. They are most frequently found within Type D. Some are built on irregular shaped plots of land and have been extensively modernised, with the new building work sometimes incorporating the older structures.

Within the intermediate type are houses with concealed entrances: these are dwellings with more than one entrance used by people other than the occupants to pass through into another dwelling. House no. 38 is used as a concealed entrance and would perhaps fit into Type D, except for its lack of symmetry. This is probably the result of its central rooms being used as a passage by other members of the Kshatriya caste in order to cross from one side of Anegondi to the other without using the main routes. House nos. 39 and 40 would also probably fit into Type D, though their interior rooms and exterior spaces have been greatly modified and extended in the last couple of decades. The same is true for House no. 41, with its unusual modern hall extending the full width of the dwelling. House no. 42, the largest of Type D, has been considerably modernised by the present occupants. Two rooms had been used as a shop and store room before being converted into a living space. The houses of this last group all have two entrances.

House no. 43 is unusual in that three of its rooms appear to have been created out of the space taken by the mansion (House no. 50). The thickness of the walls would appear to confirm this, though the present occupants have no memory of this. House no. 43 has a room overlooking the entrance, similar to the guardrooms found in the houses of Type E.

Type E: House nos. 44 to 50

The mansion houses that constitute Type E are the largest in Anegondi. They may consist of three or four rooms across, and between four and seven rows of rooms deep. Some have aligned doors and windows, and several examples are laid out around a central courtyard with a water basin. The dwellings may contain from nine to more than 20 rooms, each with a discrete function. In nearly every case, the dwellings have two entrances: a front door onto the street, and a back exit used by those wishing to be discreet. The group of houses includes the dwelling of Achyuta Deva Raya (House no. 44).

Houses of Type E were either planned by architects, or drawn up according to the *shastras*. Houses nos. 48 and 49 have aligned doors and windows, intended to permit the free flow of light through the dwelling. Both examples have an enclosed garden at the back; in each case these had been used partly as a water-buffalo byre. Other houses (nos. 45 to 47, and 50d) are based on a square design. The core of such dwellings is a group of between 9 and 12 rooms arranged around a central courtyard or verandah with a central stone basin, above which is a skylight. In each case, a well is built within the enclosure walls. The pattern of room use is clear, with the deepest room used as a kitchen. Other spaces within the square include dining room, prayer room, buttermilk-making room and child-birthing room. In two examples (House nos. 44 and 45), the front of the dwelling has a second series of rooms facing the street; these may have been inhabited by soldiers or guards in the past. Recently, these rooms have been used as granaries or as extra living accommodation.

The ruined palace (House no. 50d) also fits into Type E, and it is possible that the set of three rooms which constitute House 50e functioned as guard rooms at the front. The palace structures and administrative buildings (House nos. 50 and 51) currently have little overall symmetry of design. However, an analysis of their layouts suggests that at least part of House no. 50 was made up of a series of coordinated spaces. At present it is difficult to distinguish between the sets of rooms, especially since the property has recently been divided up into separate dwellings and rented out. (A more detailed assessment of the division of space is given in the catalogue of House no. 50.) Little remained of House no. 51: when first recorded, much of it was in ruins; by 1993, it was completely demolished.

Occupancy

A number of variables affects the size and type of houses, as is clear from the chart correlating house type, caste and occupation (see

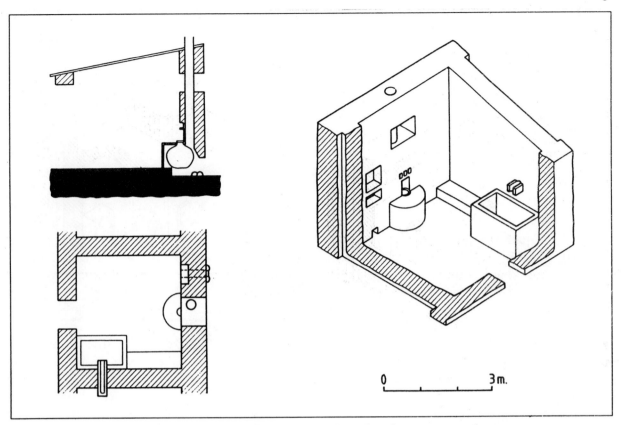

Figure 43. House no. 46: Bathroom, with enclosed copper water heater

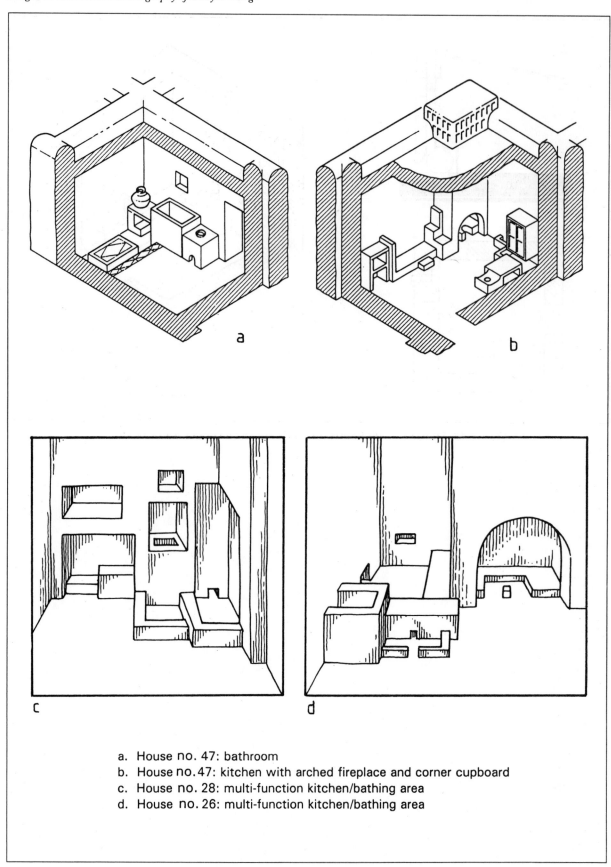

a. House no. 47: bathroom
b. House no. 47: kitchen with arched fireplace and corner cupboard
c. House no. 28: multi-function kitchen/bathing area
d. House no. 26: multi-function kitchen/bathing area

Figure 44. Internal house features

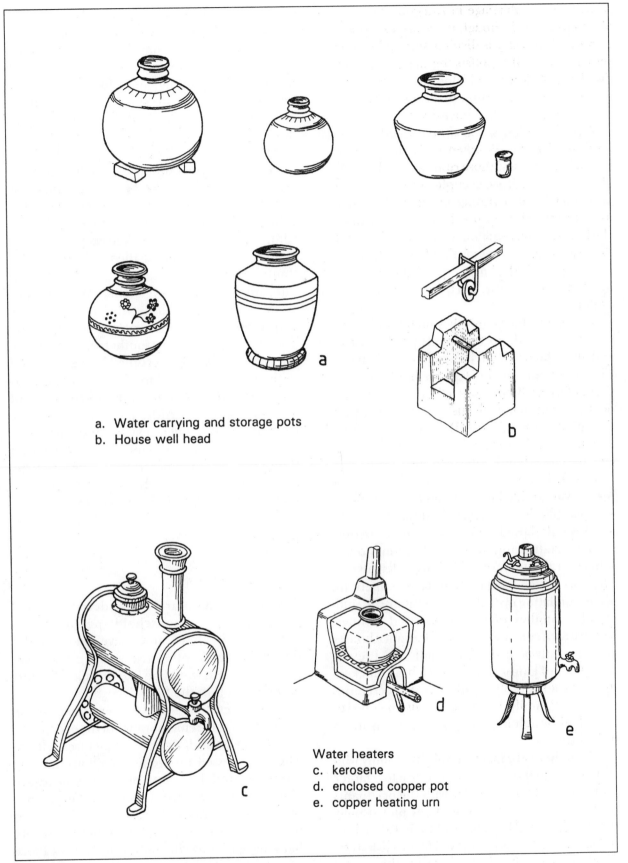

a. Water carrying and storage pots
b. House well head

Water heaters
c. kerosene
d. enclosed copper pot
e. copper heating urn

Figure 45. Domestic water: supply and heating

Appendix 1). Marriage in Anegondi is almost always patrilocal, though there are exceptions. Land and housing is divided among brothers, though quarrelling offspring may subdivide a dwelling, blocking off old doorways and opening up new ones. Kinship diagrams for house occupants is given in Appendix 2.

Type A dwellings, the simplest and smallest kind, tend to be occupied by farm labourers, house builders and those running market stalls. Houses of Type B are occupied by people of the same social and economic group, with perhaps more funds at their disposal, such as government clerks and administration workers. They include Bedarus, Kumbararus and Vaddarus, as well as Lingayats and Muslims. Type B dwellings are located around the periphery of the core settlement.

Type C dwellings, mostly situated within the core of Anegondi, are occupied by various castes and all social levels, including many Kshatriyas. The occupants of this type of house are not particularly well-off financially, including those of a Brahmana family (House no. 18). In contrast, the inhabitants of Type D houses are mostly Kshatriyas and Chetabanajigerus: they include land owners, administrative officers and a doctor.

Type E houses are also nearly all owned by Kshatriyas and Chetabanajigerus. Dwellings with aligned doorways and windows are usually architect designed, and occupied by people of high status and wealth. Mansion houses with central courtyards all belong to Kshatriyas. They are extended family houses, sometimes accommodating up to three generations, including the families of several married siblings. Kshatriyas occupying concealed entrance houses are all relatives of the Anegondi raja. Present occupants of House no. 43, which has a blocked-up doorway to no. 50, are advisors and secretaries to the royal family. House no. 50 also belongs to Type E although it is composed of many inter-linked spaces.

When there are many people in a family who wish to live together, they may move to a larger plot of land. This is the case with the occupants of House no. 42 who possess a large plot, usually the size occupied by more well-to-do Kshatriyas. In fact, the land was purchased from a Kshatriya family by five Chetabanajigeru brothers, who wanted their families to remain together.

Alternatively, the marriage of a son may result in the house being redesigned to give the younger couple their own rooms. This happened in House no. 40, where the original occupant lives in part of the dwelling, and added extra rooms on the marriage of his son. His original front door now lies in the middle of the present dwelling.

There are no areas of Anegondi that are inhabited by one caste to the exclusion of all others. However, many Muslim families live near to the Friday mosque, and people of the Scheduled Castes live near the river by the Church. Houses of many Kshatriya and Banajiga families are located along the southern Chariot Route, while Brahmanas tend to be situated within or near to the Ranganatha temple. Bedaru and Vaddaru groups have settled at the northern and southern outskirts of the village. The dwellings facing onto the southern Chariot Route are said to have been occupied by those related to the royal household in the past; today, however, they are occupied mainly by Kshatriya and Madigaru families. Although since the 1940s Brahmanas have been leaving Anegondi, selling off their land to others, the north Chariot Route is still remembered as the street of the Brahmanas. Significantly, it leads from the Ranganatha temple down to the river.

Facilities

Entrances (Figure 37)

Respectful behaviour is considered essential when entering a household: people always remove their shoes and leave them at the threshold. To do otherwise would cause great offence, since it would be like bringing the dirt of the street into the house.

It is the custom for house entrances to be used as the site of remembrance of the occupants' ancestors. Garlanded photos or pictures of those who have passed on are arranged around the doorway. Model replicas of a cow's head are placed above the front door for auspicious purposes, together with leaves from the mango tree which are threaded together to create hanging garlands. In numerous houses there are also small niches at ground level just by the entrance door, where people leave their

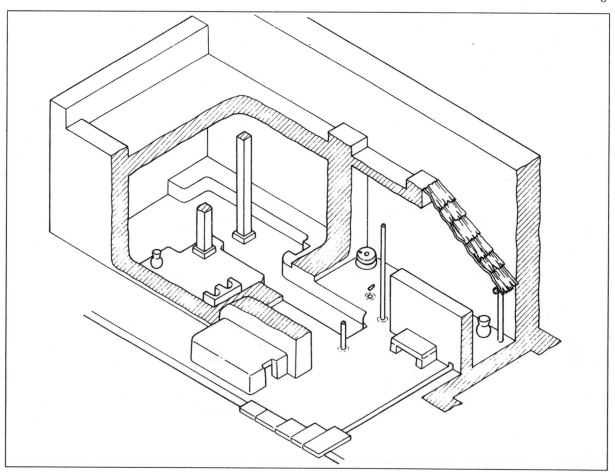

Figure 46. House no. 15: Multi-function dwelling adjoining House no. 50

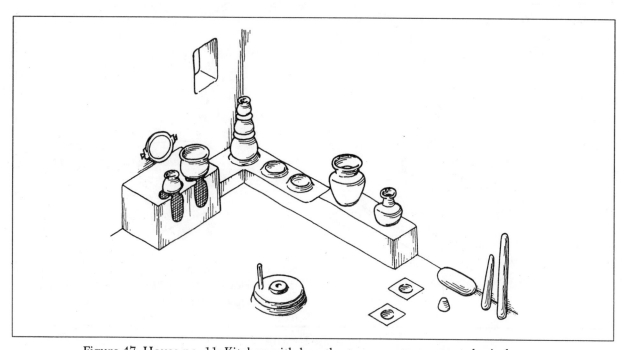

Figure 47. House no. 11: Kitchen with hearth, storage pots, quern and grindstones

Figure 48. House no. 44: Fireplace, with arch and chimney above

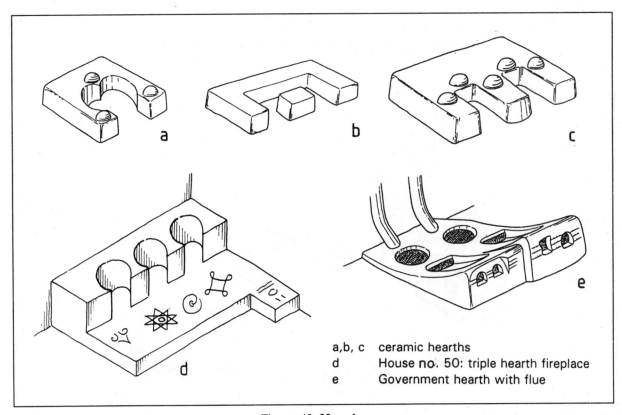

a,b, c   ceramic hearths
d   House no. 50: triple hearth fireplace
e   Government hearth with flue

Figure 49. Hearths

footwear. In smaller dwellings, such niches are used for chicken coops and are blocked at night. Often the front doorway frame is painted with red pigment and embellished with *rangoli*. In mansion houses, the threshold and door frame may be of finely carved wood. In larger homes, people sometimes step over and not onto the threshold when enterting the house, a custom common when visiting shrines.

Ventilation and light (Figure 36)

Houses of types A and B either have no windows, or they have very small ones (less than 30 cm wide) to permit smoke from the hearth to leave. In such dwellings, the ventilation holes are either above the hearth or beside the front doorway. In Type A houses, the front door is often the only source of light and ventilation. Houses of Types C, D and E may have windows, but they tend to be small so as to keep out the heat of the sun. Windows on side walls facing the streets are small, meshed over, and placed high so that privacy is maintained. House no. 46 has no windows at all facing the street; instead, light is obtained from the inner courtyard and from skylights in the roof. Skylights are either round, square or rectangular; those over the central courtyard of mansions like House no. 44 are elaborately designed. Rooftop ventilation chimneys are built over hearths in the kitchens of larger houses.

Private spaces

Larger houses in Types D and E have various levels of privacy, where residents, visiting family members and others can or cannot enter. Some dwellings also have a separate gateway off the main street used by women to enter and leave discreetly. In House no. 48, the male head took up a government position, and altered the position of a doorway into his office so that visitors would not need to walk through the private areas of his family dwelling. In many houses, the front verandah is considered the least private zone: if the entrance door or gate is open, then this area can be observed from the street. Beyond this zone is the inner courtyard or hall, which is where family and friends are received. In many houses, this is considered the main living quarters, where much of the daily social activity takes place. The courtyard is either open to the air, or has a central skylight so that there is sufficient ventilation and the space is pleasantly cool. Some houses of Type C have verandahs, but in those of Types A and B the verandah is usually just a sleeping platform outside the main dwelling, which faces the street. These smaller houses have the least well-ventilated privacy since they lack gardens, courtyards, enclosed yards and open rooftops in which to carry out their daily activities. In most houses, the kitchen and the prayer room are considered to be the most private areas.

Achyuta Deva Raya's mansion (House no. 44) has four levels of audience: the front plinth which is totally public and open to the street; the first courtyard where those seeking a meeting would wait; the verandah reserved for family or close friends; and the central covered courtyard where the residing family eat in privacy, entered by invitation only. Women who visit Achyuta Deva Raya's wife at Anegondi have an audience in the inner hall. Those of certain status are seated on a mat, while others sit on the ground. Separate mats are provided for people of different status, since it is the custom that one should not sit on the same mat as one's superior, unless bidden to do so. When northern Indian female guests visit, they completely cover their head and face when passing through a room where elders are seated. This degree of *purdah* is not expected in the south.

Childbirth rooms (Figures 38 and 39)

Rooms reserved for childbirth are found in House nos. 44 j, 45 h, 46 i and 49 h. During her confinement, the expectant mother stays in a room without light but on the 11th day after giving birth she is allowed to cross the threshold into the light. In larger dwellings with a central courtyard, there is a basin in the middle which when not in use is filled with ash and cow dung, and usually has *rangoli* designs drawn on the top. Inside the drain is a platform made of clay, dung and ash, with a surface design of red squares. This drain or basin is used during the 'coming out' ceremony after a mother has given birth.

During this ceremony, four spears are set into four holes beside the central basin, and another four spears are lashed on horizontally at the upper shafts. Leaves of the coconut palm are hung between to form a wall, and betel-nut leaves are placed at the edges of the drain; the roof is formed of coconut leaves. The whole area is bedecked in flowers, and coconuts covered in cloths are hung from the roof both on the 11th day of confinement and at the time of marriage. Sitting on the central platform of the drain, the new mother washes her arms and legs in the open for the first time since her confinement. Relatives participate in this celebration, and all share a common meal.

Prayer rooms (Figures 40 to 42)

Smaller dwellings of Types A, B or C, with multi-functional rooms, generally have a prayer shelf or niche in a corner which serves as the focus of their devotions. Often the prayer area is in or next to the kitchen, since this too is considered a sacred space. Dwellings of Type D and E have dedicated prayer rooms. Images of deities are displayed on a low plinth, or a series of stepped platforms. Artefacts associated with prayer, such as lamps, bells, incense holders and *kumkuma* pots, are placed nearby. Often the deities are garlanded as part of the prayer ritual; sometimes they are lit by a single bulb. House no. 30 has a 75 cm high stone *lingam* in the prayer room. Muslim and Christian homes also always have an area within the home dedicated for worship.

Sleeping areas

In many houses, whatever the size, there is no sleeping room. People sleep on a mat, covered with a blanket or shawl depending on the season. The choice is between the inner hall, the verandah, the roof, or a platform facing the street. Only some of the larger dwellings of Types D and E have a function specific room containing beds; some have huge double beds made of carved wood.

Bathrooms (Figures 43 to 45)

Dwellings of Types A and B usually have no inner bathrooms; the occupants use an unroofed but enclosed space within the exterior walls of their homes. In other cases, the bathroom is indicated by the presence of rounded stones on

which water is heated outside the house. Inside latrines are of the squat kind, and those who do not have such facilities use the banks of the river or the derelict area within the citadel. If families of two brothers share a common enclosure wall, then there are usually two bathrooms present (House nos. 11 and 12). In homes of Type C, the bathroom is often the same room as the kitchen, the latter having a water reservoir, drain, or a low walled bath with a hole through the wall, as in House no. 44. Type D and E houses usually have single purpose bathrooms where the occupants may heat water by means of electric urns, solid fuel copper pots (the most common in larger houses), or freestanding copper urns.

Kitchens (Figures 44 to 48)

In mansion houses, the kitchen is often the deepest and most private room. Eating is usually conducted in a clear space devoid of features beside or near to the kitchen. The only requirements are small fibre mats on which the family is seated, and which are rolled up when not in use. If the kitchen is a large room, people eat inside. Only the largest dwellings have table and chairs whereby the occupants eat beyond the confines of the kitchen. Preparation and eating of food requires privacy: the author was never permitted to enter a house if the occupants were preparing a meal. Cooking and eating of food involves many proscriptions: food is cooked and served by relatives. Only those of the Brahmana caste cook food in restaurants, though the Lingayat priests also run cafes.

Ideally, women may not go into the kitchen or prayer room for four days during their monthly period. Only on the fifth day, after they have taken a bath and oiled their hair, may they enter the kitchen. In the past, in joint families, women having a period did not touch anything, for if they did no one else would use it. Nowdays, in a nuclear family, if the woman does not work there is no one else to do her chores.

Hearths (Figure 49)

Most households in Anegondi are vegetarian, and have only a single hearth. Several houses, however, have a fireplace for cooking mutton; some larger dwellings have two or three hearths. Older or more devotional members of a

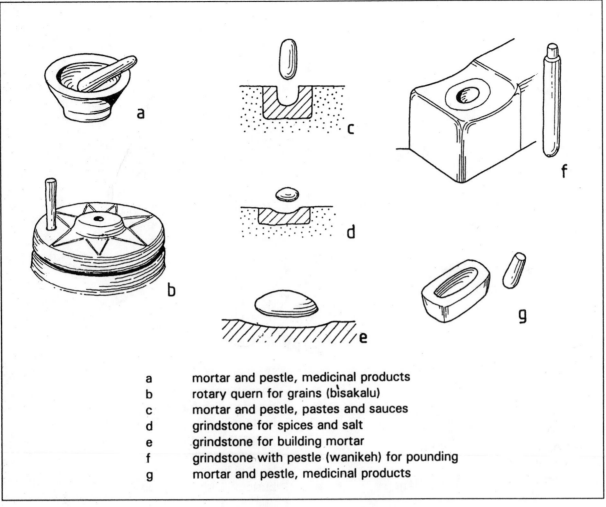

a   mortar and pestle, medicinal products
b   rotary quern for grains (bisakalu)
c   mortar and pestle, pastes and sauces
d   grindstone for spices and salt
e   grindstone for building mortar
f   grindstone with pestle (wanikeh) for pounding
g   mortar and pestle, medicinal products

Figure 50. Grinding equipment

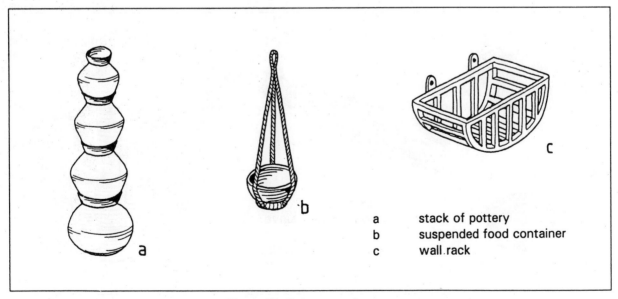

a   stack of pottery
b   suspended food container
c   wall rack

Figure 51. Storage equipment

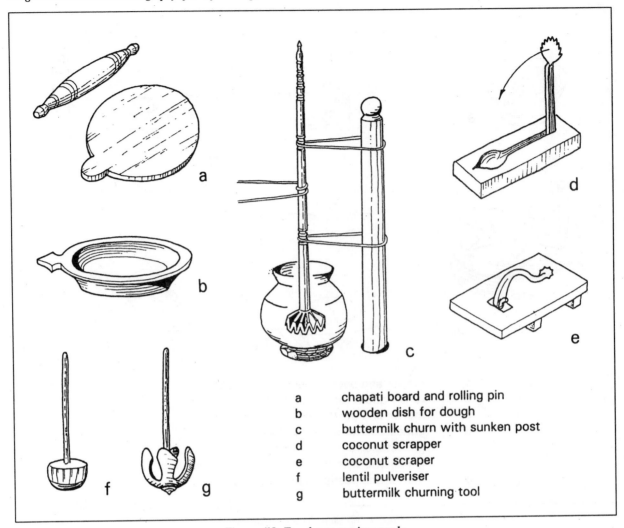

a	chapati board and rolling pin
b	wooden dish for dough
c	buttermilk churn with sunken post
d	coconut scrapper
e	coconut scraper
f	lentil pulveriser
g	buttermilk churning tool

Figure 52. Food processing tools

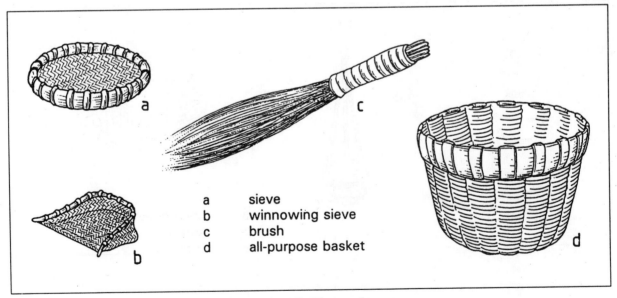

a	sieve
b	winnowing sieve
c	brush
d	all-purpose basket

Figure 53. Fibre tools

household insist that meat cooking must be separated from vegetarian, with its own pots and implements. It is a custom for some members of the Kshatriya caste to eat meat. Some men are partial to meat, and go out hunting in the hills behind the village. Beef is never eaten, only mutton or chicken or wild animals: porcupine is trapped in the hills.

Hearths are of various kinds. Most people have either a clay or ceramic hearth, and use wood or dried cow dung as fuel; some of the wealthier houses have kerosene burners. Ceramic burners are bought ready-made from potters in Kamalapuram, or from itinerant craftsmen who come seasonally to Anegondi with their wares. Hearths are generally installed as fixtures, and in houses of Types C, D and E the hearth is built with a skylight or smoke vent above. Houses of meat-eating people have a meat hearth and separate implements in a different part of the house. In house Types D and E, the cooking area is often set up behind a large archway or an arched chimney. In some of the smaller homes, it is screened from view by a low wall, or a curtain (known as *purdah*). In 1990, when the occupants of House nos. 1, 2 and 3 were shifted to new dwellings to the south of the village, each house had a new style hearth that was supposed to conserve fuel and remove the smoke through the roof. However, the women did not like the new hearth since they could not make bread on it; as a result, they each had a traditional hearth built in the old way.

Grindstones (Figure 50)

Many houses employ grindstones, known by different names according to their functions. In smaller houses, the grindstone is set into the floor as a fixture. The *wanakeh* is used to crush food to a powder or dry paste, whereas the *rubbughundu* is used for wet foods. The shallow *waralu* is used for crushing small quantities of dry spices and salt using an iron beater (*harih*). The *bisakalu* is used for crushing grains, such as sorghum, millet or rice, and has a notched side and is turned with a stick. A *waralu* is used in combination with a *wanakeh* for various purposes: to crush cloves and cinnamon to a dry powder; to crush coconut, garlic, salt and red chilli to a smooth paste; to pound coriander, garlic, salt,

and ginger to a green paste. It is said that coconut crushed with water to a paste takes away strong smells. A deep *waralu* is used with a *rubbughundu* to pound chopped onion and red chilli to a liquid. In the mid 1990s, gleaming electric grinders were available in the same size and shape as a *rubbughundu*.

Kitchen implements (Figures 52 and 53)

Implements found in the kitchens of Anegondi houses include coconut scrapers, vegetable cutters, butter-milk churns, cooking pots, fibre items like sieves and brushes, and wooden *chapati* boards and rollers. A variety of instruments for making sweet and savoury snacks is also used. In the largest dwellings, cooking pots and water pots are usually made of brass or copper: copper purifies water and destroys bacteria, and for this reason it is preferred as a container for holy water in homes and temples.

Ideally, people are very careful about cleanliness and table manners. The right hand is used for eating so the left may be used for serving food. When serving from a dish onto one's plate, one has to take care not to allow the spoon to touch the plate; if it does, it is not put back in the main dish since it would pollute the contents. No one would ever take food from the plate of another. If water is poured into a cup and offered to one person, and declined, it is poured away since it cannot be offered to a second person. Such customs relating to preparation and consumption of food are adhered to rigidly by those of the Kshatriya caste in Anegondi, but other groups may be less rigorous. Earthenware pots are used for water storage, but not for eating off since this would make them polluted, and they cannot be rendered pure, even with another firing. Metal vessels are preferred since these can be cleaned with ashes and water.

The polished surface of stainless steel is ideal for eating off, but a fresh banana leaf is the preferred plate at feasts. On particularly auspicious days it was the duty of the raja to feed people that came to do prayer. In some mansion houses, there are dozens of large brass and copper cooking pots, some so huge that they alone could hold enough cooked rice to feed a group of 50 people. They are rarely used except on occasions of mass prayers and celebration when Kshatriya men serve food cooked by Brahmanas.

Storage (Figure 51)

In houses of Types A and B, people often use the space in the ridge roof for storing bedding from cross beams. In smaller dwellings, people use stacks of ceramic pottery of decreasing sizes to store food items and personal belongings. Often several stacks of these pots, with their bases painted white, are given to a couple as part of their marriage goods. In the kitchens of larger homes, women use wooden cupboards with mesh fronts to keep out insects; unused kitchen wares are hung from metal racks nailed to the walls. Sometimes vessels containing foods are hung from the roofing with rope cradles. Houses with a small room set aside as a granary usually have the door of that space raised 100 cm or more above ground level to protect the area from insects.

Exercise equipment

Among the exercise equipment found in House no. 46 is a huge circular stone wheel for men to put around their necks to strengthen their backs. (This is now displayed in the Archaeological Museum at Kamalapuram.) In the past, men practised wrestling, and wore the wheel around the neck and walked up steps with it on. In several houses, smaller stone wheels are seen; these are to used as arm weights for body building.

Courtyards

In some houses of Type E one can see from the front door through to the sacred altar (*brindavan*) in the garden. People believe that the passage of light should not be blocked; the doors should face another and wherever there is a window then this should aligned with another window or door, so that the light is unobstructed. Only two houses (nos. 48 and 49) conform to this scheme; both are dwellings of high status, wealthy occupants. Many larger houses have a sacred raised garden altar within which grows a *tulsi* plant. Once the prayer rituals inside the house are completed, water from the copper pot is poured over the plant. Eight houses

of Types D and E have wells on their properties; two have water taps. The remainder of the villagers collect water from street pumps, public wells or the river.

Numerous dwellings have cattle byres built immediately outside their homes. In some of the middle sized dwellings, such as House nos. 28 and 37, the occupants have built cattle byres in the front parts of the house. However, this is not thought of as an inconvenience, since the occupants believe it is auspicious to walk through a cattle byre to their living space. Although in other houses, cattle are no longer kept within or just outside the property, shelving and food troughs indicate that this was the practice in the past. If people have a garden attached or within their properties, they plant flowering shrubs. They pick the flowers to use as part of their daily prayer rituals, or make them into hair garlands for women and girls. Only three dwellings (House nos. 34, 35 and 36) were built within enclosure walls.

Concealed entrances

Some houses have an additional entrance which is used by other village people to pass through into another dwelling. Such houses often have land attached, and the light flowing through the dwelling is obstructed. In the past, royal women would observe *purdah* on entering and leaving dwellings. Today this is less rigorously observed: for example, women leaving House no. 50 do so by the front or back exits; they are not required use the discrete side exits any more.

Through the use of concealed entrances to dwellings, a level of privacy can be maintained by royal men and women. Houses occupied by relatives of Achyuta Deva Raya may have once been used as concealed entrances to larger dwellings or palaces, such as House nos. 21, 22 and 38. House nos. 21 and 22 have been built against the back wall of the palace House no. 44, and open into the garden behind that house which has been reserved for their use. House no. 38 is built up against the ruined palace of Narasingamma (House no. 50d), currently used as a passage way for those wanting to cross the settlement without using main routes.

House no. 43 may have been similar to these

examples, since it is clear that there is evidence of a doorway (now blocked up) through that dwelling into House no. 50. House no. 43 is occupied by a family, members of which used to act as advisors to royalty. Their dwelling backs onto the larger central palace, and the rooms in the west wing are actually inside the palace walls. It is possible that these rooms might also have allowed access to the palace without using the street.

a-d   various early defensive walls
e   later defensive wall with rebuild
f   modern domestic

0   1m.

Figure 54. Wall construction

PART TWO

Catalogue of Dwellings

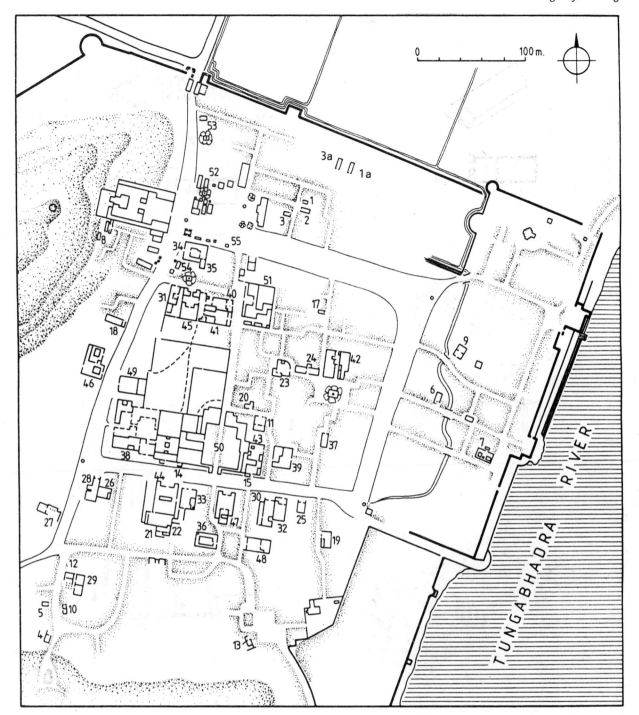

Location map of dwellings

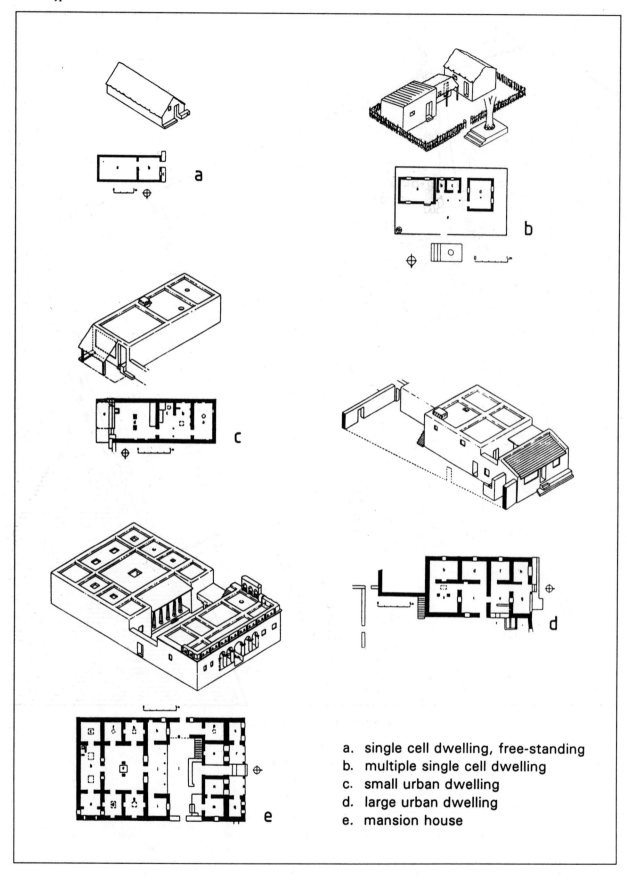

a. single cell dwelling, free-standing
b. multiple single cell dwelling
c. small urban dwelling
d. large urban dwelling
e. mansion house

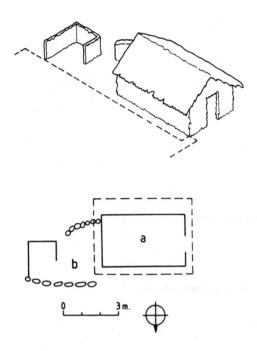

1 a	multi purpose	A newly married couple in thatch house, with a mud hearth to one side, three stone hearth in centre, and a stone bench and water pots.
1 b	yard	Area between houses, enclosed used for washing, front covered with a layer of cow dung.

This small dwelling of 12 sq m, with walls and roof of thatch, stood on the road to the east of the Panchayat building. It consisted of a single room occupied by a newly married couple who had moved there in 1987. Unusually, there was a hearth in the middle of the dwelling, as well as a regular hearth on the side wall. A small enclosed area behind (b) was used as a bathroom. By 1990 the occupants had moved to land elsewhere, and the house was in ruins, being used for storage of bikes, paints and pottery.

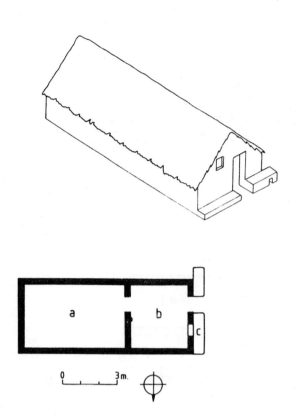

2 a multi purpose   Windowless room with a hearth, stone bench, and a grindstone.

2 b hall   Light coming from door and a single window with prayer shelf by support tree trunk, and a wooden storage stand.

2 c sleeping platform   Outside the house in the open street with a chicken coop beneath. Ground smoothed with dung and *rangoli*.

The original house recorded in 1987 (illustrated above) had a long and low thatched roof with shallow sleeping platforms at the front. It was divided into two rooms and covered an area of 32 sq m which included the verandah. The walls were all of mud, and the occupants said they had been originally built 35 years earlier. Containers hung from the ceiling, and there were many stacks of pots with their bases painted in white. The house was built on a low plinth of stones (10 cm high). Since 1988, the front plinth had been extended to create an area for sleeping and storage (c), and a low stone wall had been added. The thatch roof was supported on low walls, and the front of the house painted white. (see Plate 45)

In 1990 the occupants were asked to move. Their new house (not illustrated) is built on the edge of a banana plantation at the extreme south end of the village. In their new house, is a prayer niche at the far corner next to a raised platform containing water pots. The family has taken out the 'government fire' and installed a hearth of the old kind. A bathing area is located at the back of the hut. The floor is coated in cow dung, the walls are white, and the place is immaculately clean. Pictures and photographs of ancestors are displayed above the front door. The plot available next door is for the occupants of House no. 1 who are at present living with them.

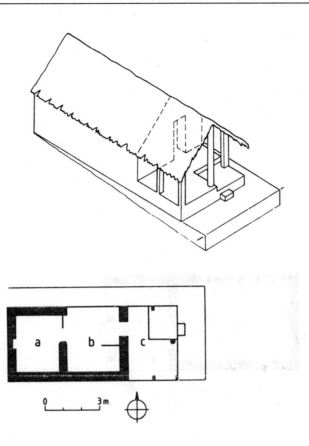

3 a multi purpose   A windowless room with hearth and stored firewood, a prayer niche, stacked pots, bath and drain. It was divided by mud/wicker wall

3b hall   Used for storage: goods in sacks, hanging from the roof, and in stacked pots.

3c verandah   Open on three sides with thatched roof, grindstone, and a sleeping platform.

The original house recorded in 1987 (illustrated above) was a small thatched dwelling of 32 sq m built north of Anegondi centre, and east of the Panchayat building. The dwelling had been constructed on a concrete covered plinth which was polished and had incised decoration. It must have been the floor surface of an older building related to the Panchayat behind. It had a low covered verandah and two back rooms. Part of the wall was of plastered wicker. The dwelling was painted white inside, with a low shelf containing stacks of pots. A depression in the floor served as the bathing area. Foodstuffs were stored in baskets hanging from the roof. One woman in the house worked with school teachers at the local nursery. The back wall was of stone and a mud cement mix and two forked-stone pillars held up the roof poles. The sides were thatch with a mud and stone face, and there was a small shelter for chickens built as part of the later dwelling. (see Plate 46)

The occupants were asked to move in 1990. The new house (not illustrated) is built on the edge of a banana plantation at the extreme south of the village. There, the kitchen floor is slightly raised, and the family stores its bedding in the rafters above the front door. A bathing area is built at the back, and the outside walls of the house are painted white.

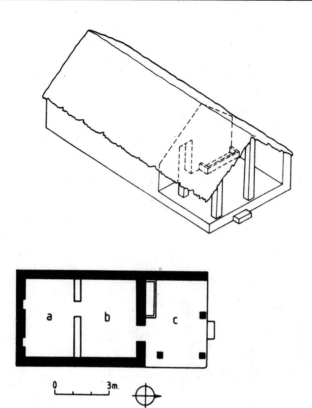

4 a kitchen	A windowless room with hearth, pot stack, prayer shelf, stored firewood (Muslim family).
4 b multi-purpose	Room with huge water storage tank and light from door. Perhaps used as a sleeping area. Entrance is opposite a blank wall.
4 c cattle shed	On a raised plinth with a thatched roof and a food trough.

This small thatched dwelling of 53 sq m is built in an area south of Anegondi, between the roads leading to Talarighat and Chintamani. It belongs to a couple who have converted to Islam who migrated here 20 years earlier from Kosigy in Andhra Pradesh. The house consists of two covered rooms and a verandah. Two huge bullocks (used to pull a cart) tied to the verandah are fed straw in a raised trough. The walls are of stone, the front painted white with a red door. The house is built on a low plinth of roughly hewn stones, and the verandah is covered in a layer of cow dung.

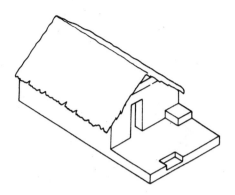

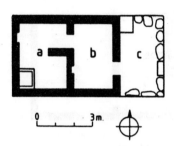

5 a multi purpose   Room with bath, drain, hearth plus raised shelf hidden by a low wall, a prayer niche, and a flat grindstone.

5 b hall   Area with white walls and entrance opposite a blank wall with deep grindstone outlined in white.

5 c verandah   Unroofed sleeping platform, with a chicken coop, and shallow grindstone.

This small dwelling consists simply of two rooms and a verandah. The entrance door faces a blank wall so that light is obstructed, but the privacy of the inner room, the kitchen and store is protected. The hearth and water pots are protected from view by a low inner wall. The house is built on a platform of two rows of stones which extend outwards to create a sleeping platform with a top surface coated in dung (c). The house has a stone façade, painted white, with a red door frame. The stone walls are covered in mud. Ventilation holes exist either side of the door. Sadly, in January 1990, the house burnt down, together with 15 others in two rows of streets. The walls and features remain, though the roof is lost.

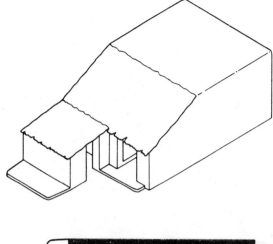

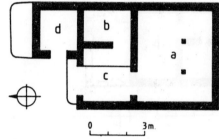

6 a multi-purpose	Room with a hearth, prayer shelf and grindstones.	
6 b bathroom	With a low shelf, and low bathing area.	
6 c hall	With one door to street and a raised sleeping platform.	
6 d kitchen	Having a second hearth, and stacked pots (a second family?)	

This dwelling is situated on a side street leading off the eastern Chariot Route. It covers an area of 58 sq m. The building is made of rough stone blocks, and the walls are plastered with mud and dung. The threshold to the front door is painted red. The house is dark, with no ventilation or light in the back room. The grinding quern is permanently set in the ground. In 1988, the wall that enclosed the kitchen was removed and the area used as a wood store. In 1990, the front wall of the house was removed, leaving a covered area for a cattle shelter with freshly harvested straw piled high on the roof.

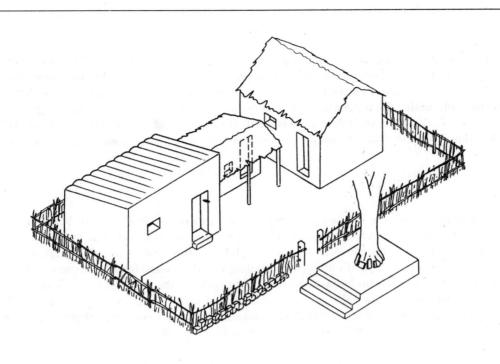

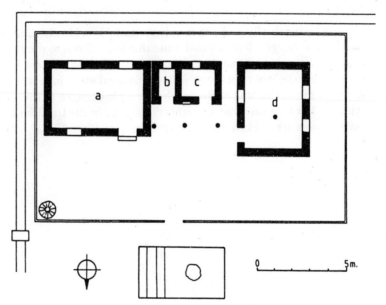

7 a multi-functional   living and sleeping area

7 b bathroom

7 c kitchen   unused

7 d storage room   used as a kitchen and guest room

7 e yard   with chicken coop

House no. 7

The Karnataka Government helped with the construction of this house by giving a 2,000 rupees loan. The family had to build the house foundation, and the government helped with the superstructure. The occupant said that his father came to Anegondi some 50 years back. The family name is Kandagal, which is also the name of the village from which his ancestors come. The house, which measures some 30 by 70 m, is built of stone blocks and then whitewashed. The compound is enclosed with a low straw surround. Outside the house is a tree shading stone images of deities; this is known as the Durgamma shrine.

House no. 8

This house is situated beside the Ranganatha temple in an area called Singer Gunti beneath the foothills which rise above Anegondi. A nearby pond is a quarry for building materials; around it lives a mixed community with different castes. Many households have cattle next to their dwellings. In this family, the eldest brother and his family live in one dwelling (b), the second brother in the adjoining room (c), and a third married brother has a dwelling to the south of the compound (e). The house of their divorced sister (d) has low walls, stone at the front and thatch for the other walls and roof. There is a hearth inside. The other houses are built of stone, the floors are covered with purifying cow dung, and the walls whitewashed and immaculately clean. (see Plate 59)

House no. 9

This south facing dwelling of 124 sq m is occupied by a Muslim family. It is built on a side road to the east of central Anegondi on a small route that leads down to the river. The dwelling is built of stone and has enclosure walls plastered in mud and dung. The entrance which faces the street is coated in red matt paint; the inner enclosure walls are painted with a lime wash. The rear of the dwelling is stone built with a mud brick wall enclosing the yard. One length of the yard is covered by a thatch roof to provide shelter for cattle that are tethered outside by the front wall. The rear room (a) is for prayer. Groups of pots are stacked up in the kitchen. (see Plate 47)

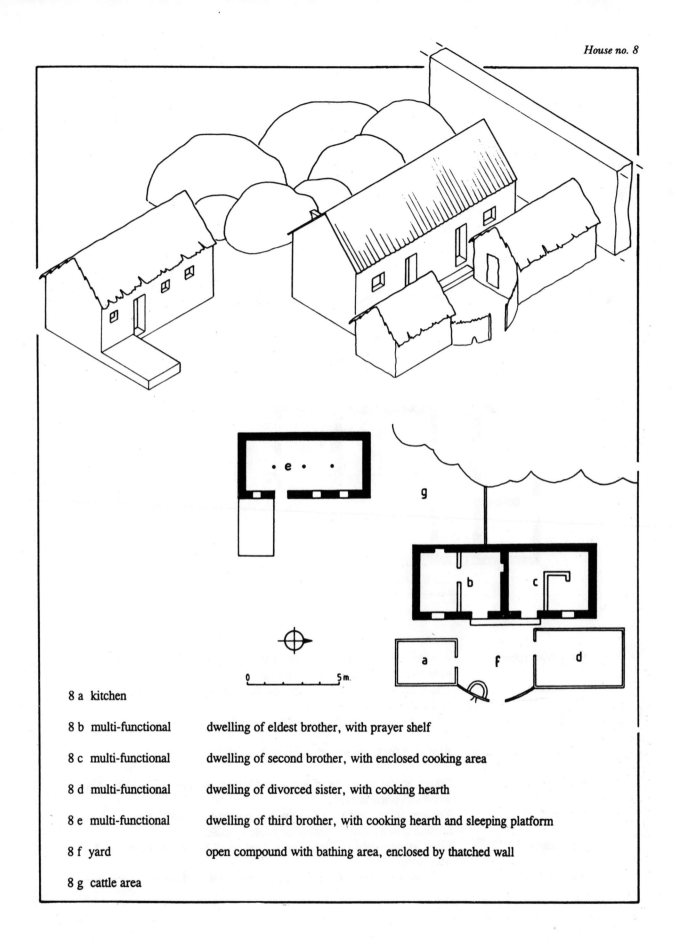

8 a kitchen

8 b multi-functional   dwelling of eldest brother, with prayer shelf

8 c multi-functional   dwelling of second brother, with enclosed cooking area

8 d multi-functional   dwelling of divorced sister, with cooking hearth

8 e multi-functional   dwelling of third brother, with cooking hearth and sleeping platform

8 f yard   open compound with bathing area, enclosed by thatched wall

8 g cattle area

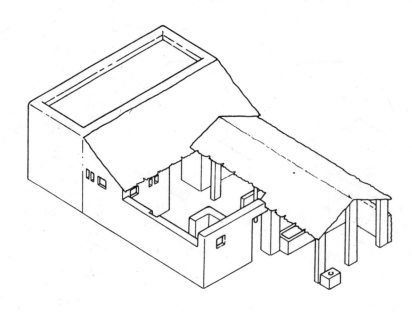

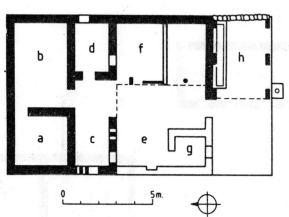

9 a prayer room	A windowless room at the back of the house with a skylight. Entry was forbidden, it was also used for storage
9 b kitchen	The walls are painted white and the floor left brown, it is used for food preparation and storage.
9 c hall	A living space, painted white with a grindstone.
9 d store room	Also used for cooking with a double hearth.
9 e yard	Giving access to whole of house and street, the area by gate used for wood and straw storage.
9 f kitchen	The area is screened with sacking, has thatched roof and a second hearth. Muslim family, outside hearth for cooking meat?
9 g bathroom	Black granite slabs on floor and a third small hearth for heating water, pot present.
9 h cattle shed	Thatched roof with a food trough, beyond outer walls of house by street.

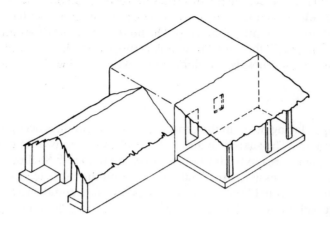

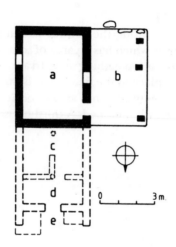

10 a	multi-purpose	Room painted white except by the fire, with a hearth, prayer shelf and light bulb. Stone house on same site as straw (burnt down)
10 b	verandah	Covered with thatch and open on three sides.
10 c	kitchen	room with screened hearth
10 d	living room	with grindstone
10 e	sleeping platform	

House no. 10

Situated outside the settlement centre, between the Talarighat and Chintamani roads, this east-facing house was built by a young couple on the site of a straw house that had burnt down. It is a flat-roofed thick stone constuction, which is unusual in an area where most other houses have thatch roofs. The blocks are whitewashed, and the frame painted red. The house is built on a low plinth of rough stones which are coated with dung to fill the gaps. Stone pillars support the lean-to roof. An addition (c, d and e), built with a government subsidy, has dung covered floor and walls, and a thatch roof.

House no. 11

This dwelling of 135 sq m, facing north in the central part of Anegondi, is occupied by two brothers and their wives and families. The shared verandah (c) is divided into two. There are two open-air bathrooms (d and e), and an area in front where animals are tethered. Shallow and deep grinders are seen here: large shallow holes in the rock slabs are for grinding cattle feed, or sand and mortar. The front wall of this house is roughly constructed, and is covered in mud and dung. The verandah walls are painted white with brown pillars; green vines cover the thatched roof. (see Figure 47 and Plate 52)

House no. 12

The south-facing dwelling is situated outside the central settlement area, between the roads to Chintamani and Talarighat. The house, which has an area of some 60 sq m, is divided into two and is shared by members of one family. It has two bathing areas (d and e). An additional 22 sq m is taken up by a cow shed in front (f). The fireplace in the first house is unusually placed to the right of the front door. Stacked storage pots on a low mud plinth are full of rice and chillis. The house walls are made of stone blocks which have been whitewashed. A third house opposite (no. 29) belongs to a relative. (see Plate 61)

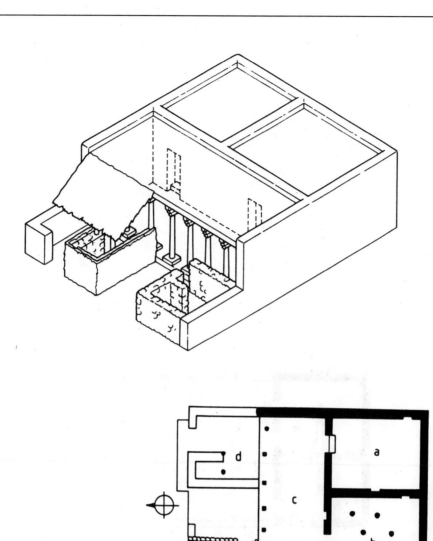

11 a multi-purpose	Room of one brother's wife with walls and features outlined in white, containing a hearth, pot stand, prayer corner, and a grindstone.
11 b multi-purpose	Room of second brother's wife with a hearth, pot stand, prayer shelf, stacked pots, and grindstones
11 c verandah	Divided into two by several crossed poles. There are two grindstones in one part, and a rotary quern in the other.
11 d bathroom	
11 e bathroom	

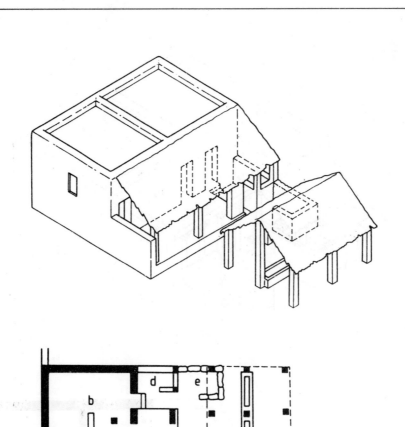

12 a	multi-purpose	Room with a hearth, stacked pots, a grinder, prayer shelf and no windows.
12 b	multi-purpose	A bare room with no windows.
12 c	verandah	With grinders embedded in ground.
12 d	bathroom	Used by elder brother
12 e	bathroom	Used by second brother
12 f	cattle shed	Large open area with troughs and thatched roofing.

House no. 13

This small, thatched roof dwelling is built near to the Jami Masjid on the route to Chintamani; the inhabitants are Muslims. Facing north, it covers an area of 40 sq m. In 1988, a thatched area (d) was added to the east wall to shelter the family's cows. The house is built close to a rise of rocky granite boulders and the inhabitants have enclosed part of the land behind their dwelling. The interior is painted white, and the stacks of clay pots all have white bases; the area around the hearth, however, is painted black. A windowless prayer room (c) is situated on the side. On the outer verandah every stone is outlined in white. The interior floor is covered with a random pattern of polished black stones. In 1990, there was very little remaining of this dwelling: only the front façade, painted white, with a verandah plastered with mud and dung still stood. The main cross beam that would have supported the roof over rooms a, b and c was still *in situ*, but was burnt. (see Plate 44)

To the immediate west, on the same plot, is a new house constructed of rough hewn blocks with a thatch front (not illustrated). It has a combination concrete and mud floor, whitewashed walls, and a flat roof. The verandah has a thatched roof, open on one side. The kitchen is in the area that used to house the cows. It is a government built house obtained with Income Certificate proof, as is the empty plot outside, but the owner does not have the means to fund extra construction. At the back is a water reservoir and a bathing area.

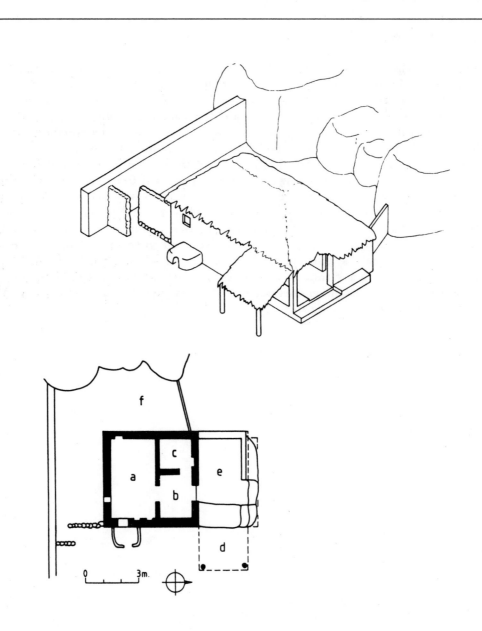

13 a	multi-purpose	The interior was all white, kitchen and bathroom also used for sleeping, with a wooden stand and window by hearth.
13 b	hall	Giving access to rest of house and street, with a sleeping area and grindstone.
13 c	prayer room	Entry was forbidden, there were no windows and no objects visible (a Muslim family).
13 d	cattle shed	Having a thatched roof: newly made between 1987 & 88.
13 e	verandah	Every stone on the ground was outlined in white, it was used as a living area.
13 f	yard	An enclosed area at back of house.

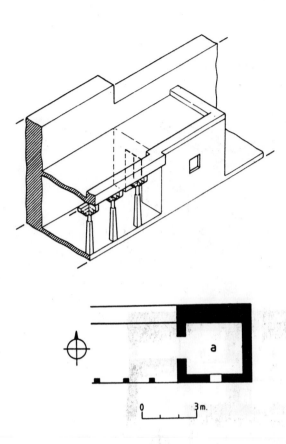

14 a multi purpose   With a hearth, bath, prayer corner, living room, outside sleeping. Room
                          used to be a store or guard's for palace behind.

This small dwelling of some 15 sq m may once have been a sentry room for men guarding the royal
palace to the north; alternatively, it could have been used as a store room. It is now occupied by a
woman and her two daughters who work in the palace opposite (House no. 44).

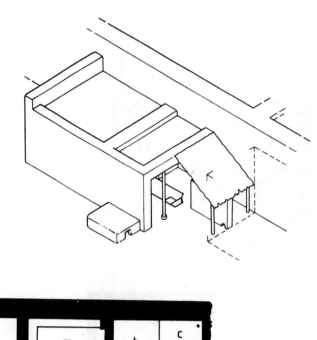

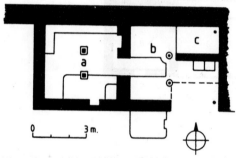

15 a multi-purpose	A room with the cooking area outlined in white and other features in red, with a hearth and prayer corner.
15 b hall	Living room which faces onto street, with grindstones, a partitioned bathroom, and a hen house.
15 c bathroom	With a drain running through to street.

This 44 sq m dwelling faces onto the northern Chariot Route, and backs onto the old palace wall (House no. 50). There is a bathroom under the sloping thatch roof, and a stone chicken shelter beside the road. The floor is covered with a layer of cow dung and it is immaculately clean. The cooking area (a) and shelf around the room are outlined in white, while the hall (b) is limited in red. The kitchen has a floor of black granite stones; these are used as a cutting surface and can easily be wiped clean. (see Figure 46 and Plate 41)

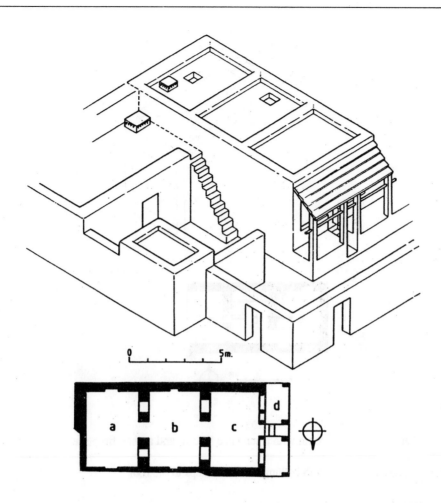

16 a kitchen   With a stone hearth and a skylight.

16 b hall   One end is used as a store, the other for sleeping, with a skylight.

16 c verandah   Enclosed, on plinth, with steps leading down to yard of 41 **(t)**

16 d sleeping platform

This small dwelling of 52 sq m, sharing a side wall with House no. 41, faces west onto the enclosed pathway. It also shares a wall with House no. 40, but the occupants are not related. The dwelling belongs to a man with seven daughters.

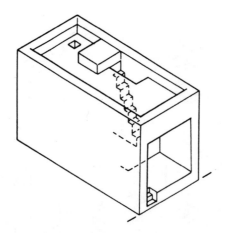

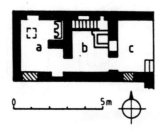

17 a kitchen   room with a screened hearth, and arched fireplace

17 b living room   with bathing area, and steps to the roof

17 c verandah

This town house has two enclosed rooms and one verandah with steps up to the roof. There is black slab flooring throughout. The walls are plastered and flat. The ceiling is of stone slabs supported on wooden beams. One room (b) has access to the roof with an open skylight and an internal wooden ladder: a bath and water storage area are also found here. In the back room (a) is a huge arched fireplace.

The occupant of the house originally came from Morigery village in Bellary district in order to marry. This is unusual since a husband rarely moves to the wife's village, but in this case her father held an important position within Anegondi. Furthermore, the husband was given land which yielded cash and bags of paddy, and was able to find work as an electrician. The occupant is also an agent and a scribe, writing letters and official documents for those who are illiterate.

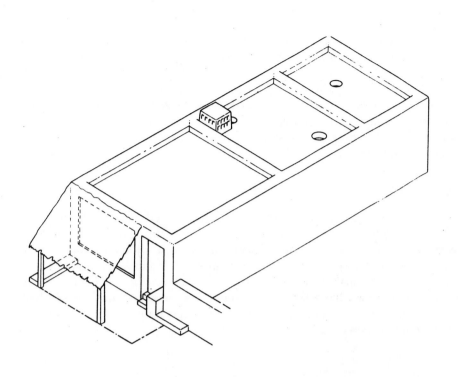

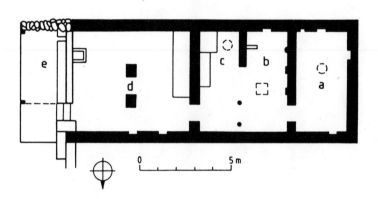

18 a	prayer room	Also used as a store room and dressing room. It has a skylight and no windows.
18 b	kitchen	A huge arched hearth in the corner. Rest of room is a hall giving access to back and front of house.
18 c	bathroom	With a bath, water storage basin, water heater, and skylight. Rest of room is a hallway
18 d	living room	A living room also for storing goods with access to the street and very wide rooms. Bathing area in corner.
18 e	cattle shed	Thatch covered

House no. 18

This dwelling of 123 sq m faces onto the western Chariot Route leading towards the Gangavati gate, which is a street of merchants. The occupants are landowners. The house is deep, with the rear space (a) used as a prayer room and dressing room. The central space is divided into kitchen (b) and bathroom (c), while the front space (d) is for living and receiving guests. A covered cattle shed for water buffalo (e) faces the street. This house is made from rough blocks of stone, whitewashed. The flooring is covered in a layer of cow dung, and in some rooms the roof is supported by rounded wooden pillars. A second bathing area exists in the corner of room (d). A drain runs in front of the house door, covered by stone slabs. (see Plate 42)

House no. 19

This simple narrow house is located off a side road on the southern Chariot Route. The entire plot once belonged to the householder's family, though now he occupies only an area of 42 sq m. The house is raised up, and must have been built on a pile of rubble; it adjoins an empty ruined plot. The house is owned by a butcher, one of several butcher families living in Anegondi. It is constructed of unshaped rough stones, painted white inside. Two flat stones have been set at the threshold to the kitchen (b). The floor surface has a layer of cow dung and the hearth has been embellished with red and yellow *kumkuma* dots. The entrance doorway has a white frame, with red painted inner wood, and a flower pattern in yellow dots.

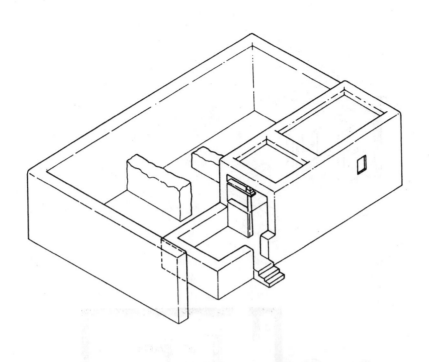

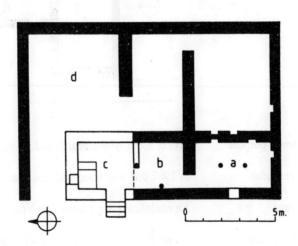

19 a multi-purpose   With a prayer shelf and grindstone

19 b kitchen   A hearth in a hall leading to room a

19 c yard   With a bathing area and steps to street, and a chicken coop.

19 d yard   Ruined area occupied by man's family in past, now abandoned.

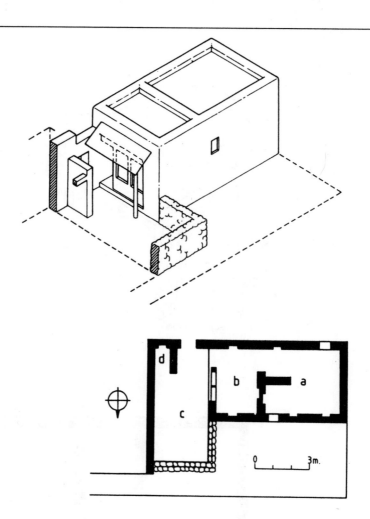

20 a multi purpose   Living room with a hearth and prayer shelf

20 b verandah   In 1987 this was open with columns, by 1988 it was an enclosed room.

20 c yard   An enclosed space between several houses.

20 d bathroom   An enclosed area within yard with black slab flooring.

This small east-facing dwelling of 58 sq m is built in the space between three much larger houses within the central square of Anegondi. The house is occupied by a young man and his wife, and is very neatly kept. It incorporates a courtard defined by a low stone wall (c), with an open roofed bathroom (d) in one corner. During 1988, the house was modified and the verandah (b) was enclosed to create a second room. (see Plate 43)

House nos. 21 and 22

In the south-east corner of the palace dwelling (House no. 44) are the houses of two brothers, whose mother is a cousin of Achyuta Deva Raya's mother. These two interlocking dwellings cover an area of approximately 140 sq m, though the families also occupy the garden (288 sq m) which backs onto House no. 44. The location of these houses against the wall of the palace suggests that in the past they might have been used as concealed entrances. Women from the two houses are responsible for maintaining Achyuta Deva Raya's properties in both Hospet and Anegondi.

The walls of House nos. 21 and 22 are plastered with dung and painted white, with a red line marking the edges of the floor and walls. The long building in the garden (g) is used as a latrine, and is built of roughly hewn stones. In the past the room was divided into two, and had also been an outside latrine, for the remaining white ceramic WCs are still present. A disused *brindavan* is seen in the garden. (see Plate 40)

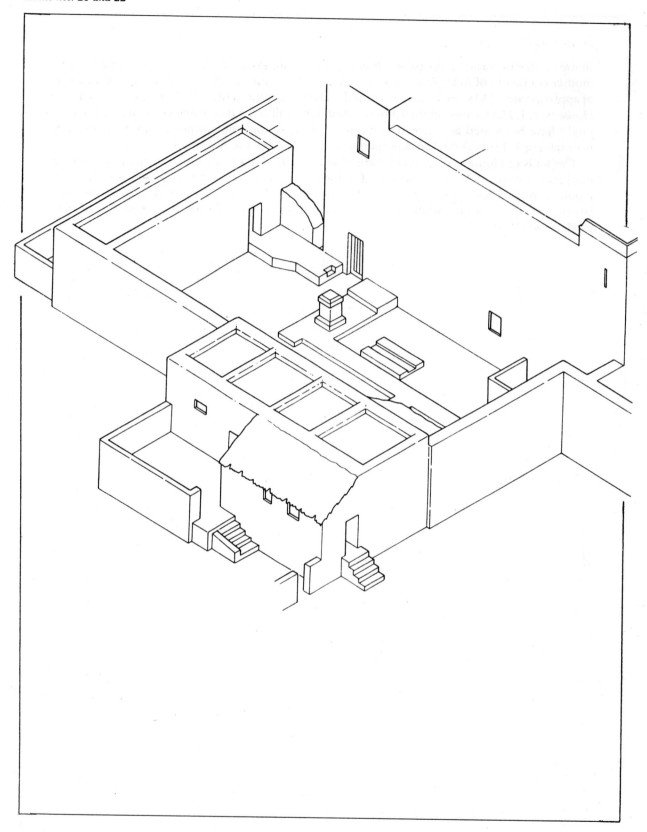

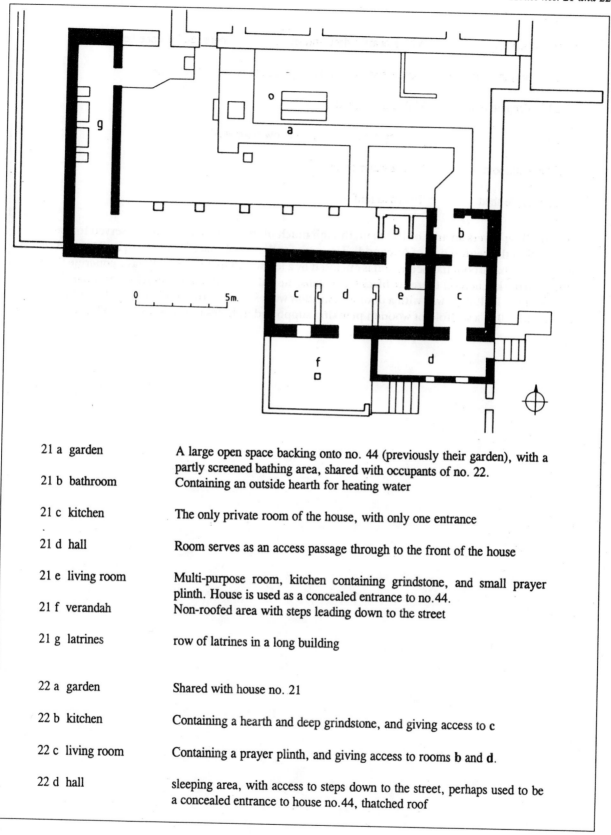

21 a garden	A large open space backing onto no. 44 (previously their garden), with a partly screened bathing area, shared with occupants of no. 22.
21 b bathroom	Containing an outside hearth for heating water
21 c kitchen	The only private room of the house, with only one entrance
21 d hall	Room serves as an access passage through to the front of the house
21 e living room	Multi-purpose room, kitchen containing grindstone, and small prayer plinth. House is used as a concealed entrance to no.44.
21 f verandah	Non-roofed area with steps leading down to the street
21 g latrines	row of latrines in a long building
22 a garden	Shared with house no. 21
22 b kitchen	Containing a hearth and deep grindstone, and giving access to c
22 c living room	Containing a prayer plinth, and giving access to rooms **b** and **d**.
22 d hall	sleeping area, with access to steps down to the street, perhaps used to be a concealed entrance to house no.44, thatched roof

23 a	kitchen	With a hearth, deep and shallow grindstones, and a stone bench.
23 b	prayer room/store	A prayer shelf, also having stacked pottery for storage.
23 c	sleeping room	With a deep grinder
23 d	yard	An open area enclosed by a low stone wall.
23 e	bathroom	With a water basin.
23 f	cattle shed	Thatched roof

This dwelling covers an area of 190 sq m, though much of this space is open and reserved for cattle. It lies within the central part of Anegondi. The occupant's roofed space is only 50 sq m. The yard (d) in which the bathroom has been built is enclosed by a low wall. The house itself has a concrete floor, though in the kitchen (a) there are black stone slabs; the walls of square stone blocks are immaculately whitewashed. In 1990, a wall with a door and window was extended from the kitchen. The additions were made using a scaffold of wooden planking supported in holes in the walls. (see Plate 38)

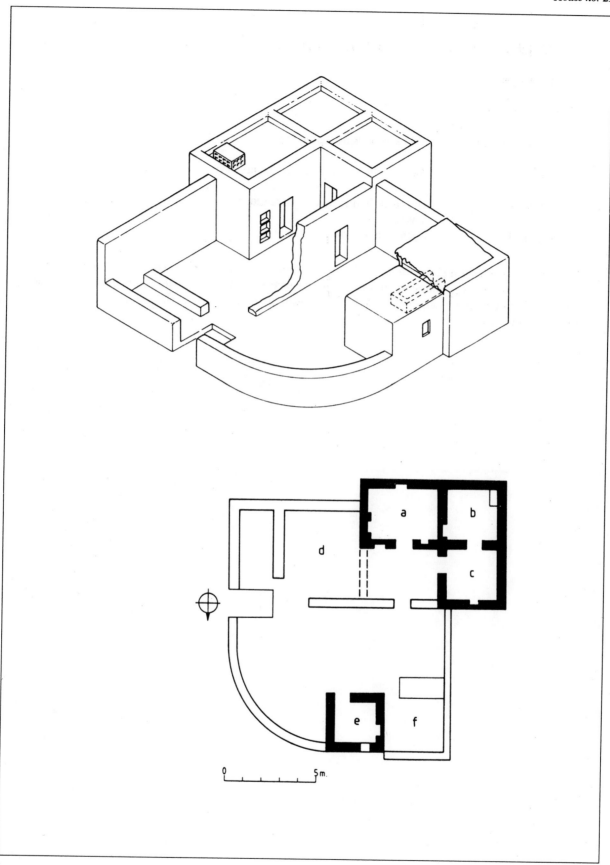

117

24 a	kitchen/bathroom	With a large arched hearth, a stone basin, and a water heater.
24 b	prayer room	
24 c	store room	
24 d	living room	With a stone bench and grinder
24 e	kitchen	Occupied by second married couple, having a prayer shelf.
24 f	verandah	The main living area: it is raised on a plinth is covered and has steps down to street.
24 g	cattle shed	Open area for cows

This west facing dwelling is located within the central part of Anegondi. It covers 398 sq m, with an enclosed cattle shed (g) taking up almost as much space as the living quarters. The house has stone walls and wooden pillars. On the verandah (f), the walls are painted green, the pillars blue and green, and the capitals bright red.

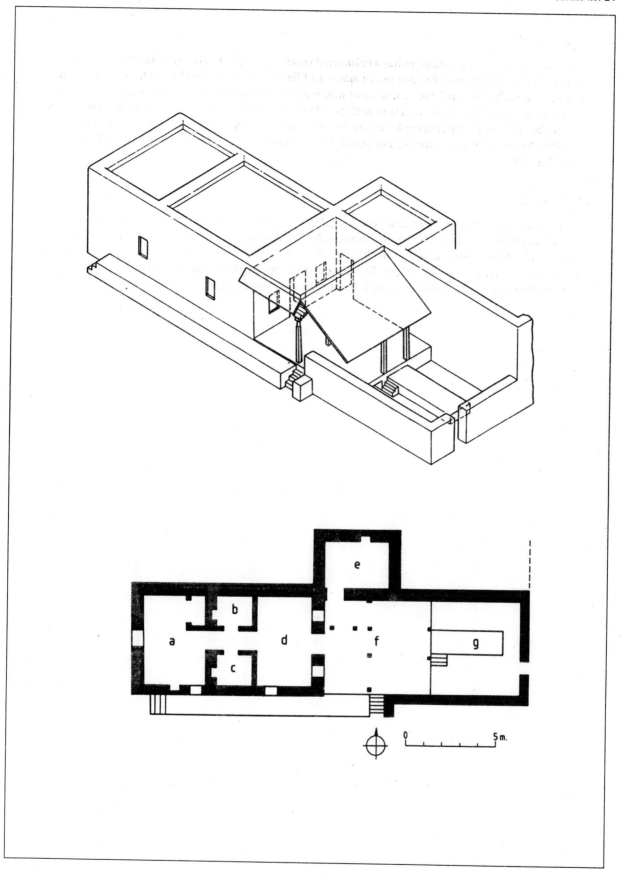

House no. 25

This compact dwelling of 85 sq m has a columned verandah facing north onto the southern Chariot Route. The house makes effective use of space and light, with all of the doors aligned. In the hall-way (c) is a high shelf, indicating that cows may have been tethered here in the past.

A woman once lived here, together with her three married sons and their wives. But she died in November 1987, and the remainder of the family moved from Anegondi back to their native place. By 1988, the property was empty and stripped of its contents, except for a steel water jar in the kitchen. (see Plate 33)

House no. 26

This dwelling of 119 sq m faces east onto a small side street which runs parallel to the road leading to the Talarighat crossing. It is rented out to professional people who work in Anegondi. Two rooms at the back of the house (a and b) are kept padlocked by the owners. The prayer room (a) has an amber light hanging from the ceiling. The floor at the entrance door is decorated with a red polished, diamond pattern surrounded by a black band. (see also Figure 44.d)

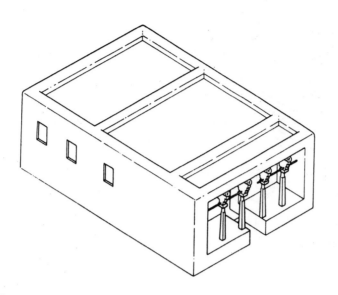

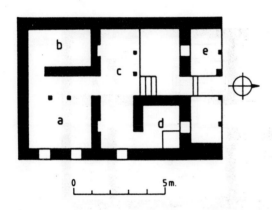

25 a	kitchen	With a hearth and deep grinder
25 b	prayer room	
25 c	hallway	Lower area possibly for cows in past, with a grinder and steps to entrance.
25 d	bathroom	Low basin and drain
25 e	verandah	Enclosed and columned, raised on plinth

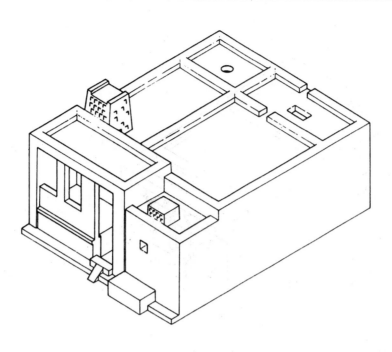

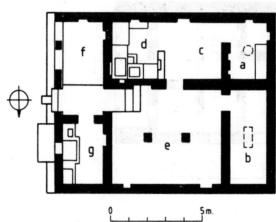

26 a	prayer room	With a skylight and deities in a wall niche
26 b	store room	Kept locked by the owners: the property is rented.
26 c	eating room	Giving access to kitchen
26 d	kitchen/bathroom	With a hearth, bath, water storage basin.
26 e	living room	It has a red polished diamond on the floor, and an exit to street.
26 f	verandah	Screened verandah on a plinth, with rotary quern and deep grinder embedded.
26 g	store room	Once used as a bathroom

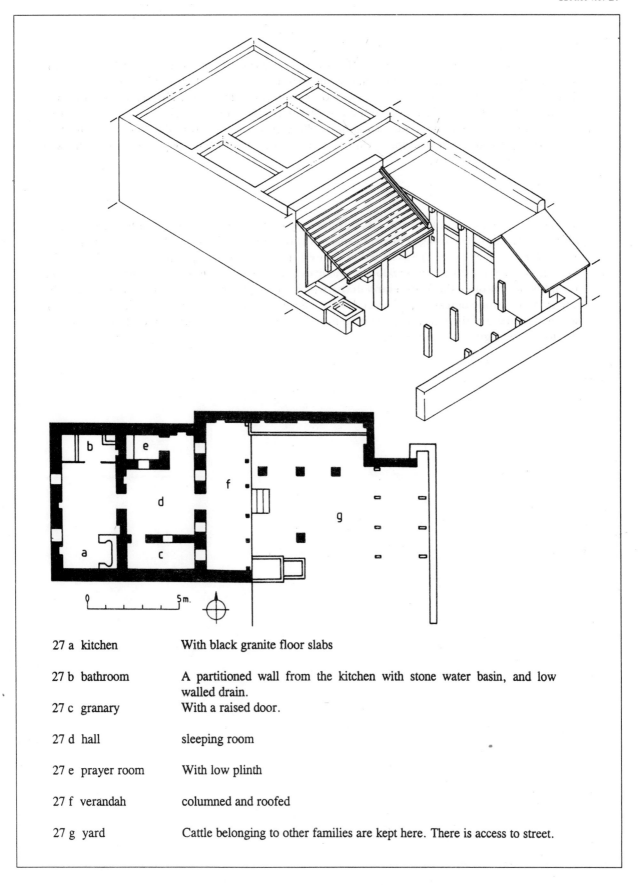

27 a	kitchen	With black granite floor slabs
27 b	bathroom	A partitioned wall from the kitchen with stone water basin, and low walled drain.
27 c	granary	With a raised door.
27 d	hall	sleeping room
27 e	prayer room	With low plinth
27 f	verandah	columned and roofed
27 g	yard	Cattle belonging to other families are kept here. There is access to street.

House no. 27

This house is occupied by a doctor and his family. It faces east and covers an area of 174 sq m. It is situated on the road which leads to the Talarighat crossing. The house is entered through a gateway which leads into the cattle-yard (g), shared with other non-related families. This serves as a cow shed where animals are tethered, and where the doctor keeps his motorbike. The house is raised on a plinth, and to one side is another quite separate dwelling. It is stone built with flat plastered walls, with a red tiled sloping roof. The interior is whitewashed throughout, with black polished stone slabs in the kitchen and hall (a and d).

House no. 28

Occupied by the families of two brothers, this dwelling of 202 sq m faces north onto the route that leads to the Talarighat crossing. The living space is entered through the cattle shed housing water-buffalo. In 1988 a new room (i) was added to the west side of the dwelling with a door leading to the street. This is used as a surgery by the doctor who lives in House no. 27. Before this, the only entrance to the house was through the front verandah (h), which meant passing through the cow shed (g). The house is built of stone blocks with plastered walls. The verandah is painted in bright blue with deep maroon at the base of the walls, and a white plinth. Photos of deceased relatives are hung above the front door. (see Figure 44.c and Plate 35)

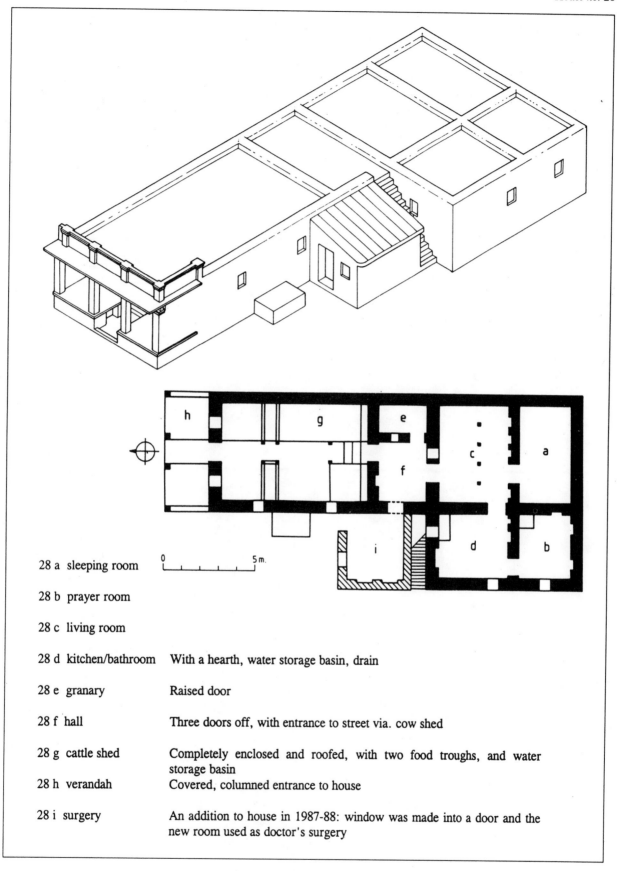

28 a sleeping room

28 b prayer room

28 c living room

28 d kitchen/bathroom   With a hearth, water storage basin, drain

28 e granary   Raised door

28 f hall   Three doors off, with entrance to street via. cow shed

28 g cattle shed   Completely enclosed and roofed, with two food troughs, and water storage basin

28 h verandah   Covered, columned entrance to house

28 i surgery   An addition to house in 1987-88: window was made into a door and the new room used as doctor's surgery

House no. 29

This house consists of two identical dwellings built for the families of two brothers. One brother is assistant to the village accountant, as well as being a local administrator and holding the hereditary post of the Valmiki community. The two families now live in only one dwelling, using the second dwelling as a cow shed (e). The rooms are finely decorated with painted walls and a smooth concrete floor. The house faces no. 12 which belongs to relatives.

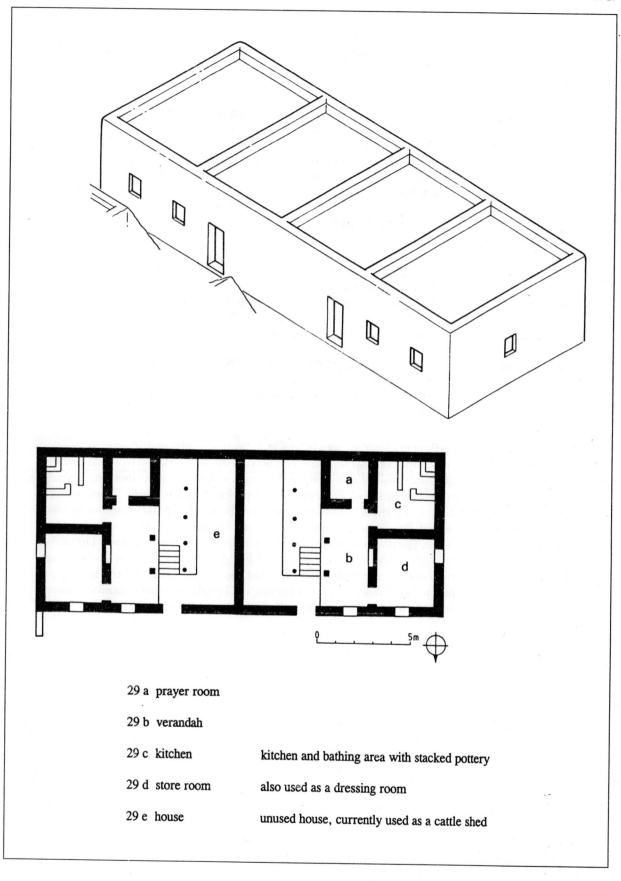

29 a   prayer room

29 b   verandah

29 c   kitchen   kitchen and bathing area with stacked pottery

29 d   store room   also used as a dressing room

29 e   house   unused house, currently used as a cattle shed

30 a bathroom	With a stone basin, a huge water storage pot, and an open hearth for heating water
30 b store room	
30 c cattle shed	now with no roof and without cows, back gate to street
30 d yard	An open rectangular space within house, totally enclosed, with a back gate to street. It has steps up to the roof and flowers.
30 e hall	Four doors lead off, one to cattle area, another to yard d, it has stone benches and a skylight.
30 f kitchen	With skylight by hearth, vertical posts by walls like remnants of a previous construction.
30 g sleeping room	
30 h prayer room	A bare room with *rangoli* on floor, and a 2' *lingam* tied with green bangles, large ceramic brazier.
30 i hallway	Three doors off, giving access to rest of house.
30 j granary	With a trap door 3' off the ground
30 k store room	hen's room, changed doorway from 1987 to 88, from access to **i,** to access onto **l**
30 l entrance verandah	On a raised plinth with steps leading up to house, columned and painted brown.

This long narrow dark dwelling encloses an area of 244 sq m, with an addtional 76 sq m as an open cattle shed (c). The remains of another cow shed are seen beyond the west wall, but this has now been turned into a garden planted with flowers. A small open courtyard at the back of the dwelling has steps leading to the roof. A covered verandah (l) faces onto the southern Chariot Route. The flooring is of rough unpolished concrete, and there is a double row of rough wooden pillars running through the house supporting the roof. Rough stone walls have been plastered with whitewash, and the wall base picked out with a red line. The doorway to the granary (j) is 50 cm above ground level. The prayer room (h) contains a 1.5 m high *lingam* decorated with green bangles (for the goddess Thaiyamma), and is surrounded by prints of different deities. The floor of the prayer room and the hall (i) are covered with a carpet of painted *rangoli* drawings during Pongal. The door from one room was moved in 1987; in 1988 it opened directly onto the verandah (l). The occupant used to be a herbal doctor. (see Plate 31)

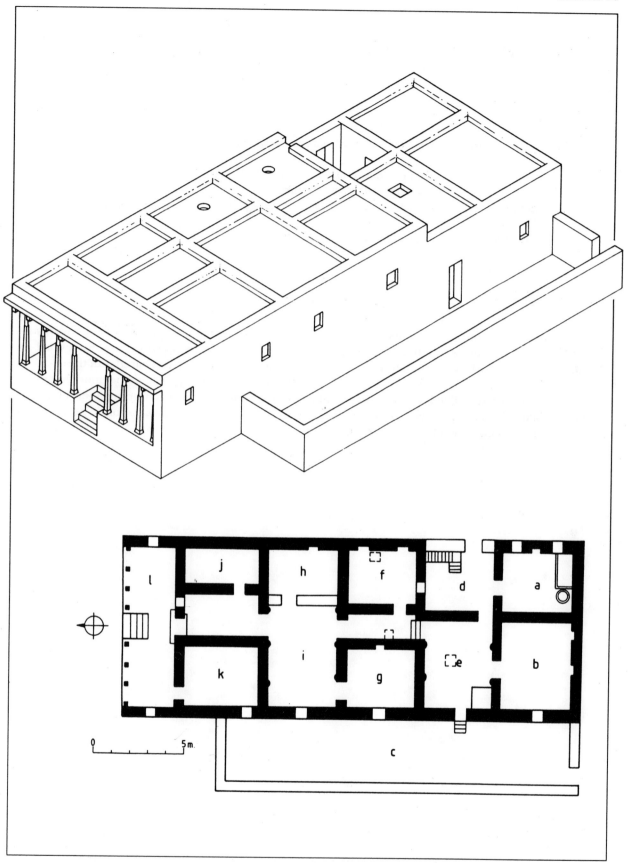

House no. 30

129

31 a	kitchen (1)	With a large hearth, a stone water basin, bath, drain pipe, and a grindstone
31 b	prayer room	low plinth, also used as dressing room
31 c	hall	Four doors off giving access to shared yard.
31 d	dressing room	With a red polished diamond on the floor
31 e	yard	Giving access to the street, open roofed and divided by a low wall, to a bathroom with drain and tank.
31 f	kitchen (2)	For mutton cooking: four members of the house are meat eaters
31 g	verandah	With large windows onto street
31 h	sleeping room	
31 i	bathroom	

This dwelling of about 145 sq m shares an open area of approximately 150 sq m with the occupants of House no. 45, from where steps lead to the roof. This house is mostly roofed, except for a small yard (e) behind the front verandah. The covered bathroom in room (i) is also shared with the occupants of House no. 45. The dressing room (d) is distinguished by a red polished, diamond design on the concrete floor. The house includes a 'mutton cooking area' (f), since four members of the family eat meat. (Usually, non-meat-eating relations insist that meat-eaters cook at outside hearths.) Black slab flooring is used for several rooms (a-d).

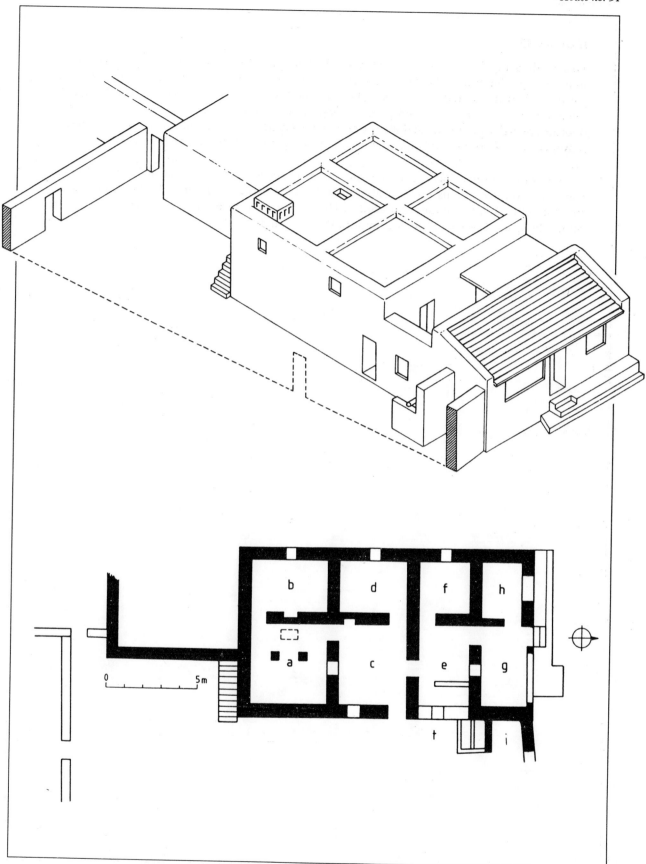

House no. 31

0   5m

b   d   f   h

a   c   e   g

t   i

131

House no. 32

This north facing dwelling, with a small low walled enclosed garden in front (f), is situated on the southern Chariot Route. The dwelling of 231 sq m has been divided into two, with the western wing partitioned off and rented out to a young headmaster, his wife and son who come from Bijapur. The remainder of the house has been partially modernised. Some rooms (a-c) have black slab stone flooring and white plastered flat walls; the door to the kitchen (b) has a yellow door frame. There are prayer corners in two of the rooms (c and g). The occupants believe that the house is about 80 years old.

This house unusually belongs to the wife: she had been an only child, and she and her husband had taken over her parents' dwelling after their deaths. The interior is wide, and contains a circular structure of basketry used for grain storage. The owners are considering constructing extra rooms within the space. Cooking is carried out with solid fuel and paraffin.

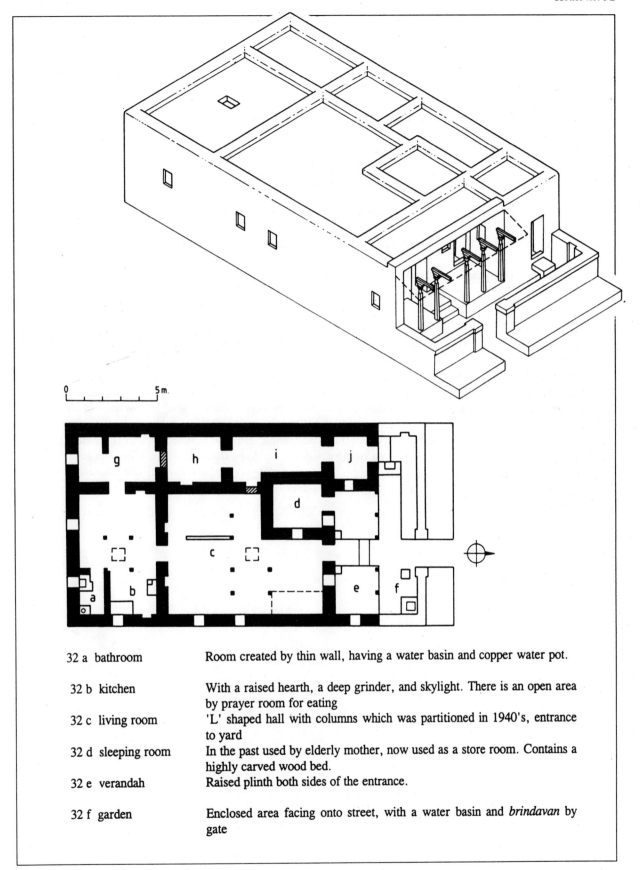

32 a	bathroom	Room created by thin wall, having a water basin and copper water pot.
32 b	kitchen	With a raised hearth, a deep grinder, and skylight. There is an open area by prayer room for eating
32 c	living room	'L' shaped hall with columns which was partitioned in 1940's, entrance to yard
32 d	sleeping room	In the past used by elderly mother, now used as a store room. Contains a highly carved wood bed.
32 e	verandah	Raised plinth both sides of the entrance.
32 f	garden	Enclosed area facing onto street, with a water basin and *brindavan* by gate

33 a	bathroom	
33 b	yard	Open area with steps leading up to the roof, drain
33 c	prayer room	used by mother as sleeping room in 1990
33 d	living room	Quarrelling brothers have split the house of their father. Occupied by first brother and his wife.
33 e	living room	Occupied by elderly man and woman, parents of three brothers.
33 f	living room	Occupied by second brother and his wife, with a hearth and quern-stone.
33 g	living room	Occupied by third brother and his wife, hearth for cooking and prayer area
33 h	multi-purpose	Living room and bathroom of third brother, access to room g, steps to street.

With an area of 235 sq m, this dwelling faces onto the southern Chariot Route. At the back of the house is an enclosed yard (b) with black slab flooring, off which are the latrine and bathroom (a). In the past, the back room of the house was used as a kitchen for a school established by Achyuta Deva Raya's wife; it could be reached through a side door. The walls are whitewashed and the floors concrete. In the corner of room (e) is a chicken coop, and room (d) is used by the elderly mother having a hearth, prayer shelf and stand for water pots. Room (c), which was once a prayer room, is now used by an older female occupant for sleeping.

This house, is occupied by three brothers and their elderly mother. Friction amongst the occupants has resulted in the dwelling being divided into three discrete units. Windows have been made into doors, so that each brother has his own independent entrance to his home. Doorways have also been blocked up so that each householder has his own kitchen for his respective wife and children.

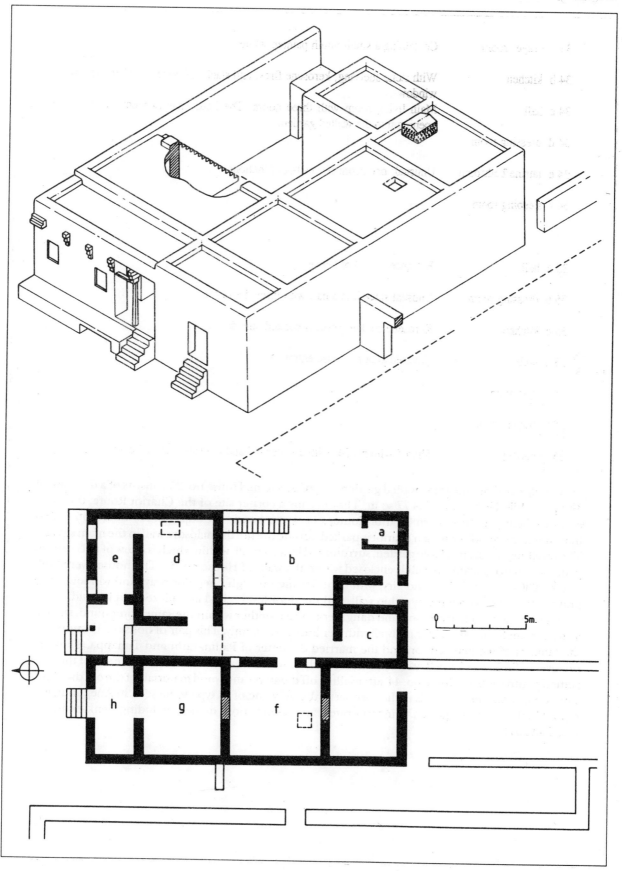

34 a	prayer room	Containing a small plinth painted white
34 b	kitchen	With stone shelving, kerosene fires, and stacks of pottery. There are two windows.
34 c	hall	Main living room with three doors. The house has two entrances both opening into the walled garden.
34 d	dressing room	
34 e	latrine/bathroom	Unusual: one room serves both functions
34 f	sleeping room	

35 a	hall	Entrance to rest of house
35 b	dressing room	Unusual since it is a hall with three doors off
35 c	kitchen	Kerosene cooker: meat is cooked outside
35 d	well	Covered area by house entrance
35 e	bathroom	
35 f	prayer room	
35 g	garden	Shared with no.34, with a water tap and a meat-cooking hearth

Two dwellings share the same walled garden plot of 318 sq m: House no. 35 consists of a dwelling of 39 sq m, while House no. 34 is 77 sq m. They occupy a corner site of the Chariot Route, the main entrance being on the eastern Chariot Route; a back exit beside the adjacent House no. 36 is used by women. Anegondi's wooden chariot is parked outside the north enclosure wall in the main square. The dwellings are set in a large garden, surrounded by a low wall, within which is a row of tall coconut palms and papaya plants. A well is enclosed within the walls of House no. 35. The houses were built in the 1930s and are bright and airy, with light flowing through open doorways and windows. The prayer room (f) is screened by a thin wall, and the floor level raised and picked out in mud.

It is unusual for a married son and daughter to live together within the same compound, since it is the custom for the daughter to dwell with her husband's family. This pair of houses is occupied by the families of the married son and the married daughter of Padmavathi and Timappa. They are relatives of Sri Ranga Deva Raya who had originally moved here in the 1930s from the site of the now ruined plinth south of House no. 44, after selling off the stone and wood materials of the old dwelling. The stone *brindavan* from this earlier property, the only one of its type to be seen in Anegondi, was rebuilt in the common garden. It incorporates carvings of various deities, including Venkateshvara. (see Plate 37)

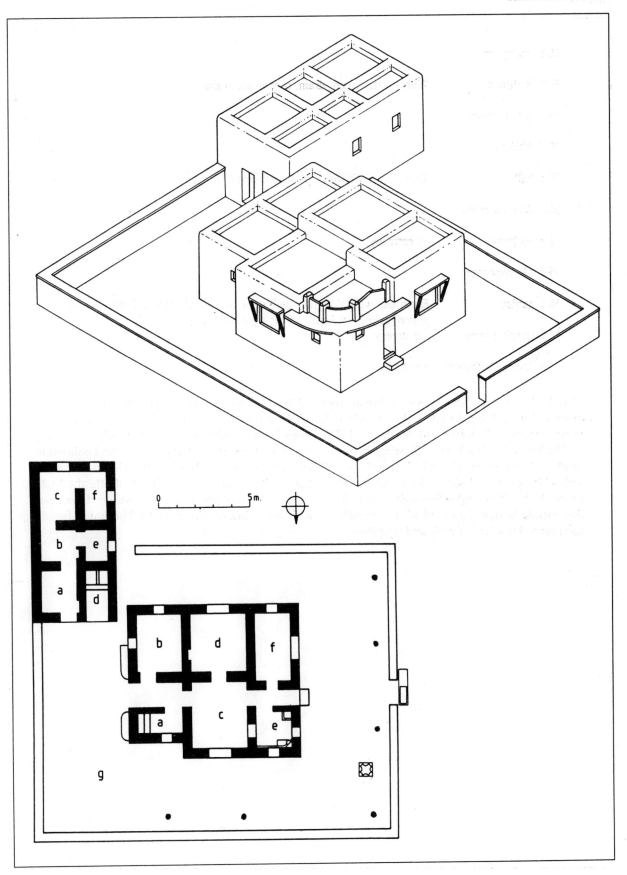

36 a eating room

36 b bathroom   With a water basin, drain, copper pot in situ

36 c prayer room

36 d kitchen

36 e hall   Three doors off with a passage to rest of house.

36 f dressing room

36 g hallway   by entrance

36 h sleeping room

36 i garden   Enclosed, with a latrine, and steps to second storey. House is newly painted in polyurethane and has a gate to street and *brindavan*.

36 j sleeping room   top storey

36 k latrine, bathroom   top storey

This double-storeyed dwelling covering an area of 235 sq km was constructed in 1977 to the design of an architect. It is painted on the outside with pastel colours. A stairway on the south side ascends to two rooms and a water tank on the roof. The house is enclosed by a low garden wall.

The house has black stone flooring throughout, and all the walls are flat plastered and painted in bright colours: rooms (f) and (d) have blue walls and purple doors with yellow thresholds enlivened with white painted designs; the prayer room (c) has a yellow and orange painted plinth; the bathroom (b) has blue and yellow walls; the hall (e) has walls painted green and red, with red flooring; the outside latrine is painted white, though the walls are ochre on the outside. The house façade has painted borders of pink and turquoise.

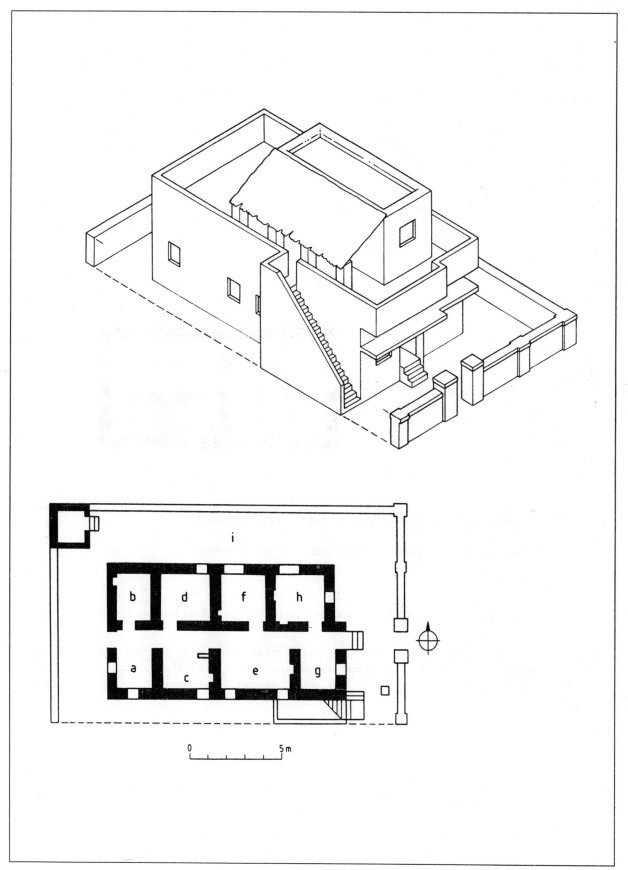

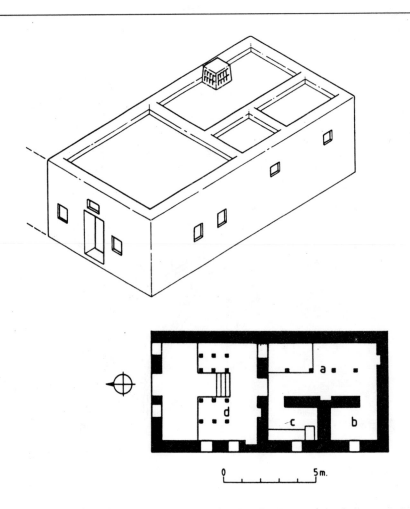

37 a kitchen/living room With a hearth, offering access to other rooms

37 b prayer room   Room with a low shelf, also used for storage.

37 c bathroom

37 d cattle shed   A completely enclosed and roofed area with an entrance to street.

This north facing dwelling within central Anegondi covers an area of 84 sq m. The house is entered through the cattle shed (d) which occupies the same amount of space as the accommodation. The house is built of roughly hewn blocks which have been whitewashed; the interior columns are painted brown.

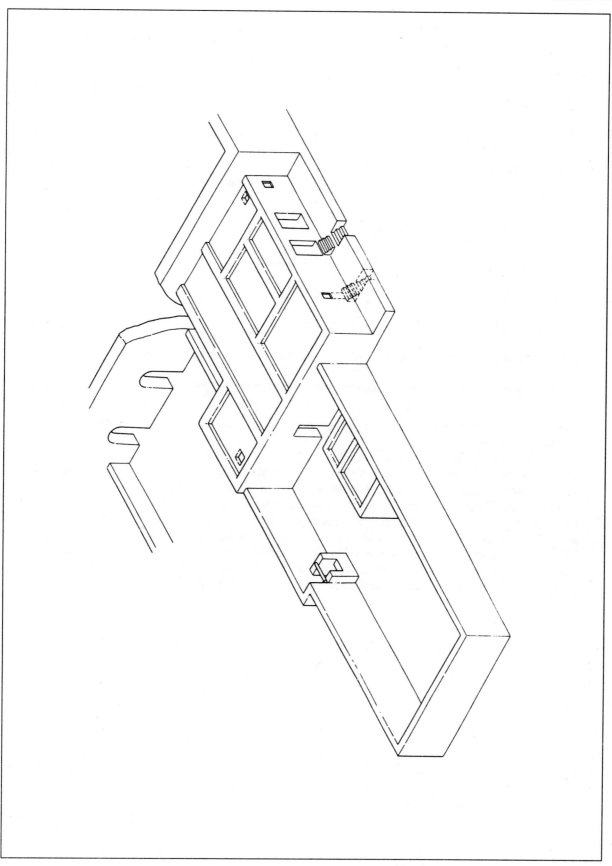

38 a	garden	large garden backing onto the palm enclosure, well present by one wall
38 b	bathroom	
38 c	latrine	
38 d	prayer room	With a skylight, also used for storage, has a stack of pottery
38 e	open yard	Possibly used in past for access to palace of Narasingamma. Currently used by many women as through route to traverse village.
38 f	hallway	Access passage to garden and through route, seven doors leading off, a concealed entrance in past?
38 g	granary	store room
38 h	kitchen/living room	Used by the wife of first brother.
38 i	hallway	Access room to street and to rest of dwelling
38 j	entrance verandah	With steps leading to street
38 k	kitchen/living room	Used by wife of second brother, containing hearth, stone basin, grindstone, and prayer shelf.
38 l	sleeping platform	Facing onto the street, with steps leading down

This dwelling in central Anegondi, almost opposite House no. 44, is occupied by descendants of Narasingamma (the 7th Pensioner of Anegondi who ruled after her husband's death from 1883 to 1889). The house shares a wall with her palace (House no. 50d) which lies in ruins, and may have served as a concealed entrance. Women related to the royal household regularly use the house as an access route to reach the other side of the village without using the main chariot roads.

The heads of this house are two brothers, one of whom is the boat contractor responsible for ferrying people across the Tungabhadra to Talarighat. The dwelling covers an area of 206 sq m, with an additional enclosed garden of 270 sq m (a), with a well against one wall, and latrines and a bathroom opposite. The house was altered in 1990: a window was converted into a door, and a plinth was added with steps leading down to the street. These changes were made so that the family occupying one side of the house would not disturb their brother's family.

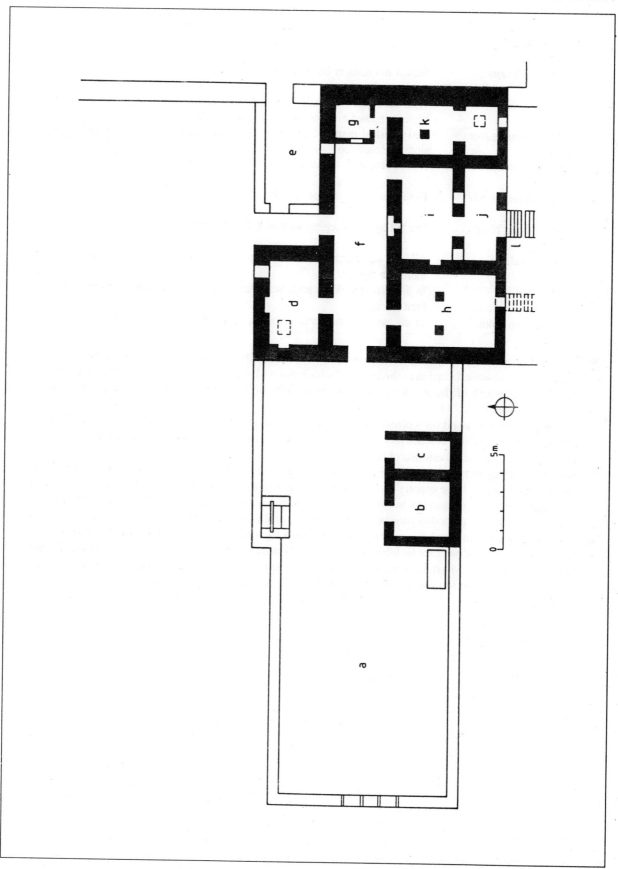

39 a latrine

39 b bathroom — With a stone water basin, copper water heater

39 c garden — With back gate (originally this was house front), methane gas tank, water basin, screened area for meat cooking outside, *brindavan*

39 d sleeping room — Red polished diamond shape on floor, this room and e is covered by a sloping thatch roof

39 e verandah — Raised area with a thatch roof and polished floor

39 f prayer room — Deities are on raised plinth, skylight

39 g living room — For sitting and sleeping, also as hall to entrance

39 h kitchen — All gas and electric, with a deep grinder. There are no windows but there is a skylight.

39 i hall — In the past area down steps was a cattle shed with a high shelf for animal feed storage

39 j store room — In the past a kitchen with grinders, now used for food storage

This dwelling of 290 sq m is located near to the southern Chariot Route. It was modernised in the 1980s, and has a walled garden at the back, off which open a latrine (a) and bathroom (b). A *brindavan* stands to the north of the garden gate. Only two-thirds of the dwelling has a regular roof; the remainder is thatched.

The building is raised on a plinth, and is built of stone with white finely plastered walls. There is a white painted outline at floor level and around the grindstone. The door to the kitchen (h) has a yellow threshold; the thresholds of the front and back doors are painted red. The doors are of heavy carved wood with brass knobs. There is black slab flooring in rooms (g), (h) and (j). Wooden columns are painted in a pale olive green polyurethane. The bedroom (d), kitchen and verandah (e) have red polished wax floors; that in the bedroom is adorned with a diamond pattern. A similar red diamond design is seen on the path that runs between the house and gate. Photographs of the family's ancestors and relatives are hung in the corner of room (g), with a green light positioned over the photograph of the wife's father. Power for lighting and cooking comes from methane fuel stored in a circular gas tank in the yard. But when the current fails, the occupants use a small clay hearth outside the house. In the hall (i) is a wooden swing hanging from the roof. A cow shed was once situated here on a lower landing.

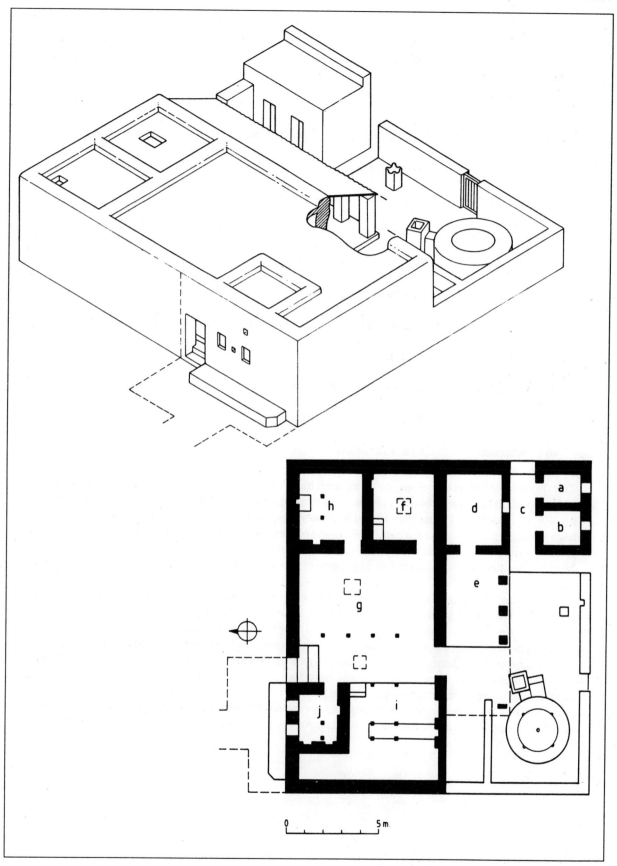

40 a	garden	With steps to roof and access to bathroom. It has a tree and a wide back entrance.
40 b	bathroom	
40 c	kitchen	Painted green with a huge arched hearth, a water storage basin, and a grindstone.
40 d	hallway	Four doors off, with a hole in ground for a buttermilk stand
40 e	prayer room	Deities on a plinth.
40 f	living room	living room with television
40 g	granary	With a raised door, 1.5 metres above floor level.
40 h	store room	Store room for boxes and clothes
40 i	sleeping room	with ceiling fans
40 j	sleeping room	with ceiling fans, and floral pattern on concrete floor
40 k	unknown	storeroom?
40 l	verandah	On a low plinth and roofed.
40 m	yard	With a front gate to street.
40 n	bathroom	with water heater

This dwelling of 206 sq m, belonging to the merchant Venkat Reddy, is located within the central part of Anegondi. It faces east towards a pathway running from the back entrance of the old palace (House no. 50); it also adjoins House nos. 16 and 41. Low walls at the front enclose the yard (m), while at the back is a small garden (a) with a bathroom in one corner (b), and steps leading to the roof. The house is well painted and well maintained, with mattresses and beds, and a grain storage area (g). A huge hearth is located in the kitchen (c). Light passes through the dwelling from the front to the back doors.

In the past, the house consisted only of rooms (a) to (h), with the front door at the entrance to room (f). They were built by Venkat Reddy for his own use and that of his family. When his son married in the 1960s, rooms (i) to (n) were added. These have black slab flooring at the entrance and at the verandah, whereas the original part of the house had concrete flooring. The floor of the sleeping room (i) is distinguished by a red painted diamond design, while that of room (j) has an incised circular floral pattern. Both rooms have fine varnished bamboo wood ceilings and ceiling fans. The walls are plastered throughout, and painted in deep green polyurethane. The original front door is still *in situ* between rooms (f) and (h). In the back yard are a coconut palm and two jasmine shrubs. Mango leaves are hung on a thread above the doorways at festival times. (see Plate 55)

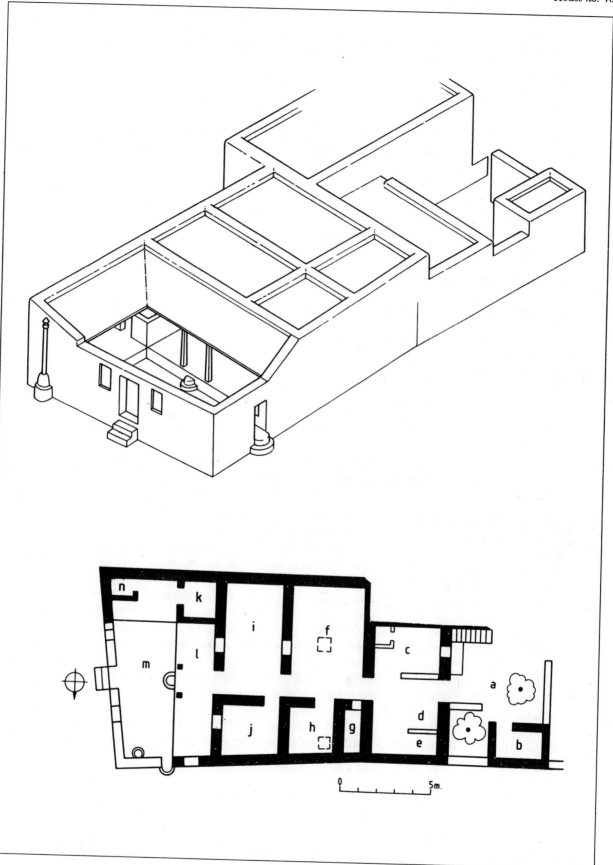

41 a yard	Through-route used by relatives in house nos. 31, 45, access to houses nos.16, 40
41 bc latrines	
41 d bathroom	
41 e yard	Plot of land bought piecemeal from three families, open roofed with steps to roof and a *brindavan*.
41 fg exercise room	For weightlifting and wrestling, now used for sleeping.
41 h kitchen	With a hearth, grindstone, and drain. In 1988 stone basin was built.
41 i hallway	Four doors off, it was also used as a dining room.
41 j prayer room	skylight
41 k store room	A granary with pottery in stacks.
41 l hall	Three doors off, used as living and dining room.
41 m sleeping room	
41 n hall	Four doors off giving access to garden and street.
41 o sleeping room	
41 p garden	Low walled garden giving access to the street, built 1988. In 1987 house consisted of rooms **h, i, j, k** and **l**.

In 1987, this dwelling covered an area of only 94 sq m, but extensive rebuilding meant that by 1988 it was enlarged to 322 sq m. The house is occupied by relatives of those in House nos. 31 and 45, and was built up piecemeal as the inhabitants could afford. In 1987 it consisted of a verandah the length of the house, and four other rooms in a row: kitchen, dining hall, prayer room, and a store (h-k). The old parts are rooms (a-g), and the new are rooms (h-l). Rooms (m-o) have black stone flooring while the remainder have concrete flooring. The walls are plastered and given a white lime wash, and there is a painted *rangoli* design at the entrance of room (n). A double row of rooms and a walled front with polished red steps have been added, while the back portion of the house remains the same. The rooms (f and g) are used for body-building exercises such as wrestling and weight-lifting.

A low-walled garden (p) marks the east entrance; the back entrance opens into a small yard (e) surrounded by other rooms; a flight of stairs lead up to the roof and a small *brindavan* (Plate 17). Further to the back is an enclosed yard (a) adjoining the outer walls of House no. 45. This is used as a through route by members of related families when crossing from one side of the village to the other. (It is more or less aligned with the front door of House no. 44, through House no. 38, and leads to the rear entrancse of House nos. 34 and 35.) Older family members remember a gateway being built along this route. (see Plate 39)

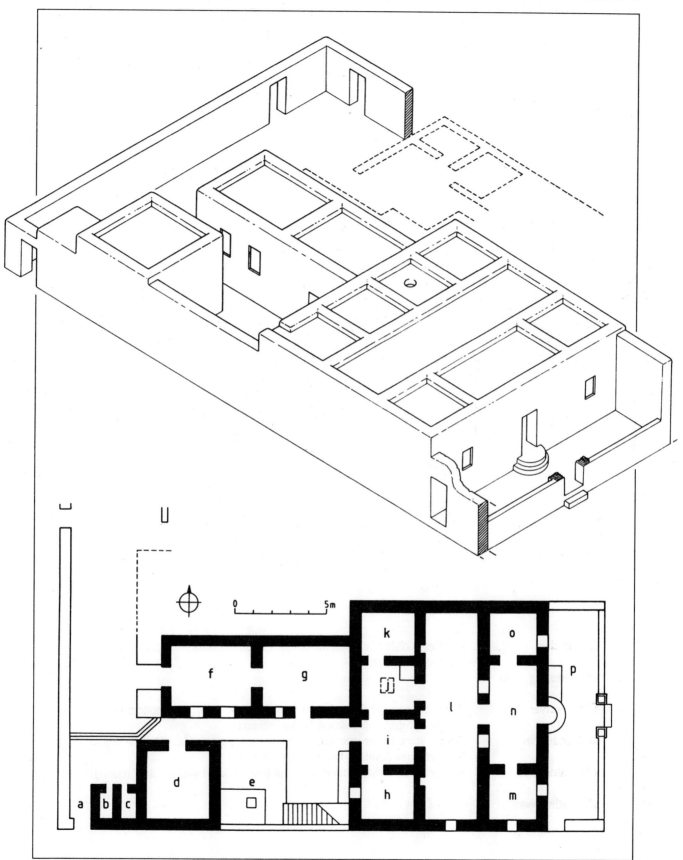

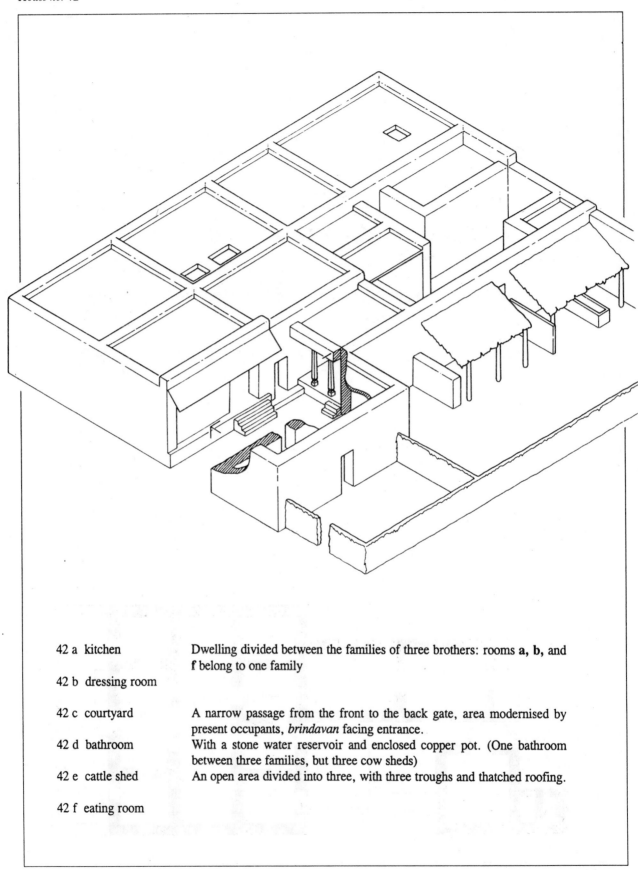

42 a	kitchen	Dwelling divided between the families of three brothers: rooms **a, b,** and **f** belong to one family
42 b	dressing room	
42 c	courtyard	A narrow passage from the front to the back gate, area modernised by present occupants, *brindavan* facing entrance.
42 d	bathroom	With a stone water reservoir and enclosed copper pot. (One bathroom between three families, but three cow sheds)
42 e	cattle shed	An open area divided into three, with three troughs and thatched roofing.
42 f	eating room	

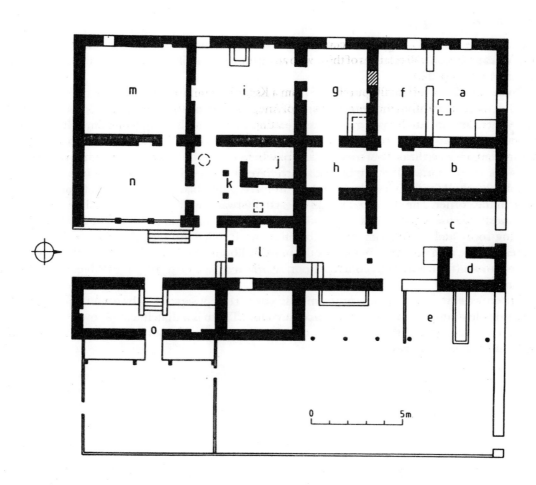

42 g kitchen	Adjoining doors between room f and i are now locked. A prayer shelf in corner.
42 h eating room	Also used for storage of foodstuffs, and as a dressing room
42 i kitchen	This is used by the eldest brother's family
42 j prayer room	
42 k sleeping room	
42 l verandah	Dwelling has been considerably modernised by present occupants
42 m store room	Changed between 1987-88, now used as a granary.
42 n sleeping room	Room used to be the front of a shop facing the street, it was changed in 1987-88
42 o cattle shed	Roofed enclosed area used for one family's cows with a back exit to land behind.

House no. 42

This large dwelling of 576 sq m is occupied by the families of three brothers (Guntakal, Krishna Murti and Venkateshwara), all relatives of those who advise the royal family. (Another brother, Ramaswamy, lives in House no. 32.)

House no. 42 was originally purchased from a Kshatriya family related to the occupants of House no. 31. It is situated within the central square of Anegondi behind the old palace (House no. 50). The main spaces are the kitchens (a, g and i) and eating areas (f and h). Only one family has a separate prayer room (j), and there is only one bathroom (d). It is said that if men are sitting in room (k), then the women can open the door of room (i) and pass between the households so as not to disturb them. The walls are of mortared square blocks, which have all been whitewashed. The interior has been completely rebuilt, with new walls, an arched fireplace, a new black stone kitchen floor, and prayer room in the corner. The threshold blocks of each doorway have been painted yellow and red. The outer west wing used to serve as a shop and store room (n), but this was altered in 1988 to serve as a sleeping room and a bathroom fronted by blue metal, roller shutters. The prayer room has flat plastered walls, with wooden columns on the outside. Rooms (i-k) and (n) have black slab flooring, whereas room (m) has a rough concrete floor. A *brindavan* in courtyard (c) is visible from the front entrance.

The entire east wing is given over to animals: cows are kept separately by each family so that the area is divided into three with a straw fence surround. There is a thatch lean-to over the cows, and three sets of eating troughs. New-born calves are kept in the dressing room. In 1990, the family owned eight bullocks and six cows.

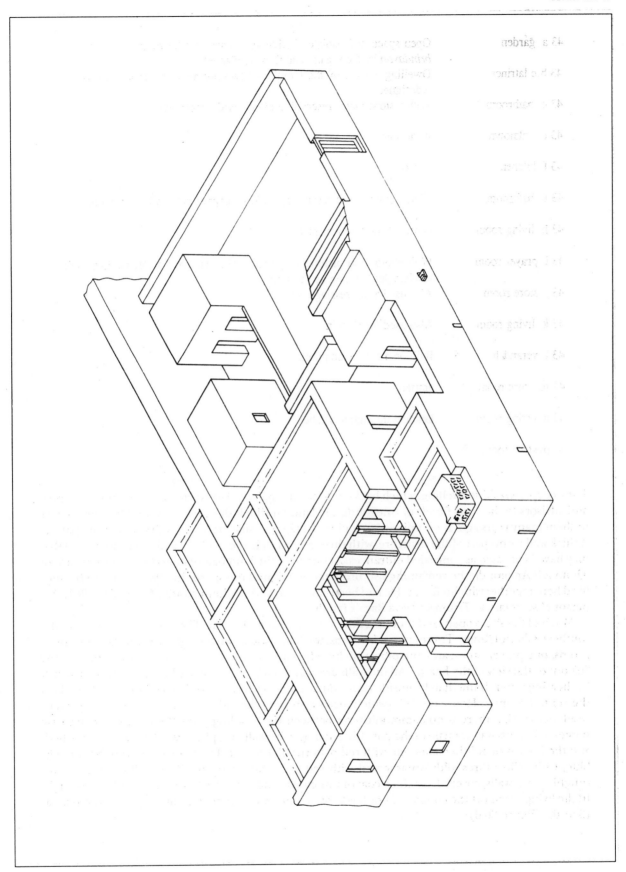

43 a	garden	Open space with isolated buildings, a back exit by room e, a water tap, *brindavan* by front gate, and flowers planted
43 b,c	latrines	Dwelling is used by the families of two brothers, the area is completely redesigned
43 d	bathroom	With a stone water reservoir and enclosed copper pot
43 e	unknown	storeroom?
43 f	kitchen	unused
43 g	bathroom	With a stone water reservoir, enclosed copper pot, and electric urn
43 h	living room	unused, with a prayer niche
43 i	prayer room	With photos and pictures of goddess Thaiyamma, an electric light bulb, and bangles hanging by the shrine.
43 j	store room	Also used as a dressing room
43 k	living room	Also used for sleeping
43 l	verandah	Built on a columned plinth
43 m	store room	unused
43 n	eating room	Leading through to kitchen
43 p	store room	

The occupants of this dwelling, which backs onto the old palace (House no. 50) were once retainers and advisors to the royal family of Anegondi; the land on which this house was built was given over to them many years ago. It occupies a large plot of 442 sq m, sharing a side wall with the old palace. A thick wall forms part of the structure, with three rooms (f, h and m) built within House no. 50 that may have been used as concealed entrances. At one time the land belonged to four brothers, two of whom left Anegondi; the remaining two brothers redesigned the space. In 1987, only one brother lived here together with his family. He had been chairman of the Administrative Council in 1961, and personal secretary to Tirumala Deva Raya's family.

Much of the site is open, and there is a flower garden (a) at the rear. The main gate faces onto the southern Chariot Route. There are two kitchens, two bathrooms, two toilets, two verandahs, two store rooms, one prayer room, and one prayer niche. The kitchen still in use (o) has a small dining area (n) out of the view of the hearth. All the walls are painted white. In one bathroom is an electric urn for heating water. Immediately outside room (f) is a wide archway, now blocked up, which leads to the central room of House no. 50k (which locals claim was the old elephant stable). (The present residents say that there is no communication between the dwellings, but the blocked-up archway suggests that this was not true in the past.) In room (k) the walls are plastered flat and whitewashed, and the floor is of polished concrete with red patterns picked out. The door frames are outlined in blue, with yellow thresholds ornamented with red and white patterns. Rooms (f) and (h) have roughly hewn walls, covered in a thick coat of whitewash, and concrete floors. The ceilings are high. In the living room (k) the concrete floor has a square incised block pattern and a polished red area. (See also Figure 36.d)

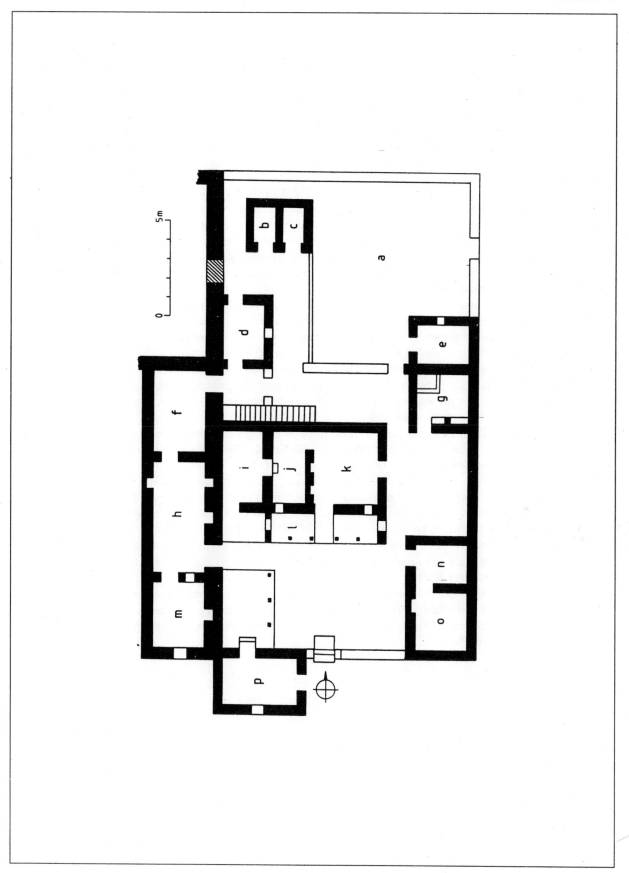

House no. 44

The Anegondi residence of Achyuta Deva Raya, this is a double-storeyed house covering an area of 570 sq m. The main entrance faces north onto the southern Chariot Route, though in the past the residence may have had several entrances. The dwelling appears to be constructed in two phases, the first of which borders the main entrance and was occupied in the past by palace guards. In order to have audience with the raja or rani, one passed through this entrance into an open courtyard which was enclosed on three sides by a columned verandah. From here, one ascended the steps of the raised verandah (m) where the raja was seated. Beyond is an inner reception court (f), to which only family and close friends are admitted. This is marked by a central water basin and an elaborate skylight, decorated in pale green paint (see Figure 36.a). The 14 rooms of the inner palace are arranged around this court. The upper rooms of this house have arched windows with the same beading as arches in the Secretariat (House no. 50i). The master bedroom on the upper storey (now unused) has a wind fan with a cord attached, which goes through a hole in the door frame and would have been pulled by a servant outside the room in the past. There are black slabs of polished stone throughout the ground floor, including the outside verandah. Some stones, particularly those at the entrances, have *rangoli* designs painted on them.

One of the deepest and most private rooms is the kitchen (a). This has black granite flooring and walls painted white with lime. There is a raised sink and a draining board; an arched fireplace is set into the rear wall (see Figure 48). Men are not permitted to enter. Room (k) used to be a bathroom, built inside due to the age of Rani Kuppamma, and room (n) served as her bedroom. Room (c) was once for milk and buttermilk preparation, but now stores some 60 huge cooking pots. (These were used in the past when the palace had to feed a large retinue of relatives, retainers and staff.) Today there is only one relative present responsible for running the property, maintaining the shrine in the prayer room, and one servant woman.

When Achyuta Deva Raya married, he and his wife lived in the house together with Rani Lal Kumari, wife of his father's brother, Durbar Raja Sri Krishna Deva Raya. Previously, it had been occupied by Krishna Deva Raya who reigned from 1871-72.

It is possible that this house was built for Rani Kuppamma who lived outside the other palace (House no. 50). Married at the age of nine, she was widowed at the age of eleven. It was the custom for women not to marry a second time, and so she had no issue. It was she who adopted her younger brother (Pampapati Raju) to be her heir, the future Sri Ranga Deva Raya. Another royal residence is indicated by the ruined plinth area to the rear of House no. 44, said to have been abandoned since the 1920s. This was once occupied both by the eldest sister of Sri Ranga Deva Raya, and by the daughter of Krishna Deva Raya.

The 'garden' area at the rear (south) of this property has been given over to two families, both relatives of Achyuta Deva Raya, who occupy House nos. 21 and 22. To the east is a cow shed, now converted into a garden. Adjoining this is House no. 33, a recent construction occupied by relatives. (see also Plates 26 to 28 and 57)

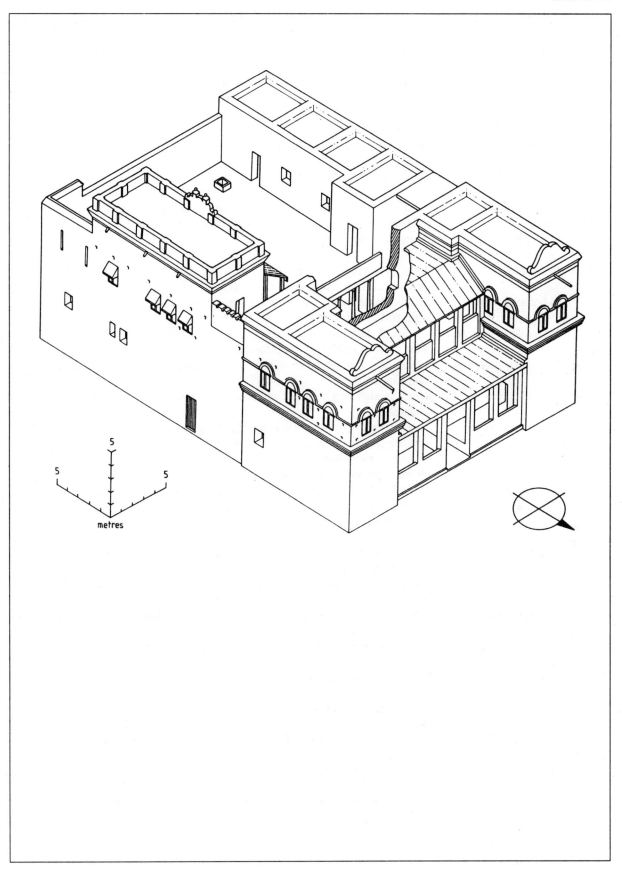

metres

44 a	kitchen	One of the deepest rooms in the house with an arched fire place, small drain, skylight
44 b	food preparation	A deep room with three doors off it. Female relatives eat in here. There are two skylights, black granite floor, and a raised sink.
44 c	buttermilk room	Now used as store for huge brass & copper pots, last used when palace fed hundreds of staff and relatives.
44 d	grinding room	Entered from room h, it has a door to the garden in south of compound
44 e	store room	Room containing boxes on stone benches.
44 f	reception court	Central covered court where relatives may have audience with the king and queen, a central skylight over stone basin, six doors off.
44 g	hallway	Gives access to room h, skylight above, two doors.
44 h	hall	Room gave access to steps (now removed) which lead to upper storey, area was lit from above, three doors off.
44 i	prayer room	Central stone plinth in Post-Empire design, carved wooden alter, representation of Nine Planets on ceiling.
44 j	child-birthing room	A dark room with one entrance, a small skylight, cupboard, and stone drain on north-east wall that leads to street.
44 k	storage room	Access only through room **h**, this was a bathroom in the past used by Rani Kuppamma.
44 l	chamber	Room through which the old cattle shed area could be reached from the verandah.
44 m	verandah	A raised seating area for those who have audience with the king. From here one can pass through to the rest of the palace.
44 n	sleeping room	In the past room was used by Rani Kuppamma. Her bathroom was built for her when she became elderly.
44 o	bathroom	Accessible from room **n**, and from steps in lower courtyard, a modern construction.
44 p	passage-way	Access to steps leading to the upper storey
44 q	courtyard	Lower courtyard where those wanting audience with the king first waited before being invited onto the raised verandah
44 rs	private quarters	Private rooms of the present king, a modern construction within the old walls.
44 t	entrance passage	Entrance to the dwelling through heavy carved doors, and a high threshold.
44 u	private quarters	Private rooms of the present queen with bathroom attached
44 v	granary	Narrow room with a raised door.
44 w	passage	Giving access to steps leading to upper storey, used by guards in the past.
44 x	plinth	Constructed on both sides of main entrance, Post-Empire design with a modern superstructure
44 y	store room	In the past used by those guarding the royal family.
44 z	garden	Area used to be a cattle shed, now a garden, it gives access to an exit at the south of the passage.

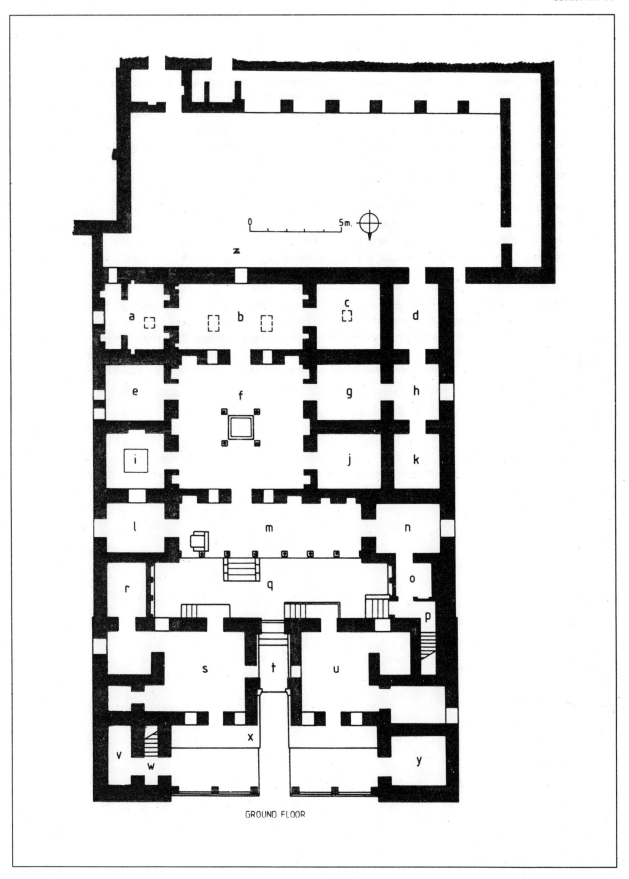

GROUND FLOOR

House no. 45

This large dwelling of 407 sq m appears to have been constructed in two phases. In front is an arched verandah (r) with an open yard (l) behind and steps leading to the roof. A second columned verandah (j) opens onto the yard. The rear of the roofed dwelling with 11 rooms is almost square; its layout may be compared with House nos. 44, 46 and 47. The dwelling is occupied by the household head, his three married sons and their families, and a daughter: a total of 18 people.

The rear of this house has black slab flooring decorated with *rangoli* designs. The walls are plastered and whitewashed. The central room (e) has a large square skylight over a stone drain of interlocking blocks, now concreted over. Three coconuts hang from the walls, one for each married couple.

The rounded columns in the front of the house have been painted light green; to the left of the plinth is a hollow wood storage area. A tall screen has been built across the doorway of the front part of the house so that there is no view through to the verandah or central hall. On the verandah (j) there are four square planks, each carved separately, with square pegs. The pillars have stone bases, and are painted brown, while the capitals are blue with silver edging. There are black stone slabs on the verandah floor, and the top part of the lower wall is painted white. A grindstone (*bisakalu*) is placed here.

A roofed area (t) between this property and House no. 31 is enclosed; it contains a bathroom, a shared well, and a washing area with chickens at the back. The open yard of this dwelling is freely passed through by family members who live in the adjoining dwellings. The house forms part of a complex of dwellings whose occupants (all Kshatriyas) are related, and whose properties are joined by pathways and doorways. Some even share the same garden space. (see Figure 41 and Plates 34, 53, 54, 56 and 58)

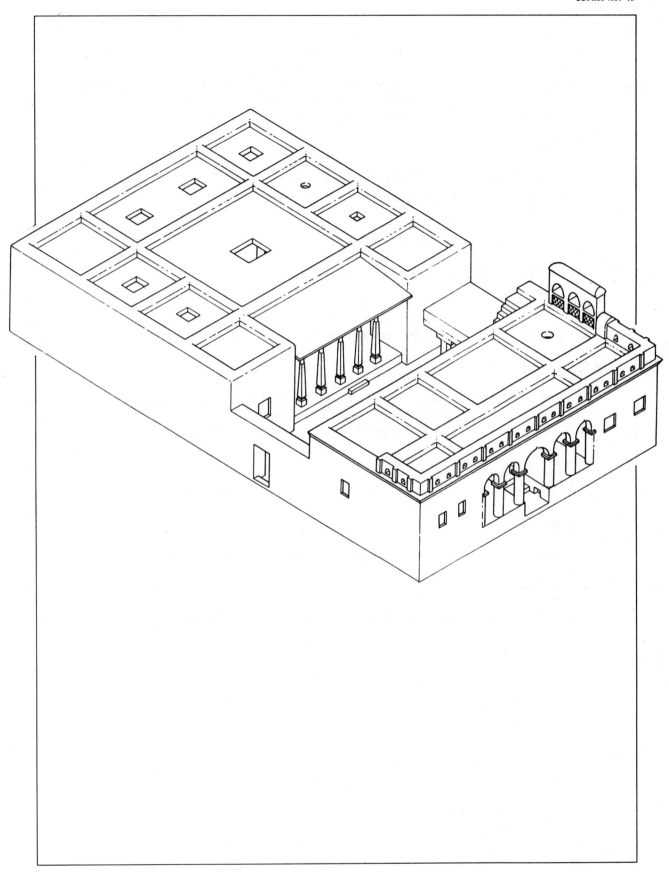

45 a	kitchen	With a large three pot clay hearth, a grindstone, and an arched fireplace
45 b	dining room	For food preparation, buttermilk churning and eating, with a drain and stone water basin. It has two skylights and access to c.
45 c	buttermilk room	With a second hearth perhaps for meat, and a skylight.
45 d	granary	
45 e	reception court	With a central stone drain and a skylight above, it has six doorways off and gives access to rest of dwelling.
45 f	storage room	With a small skylight, it is now used for storage.
45 g	prayer room	Having a raised white plinth.
45 h	child-birthing room	It is now used for wood storage.
45i	store room	
45 j	verandah	On a plinth with steps leading up to the rest of the house.
45 k	sleeping room	
45 l	yard	Obscured entrance to rest of house (dog-leg wall), the yard is used by relatives to cross town to their homes
45 m,n	living room	Elderly man and woman occupant, access to room n.
45 o	hall	On raised plinth
45 p	unknown	
45 q	unknown	
45 r	verandah	Entrance through raised columned area with steps leading to street.
45 s	unknown	
45 t	yard	This is shared with house no.31, and has a bathroom to the west, and a well.

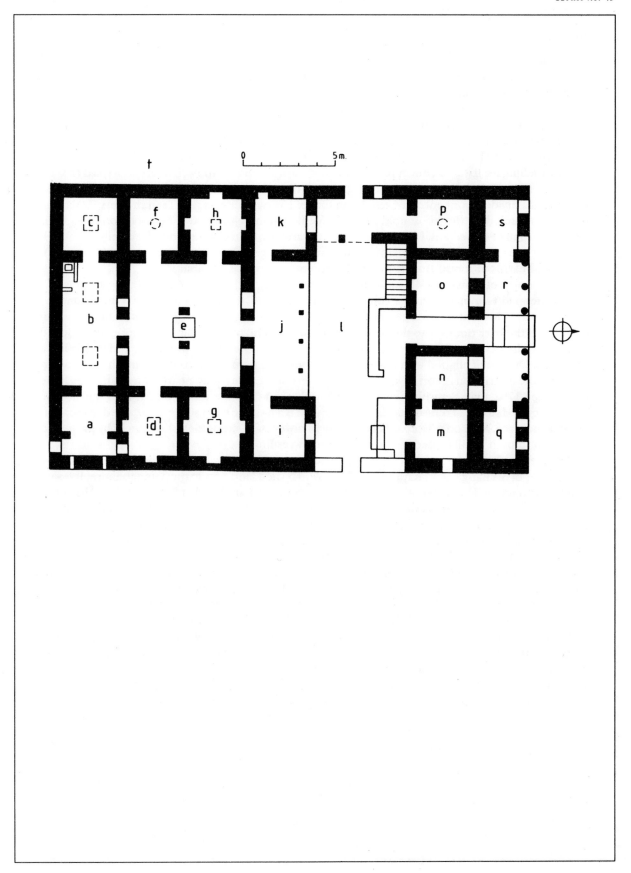

House no. 46

The house is situated on the western Chariot Route that runs from the Talarighat crossing to Gangavati gate. The owners have fields close to Pampa Sarovar. The dwelling covers 520 sq m and is divided between two main areas. The first area consists of a roofed dwelling with 12 rooms, with an open central court (n) with steps leading to the roof (see Figures 38 and 39). The second area, which adjoins the first on the north and is of almost the same size, has an enclosed open yard (l). It contains the two bathrooms (e and f, see Figure 43), latrines, and an old kitchen (d) with a red polished plinth beside the hearth. In the middle of the space stands a large hen house with a well to its south.

The dwelling itself was once occupied by two discrete households: the well in the courtyard (n) and the room (p) are all that remain of the original building. In the west wing are modern rooms. The remains of a divided front entrance, similar to that of House no. 44, can be seen in ruins. Today the house is occupied by the household head, K. Venkataramaraju, his two married sons and their families: a total of 18 persons. Four cooking hearths are distributed thoughout the dwelling, though not all are in use: some are for cooking meat. There is a vegetarian hearth and kitchen in room (t), and meat hearths in rooms (m), (p) and (d). Room (r) serves as a granary.

To the north of House no. 46, and aligned with its front wall, are the remains of a plinth with a central stepped entrance. It had a columned verandah and two rooms at either side. Room (p) remains, with a low lintel with a gap marking the position of a carving of Ganesha. At the original entrance is the back doorway to the bathrooms of no. 46. The rectangular well belonged to the old house, and the newer buildings were simply built around it. The well is still in use, and beside it is a *brindavan*. On a shelf aligned with that of room (k) outside is an old hero stone on which is carved a trident; the inscription is worn away. (Two other hero stones are found nearby, one dated 1801, the other dated 1792, together with the name Venkateshvara.) On a low plinth on the near wall are the standing carved stones of nine deities. Also in the yard is a huge circular stone with carved decoration on its upper face. Men once wore this as a collar in order to to strengthen their necks by pacing up and down steps; it is still is used by those practising wrestling.

The men in this house have access to prime land around Anegondi, since their grandfather was the brother of Sri Ranga Deva Raya (died 1918), who owned land beside the Tungabhadra. It is said that the structure of House no. 46 already existed when Venkataramaraju moved in there. His father had two wives, and he had previously been living in the area behind House no. 44. Outside in the garden to the north is an old latrine. Hung high on the walls of the verandah are numerous photographs of tiger and cheetah shoots in the Anegondi area taken in the 1940s and 1950s. Near to a pond in the families' plantation is a small Siva shrine with a black stone *lingam*.

The prayer room (k) contains a high prayer plinth, painted white, with shelves around the walls (see Figure 40). In the central court is a stone basin covered with dung and ash when not in use. A raised platform in the middle is used on the 11th day after childbirth to celebrate the 'coming out' of the new mother and child. On the other side of the verandah is the child-birthing room (i), with no light inside, but a drain in the corner. This dark room is used ordinarily as a sleeping room by Venkataramaraju. One married brother sleeps in room (a), the other in room (c). Both rooms have black slab flooring, while the floors of rooms (i), (j) and (k) are of concrete. The walls are plastered and painted white. It is said that the wooden columns in the houses are of imported Burma teak, fashioned by local carpenters. (see Plates 32, 36 and 60)

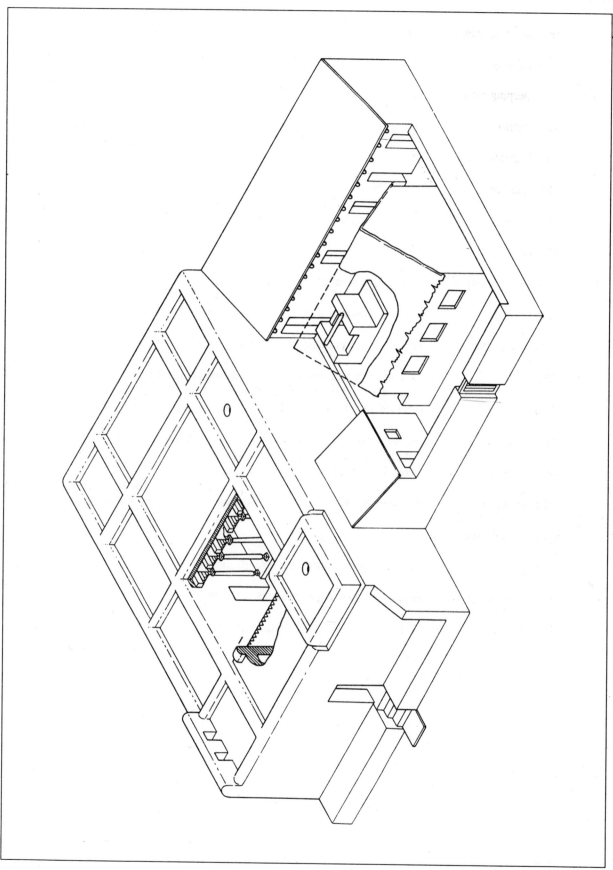

46 a	sleeping room	eldest brother
46 b	hallway	Four doors off, access to bedrooms, rest of house, and garden.
46 c	sleeping room	second eldest brother
46 d	kitchen	Now unused with part polished red floor and access to yard and garden.
46 e	bathroom	
46 f	bathroom	With a copper water heater, stone water basin, drain, and flow pipe so reservoir can be filled from outside
46 g	latrine	used by two families
46 h	latrine	
46 i	child-birthing room	With a stone drain and no light source except from doorway.
46 j	verandah	Covered columned area
46 k	prayer room	The deities are placed on a huge white stepped plinth
46 l	yard	An open area with bathrooms and latrines off it. The well is still used: beside it a prayer altar with nine stone carvings of deities.
46 m	kitchen	Used for meat cooking, with stone benches, gives access to room r
46 n	courtyard	An unroofed, open area with some flowers planted. It offers access to rest of house and has steps leading to roof.
46 o	hallway	Three doors off, giving access to kitchen t and yard
46 p	store room	A room with two doors, for fuel storage and a hearth for cooking meat
46 q	chicken house	
46 r	granary	No light source, only access through room m
46 s	entrance verandah	Entrance to dwelling from street
46 t	kitchen	With a skylight, drain, and raised hearth.

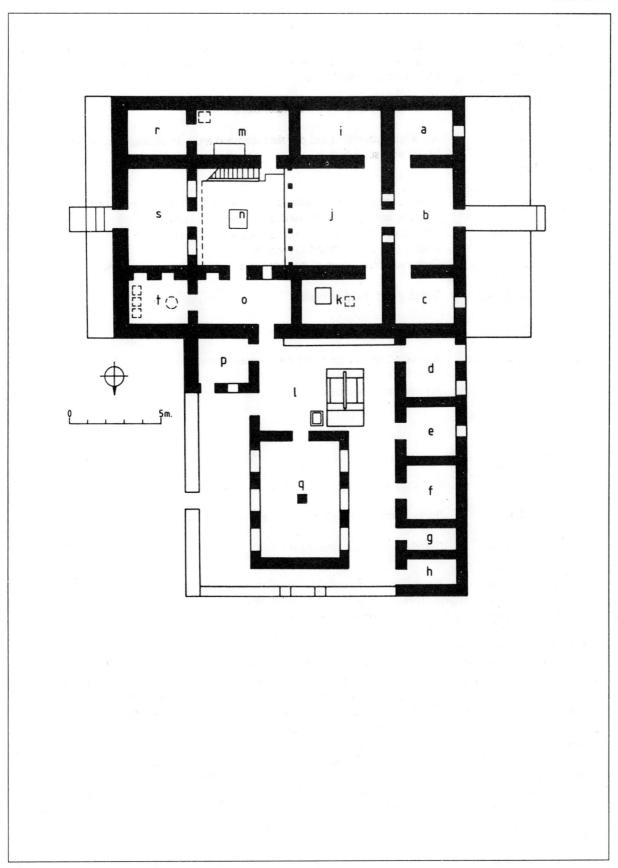

47 a	garden	Some areas planted with flowers, steps leading to the roof, a disused well, and a back gate for women. A three stone hearth for water.
47 b	chicken coop	Now used as a wood store
47 c	latrine	With foot stands and a stone water basin
47 d	bathroom	A sunken bath with a red polished diamond area, an enclosed copper pot heated with solid fuel.
47 e	sleeping room	
47 f	kitchen	A white painted room with a large arched fireplace, solid fuel and kerosene hearths, used for food preparation and eating.
47 g	living room	Four doors off, used for sitting, watching television and eating. It is divided by a thin partition to room **h**
47 h	sleeping room	Partitioned from room g, it is used as a sleeping and dressing room
47 i	sleeping room	Sleeping and dressing room
47 j	prayer room	Locked: the present occupants only rent rooms **a - i**
47 k	reception court	A covered central reception court unused except to access rooms rented at the back of the house.
47 l	store room	Rooms **l, m, n** were locked
47 m	prayer room	
47 n	store room	
47 o	store room	Currently used as a chicken house.
47 p	verandah	Street entrance through which the rest of the house is accessed.
47 q	store room	Currently used as a sleeping room.

This house lies on the southern Chariot Route. The dwelling consists of a covered area of 435 sq m, with a small garden (a) and chicken coop (b) to the rear. Within the enclosed wall of the garden is an unused well, and steps leading to the roof. In the corner of the yard is a stone quern (*rubbughundu*). The house itself is built at ground level, not on a raised plinth. There are two entrances, one at the front facing north towards the street, and another through which women enter at the back. This house has a concrete floor throughout, with red polished floors in rooms (p) and (g). The bathroom (d) is finely finished, with a red polished diamond design in the middle of the rectangular washing stone (see Figure 44.a). A large cement cistern is seen here, together with brass buckets and copper pots. Door lintels and thresholds are decorated with carved rosettes or lotus motifs; the frames are painted a blue-grey colour, except for the threshold at the main entrance which is red (see Figure 37). The door between rooms (k) and (p) is heavy with brass spikes.

The house originally belonged to Achyuta Deva Raya's biological mother and father. It was subsequently inhabited by his brothers Sri Ranga Deva Raya and Narasimha Deva Raya, who left and rented it out in the 1980s to a pharmacist and his family who come from Adoni. They occupy only half of the dwelling space: the central hall and adjoining rooms have been locked by the original owners. The new family, which is Protestant, has placed a Christian shrine in the living room (i). (see Plate 29)

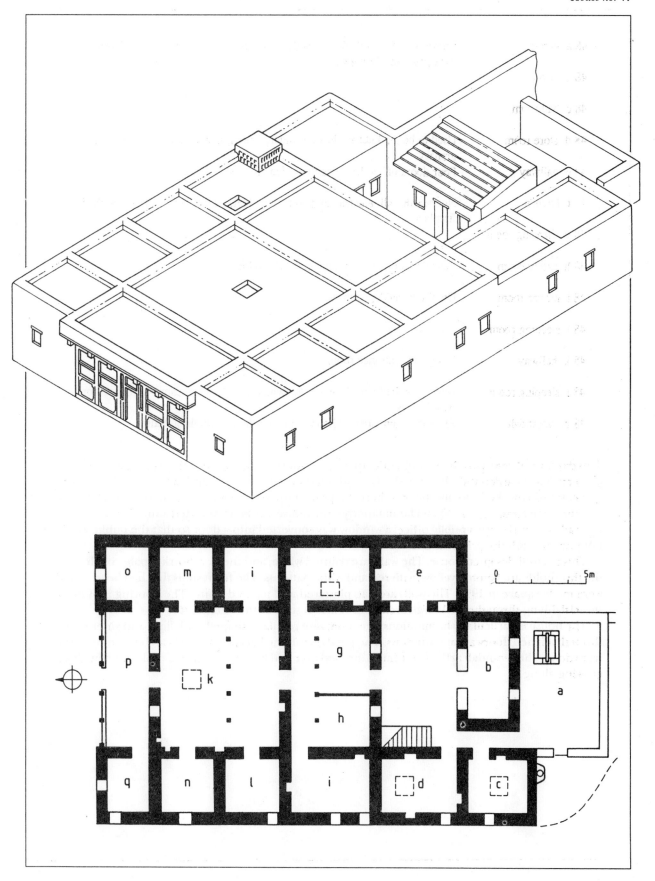

48 a	garden	Enclosed space with flower beds, steps to roof, a water storage basin, a back gate, and *brindavan*
48 b	latrine	
48 c	bathroom	
48 d	store room	Used to be the kitchen, has a grinder, drains, many stone benches, and a granary
48 e	hallway	Four doors off with access to garden and rest of house
48 f	kitchen	No hearth: all electric and kerosene fuel, stone bench, large arched fireplace
48 g	dressing room	
48 h	eating room	Four doors off, it is at the centre of dwelling
48 i	prayer room	On plinth, hidden from window by a 4' white wall
48 j	sleeping room	
48 k	hallway	Verandah, entrance room
48 l	sleeping room	New door built in place of the window. Room became an office for public visits.
48 m	verandah	Entrance from street to house, running the full width of house

This dwelling of 288 sq m is built onto a side street to the south of the village. A third of the area consists of an enclosed garden with flower beds (a), in which is situated a latrine and bathroom; the remains of a covered cow shed can also be seen here. Steps lead up to the roof where there is an elaborate chimney (see Figure 36.c). When Hanumantayya, the house owner, was elected administrative chief, he made room (l) into a public office: a window was converted into a door so that the public would not pass through the private areas.

This is a well designed house. The walls are painted white, and the woodwork is pale cobalt blue; the thresholds are painted yellow, with red and white patterns. The front steps that had been round were made square in 1990. The walls are flat, plastered and painted white. The flooring is of black stone slabbing throughout. A large arched fireplace is seen in the kitchen (f).

The house is particularly harmonious: the rooms are regularly shaped, with light and air entering through aligned doorways and windows. The *brindavan* in the back garden (a) can be seen from the front door. The verandah at the front (m) is meshed over and has a huge bush of pink bougainvillaea growing along it.

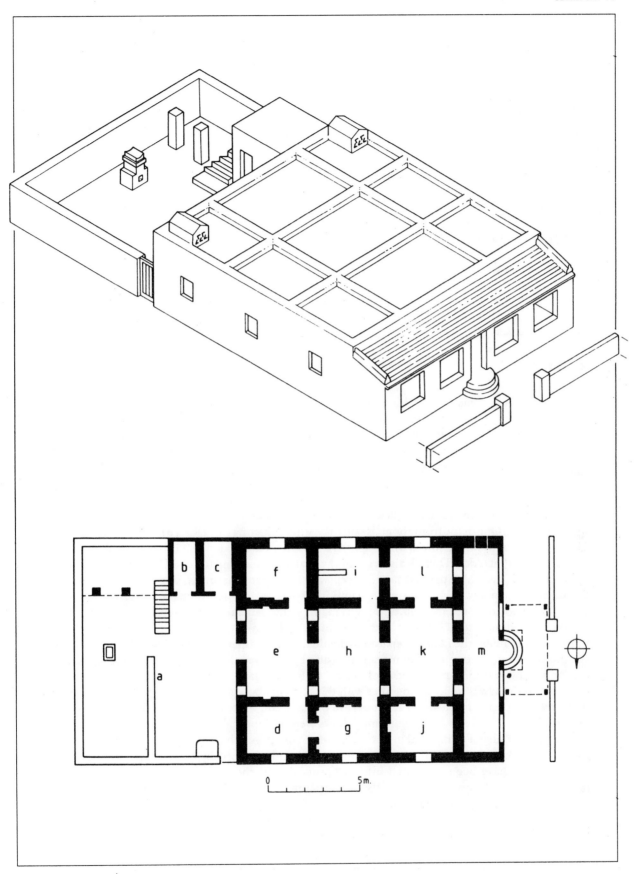

49 a	yard	enclosed yard with *brindavan*, cattle area in past, second entrance
49 b	bathroom	with water heater
49 c	dining room	with well built in and exit to yard
49 d	kitchen	
49 e	store room	for boxes
49 f	hall	entrance hall with two grindstones set in the floor
49 g	prayer room	
49 h	childbirth room	
49 i	bedroom	
49 j	verandah	
49 k	bedroom	for guests

The property is occupied by an elderly woman, her married son, and his family of two sons and two daughters. The family are from the Vaishya community, being Settys or traders; indeed, the owner's father became wealthy from selling oils and grains. In the raised verandah in the back yard (a) are hollows worn in the stone which were made by labourers grinding rice into flour. A drain passes the length of the outer area to the street. On the low plinth behind the house is a row of six grindstones where 12 people would sit crushing rice to a powder. In recent years, the area was covered with a sloping thatch roof and is now used as a cow shed. (see Plate 51)

Near to the front entrance is a guest room (k). This can be entered both from the verandah and from the house. One of the front rooms is said to be where Krishna Deva Raya came to meet the family. The floor of that room is covered with English Art Nouveau tiles dated 1896; in fact, the house might even be somewhat older. There is also a room (h) that was once used for child birthing. A well within the kitchen (d) has a blue painted cast-iron grill with floral patterns on two sides. A shelf fitted beside the well was to support a *brindavan* made of imported tiles, as well as a number of carved snake stones. The plinth had collapsed by 1990, and the remains of the *brindavan* were seen on the floor. Three carved snake stones stood in a row by the well hung with leaves.

In the early 1990s, the family prepared to divide the house up for the marriage of one of the sons. For this occasion, the dwelling was modernised and brightly painted. The old roof was stripped, and the supporting steel girders painted apple green, with stone slabs laid on top. In the central room (f), the squared drain was removed together with the skylight above. However, the walls and floor plan of the dwelling remain. The internal floors are of black and white marble, with floral decoration in the middle. The carved wooden entrance doors were stripped and re-varnished. The well in the dining room (c) has a pump so that water can be obtained from a tank in the roof, and the ancient iron railings that surrounded it have been removed and replaced by concrete. Sculptured snake stones nearby have been cemented into the ground, and the area around painted in sky blue polyurethane. The prayer room (g) is also newly painted. Water is available on tap in the bathroom. The *brindavan* outside has been remade using the older tiles with red designs and floral patterns; a *tulsi* plant grows out of the top. A circular grindstone is still set into the ground nearby. Outside, a long trough for mass cooking has been set into the raised ground. Here rows of cooking pots can be heated.

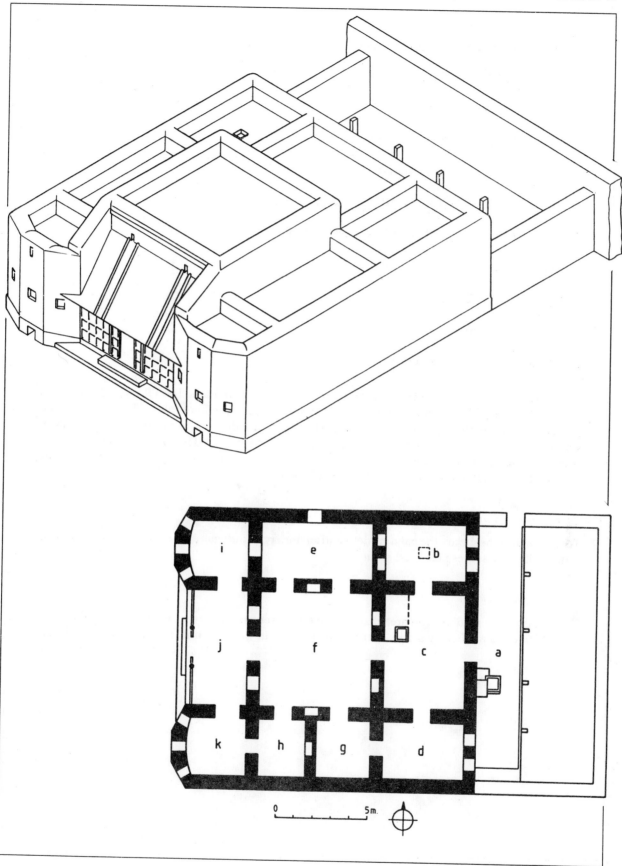

50 a	Palm garden and underground well
50 b	Servant's quarters
50 c	Demolished palace
50 d	Palace of Venkamma and Narasingamma
50 e	Living quarters of Narasingamma
50 f	Living quarters of Tirumala Deva Raya and Rama Deva Raya
50 g	Living quarters of Rama Deva Raya and family
50 h	Central Square
50 i	Secretariat and Archives Office
50 j	Cow shed
50 k	Horse and Elephant stables

This dwelling is occupied by Tirumala Deva Raya, his married son Rama Deva Raya and family, and a number of guests. The room groupings are very complex, and are here referred to by letters (a-k) per group, rather than per room. It is possible that this dwelling was originally used as an administrative centre with an arched colonnade right the way around. The only fine arched building that remains is the records office (or secretariat). The dwelling covers a large area and the distinct groups of rooms are set out below. (see Plates 48 and 49)

Palm garden and underground well (50a)

To the north of the site are the palm gardens and an underground well. At the site of the well is a shrine with small snake stones placed all around.

Servant's quarters (50b)

To the east of the gardens is an area that used to be the servants' quarters, with various structures in ruins. There is a methane gas tank in the yard, also a flour mill that only has access from the road.

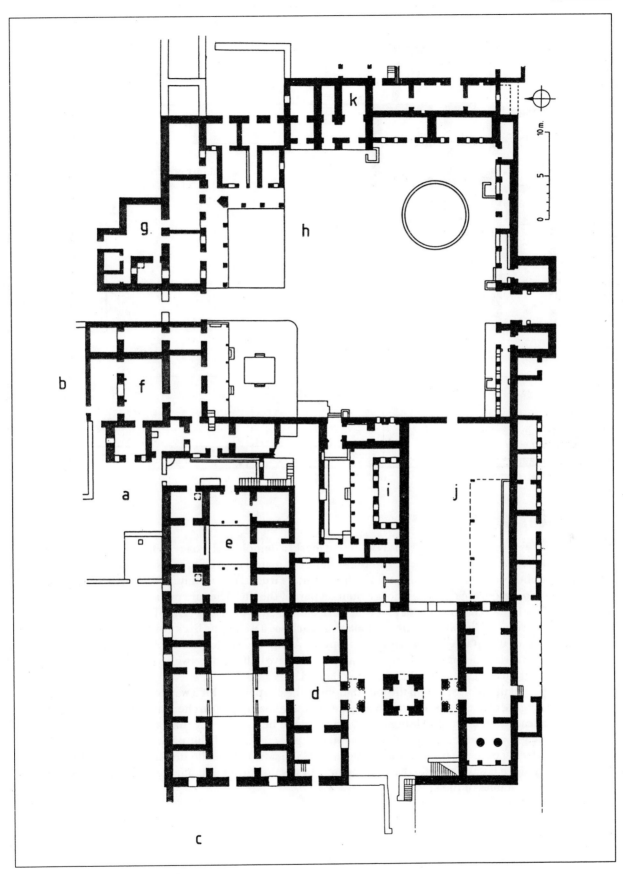

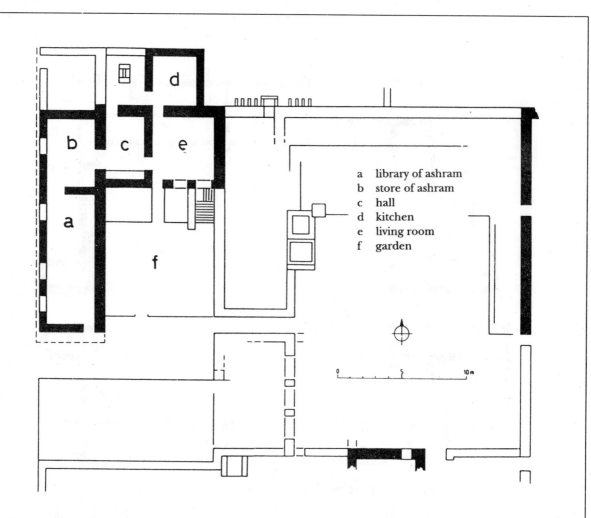

a   library of ashram
b   store of ashram
c   hall
d   kitchen
e   living room
f   garden

Demolished palace (50c)

To the far west of the dwellings is an area (c) that marks a demolished palace. When this fell into ruin, the wood and stone features were sold off as building materials. The area used to be occupied by relatives of those in House no. 34, whose mother was Tirumala Deva Raya's sister. An ashram and library for devotees of Sri Aurobindo are built on part of the site. They are maintained by a Kshatriya man called Katweh from Madhya Pradesh, unrelated to Achyuta Deva Raya. The ashram has been built using some of the walls of the old palace. It encloses a well in its back corner. The steps of the raised palace run up the side of Katweh's property. At the top is a low relief plaster elephant head, made out in incised decoration. Part of the walls inside have half-windows with a pointed arch. During the August rains of 1991, the ashram roof collapsed.

   This part of this house rests on the foundations of the old palace which was demolished in the early 1980s. Hanging over the garden wall to the east are the remains of an arched latrine. A path through this area leads to relatives in House no. 46; the passage belongs to K.Venkataramaraju. An elderly female neighbour remembers seeing a painted representation of the palace showing all of the archways facing onto the road beside House no. 49. She says that she did not know who was living in the palace since it was a closed area, entered only by royalty through its gateway. That area is said to be the horse stables of the king.

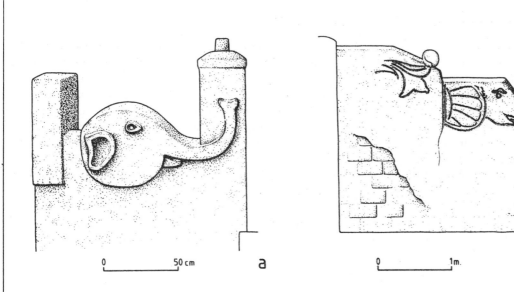

steps to the roof of House no. 46   ruined stairs of House no. 50c

Palace of Venkamma and Narasingamma (50d)

This dwelling, now standing in ruins, adjoins the previous one, and was the palace of Venkamma, the brother of Narasingamma (the 7th British Pensioner). It has no roof, though most of the walls are still standing. There are four enclosed rooms to the north, with a fifth hallway having a wooden trellis in front. The southern portion of this palace is of interest for its central arched structure. Steps lead up to the roof. Close by is the family shrine of Achyuta Deva Raya. This was robbed in 1979 when all of its images were lost. Facing the shrine is a kitchen with a huge arched chimney place; between the two is the women's entrance to the royal house. The area is still used as a passageway by women wishing to avoid the main street. Monkeys leap from the huge trees that have grown within the ruined palace walls. The rows of arched doorways, plastered walls and lamp niches indicate that it was once a splendid dwelling. (see Plate 50)

Living quarters of Narasingamma (50e)

This set of rooms in the north-west corner of the complex are said to be those of Narasingamma. The area has been much altered by the present occupants, and is used as a kitchen. The front three rooms are on a raised plinth, and may have been used as an entrance verandah for another palace, with two rooms opening off on each side. Steps descend from the plinth to an open courtyard, through which women enter the dwelling. Steps also climb up to to the second floor rooms in area (i), used by the late Harihara Deva Raya. The stone wall is faced with plaster, and has an open balustrade around the roof. In the corner of the courtyard is a triangular sink.

The rear building is square and divided into three sets of three rooms. The central room is used for eating, and is a wide open hall the full length of the dwelling, having a central sunken floor with a square skylight above. At one end is a wash basin and drain; at the other end a deep grinder. One of the rooms that opens off this space was for prayer in the past, though later it was used as a kitchen. There are the remains of three kitchens, two currently in use, one for meat cooking, the other for vegetarian cooking. The ceramic hearth in one kitchen, built to take three vessels, is decorated with *rangoli* designs when not in use. A triple-stone hearth lies nearby.

Living quarters of Tirumala Deva Raya and Rama Deva Raya (50f)

The series of rooms making up this group serves as the dwelling space of Tirumala Deva Raya and his wife Rajendra Kumari (deceased 1989). The structure was considerably altered during the 1960s so that unlike other palaces the rooms have little symmetry. Immediately to the north is a paved area leading to a large bathroom, prayer room and store room. A dining room and bedroom make up the next set of rooms, while to the south are situated the drawing room or office with chairs covered with tiger and leopard skins. All around the walls are photographs showing groups of men with slain animals or royalty riding on elephants during religious festivals. One table is draped with a bear skin, the snarling head resting on the paws in front; another table has a stuffed leopard's head. Tirumala Deva Raya's own room was once the private office of an administrator of Anegondi (the village had been an administrative centre until 1947). To the south of these rooms is a verandah facing the central square (j). Beside Tirumala Deva Raya's quarters is a raised concrete platform which may have been built for some celebration, such as the wedding of one of his daughters. There are steps leading up to the plinth which is used in the evenings as a cool sitting platform, and a place to receive visitors.

Living quarters of Rama Deva Raya (50g)

This was used in 1988 by Rama Deva Raya and the family retainers. In the near past this had been the residence of Achyuta Deva Raya's father, and more recently of Rama Deva Raya himself. The courtroom was later used as a library, and then as a dispensary. Other rooms within the complex have been used as a school or a store for paddy. Water buffalo are kept in the rear yard. The rooms form an irregular shape: in the past the rulers gave living spaces to their advisors, and some areas may have been lost in this way. Areas (g) and (f) are separated by the back gate to the premises through which the public passes. At the back entrance, the door lintel rests on two stone pillars which narrow the entrance. The remainder of the entrance is built of brick. The arcade around the central square is now partly blocked up.

Central square (50h)

The central square and gardens around which the administrative offices were built in the past are occupied by numerous visitors and lodgers. Area (h) was used as a public square when Tirumala Deva Raya was a Member of the Legislative Assembly, and included a number of administrative buildings. Left of the main gate is a door through to a room in the bastion, and a narrow passage of blocked-up archways. Here, too, is a bathing area on a plinth. To the right of the main gate is another bastion, with a doorway consisting of two blocked-up arches, a large water tank, and a grinding wheel for mortar and plaster; a massive circular grinding stone lies unused in a corner. Recently, as more arches have been blocked up, additional walls to create bathing chambers have been built. An early photograph taken here of a group of dignitaries shows an arcade plastered and painted white where people walked around. (see Figure 35)

Secretariat and Archives Office (50i)

In the past, after entering the compound through the main gate visitors would have proceeded to the public offices to the west in area (i). The secretary and cashier worked here, seated on a raised verandah with a roof supported by elaborately carved wooden beams, now sadly decayed. The state records, archives and stationery were kept in a store room at the back. The archive room was once roofed, and contains many niches and shelves. At the southern end is a latrine and bathroom for present-day occupants. The Secretariat used to be the Records Office where all the village archives were kept; it was also a treasury. Currently, it serves as a store for paddy. In the recent past it was used as a prison and still has a small window built into the door, where the guard used to sit. Two of the doorways are blocked up, though the one with the prison guard's window remains.

At one time the raised verandah was surrounded on three sides by arched colonnades. The verandah is very deep with two rows of decorated wooden columns. These are divided by the east wall. The arches in the Secretariat have a beaded rim picked out in red paint. One arch on the west side is blocked up to create a prayer room. The present occupants use the narrow corridor next to this room's entrance for cooking.

Inside, facing the steps from the verandah is a door which leads to a long narrow room with a high ceiling. The arched doorway has two narrower archways on each side. Beyond, are deep arched wall niches of the same size. The long room has cupboards with wooden doors at either end, and a tall square wall niche opposite the door. This is crammed full of thick books in southern Indian languages, Urdu and English. The Urdu books date from the time when Anegondi came under the rule of Hyderabad. Here also is a stuffed mongoose, the skin partly eaten away.

The rooms to the east used to serve as a post office, and then as a bakery. There are four blocked-up arches, though two have windows. From here, steps lead to the Secretariat's house. Recently, a thick stone wall was built on the plinth using the area where the second row of wooden columns runs. This encloses the space used as a bedroom. Tirumala Deva Raya said that he built the interior of the stone house in the early 1980s for guests or for rentals. (see Plate 30)

Cow shed (50j)

This area used to house the family's cows. The outer wall beside House no. 38, still has the remains of a stucco covering high up on the wall. Access is obtained through a gate centrally placed in the wall. The wall left of the main gate has five archways, four of which are blocked up, but with windows. The cow shed consists of four roughly hewn pillars supporting a long thatched area for cows, with a long trough (12 m) in faced stone. Protruding iron rings are for tying up the animals. The ground there is high due to the accumulation of years of dung and straw deposits. A low, blocked up arched doorway in the wall would have led to the central court of Narsingamma's palace (50d).

Horse and elephant stables (50k)

Rooms (b) and (c) may have been stables for keeping a horse or elephant. Room (a) may have been the original habitation area for grooms looking after the animals. It contains a grinder and a secondary wall division. People mention a heavy iron ring for restraining animals, but this is no longer seen. These days the family cannot afford to maintain an elephant.

In 1990, a Brahmana family from Chitradurga district occupied this brick faced dwelling. The ceiling is of wooden beams, and the floor is dung coated. The walls are plastered and whitewashed. Room (a) at the front is the same as room (c) externally; internally it is divided by a shallow arch. South of the room is a blocked-up doorway. Area (b) is a long storeroom, with arches at the back and at the side. Room (c), with its half blocked up doorway but no internal division, is used by the family. It is a bare room with a small cooking stove, and a prayer shelf on which an image of the goddess Lakshmi is placed.

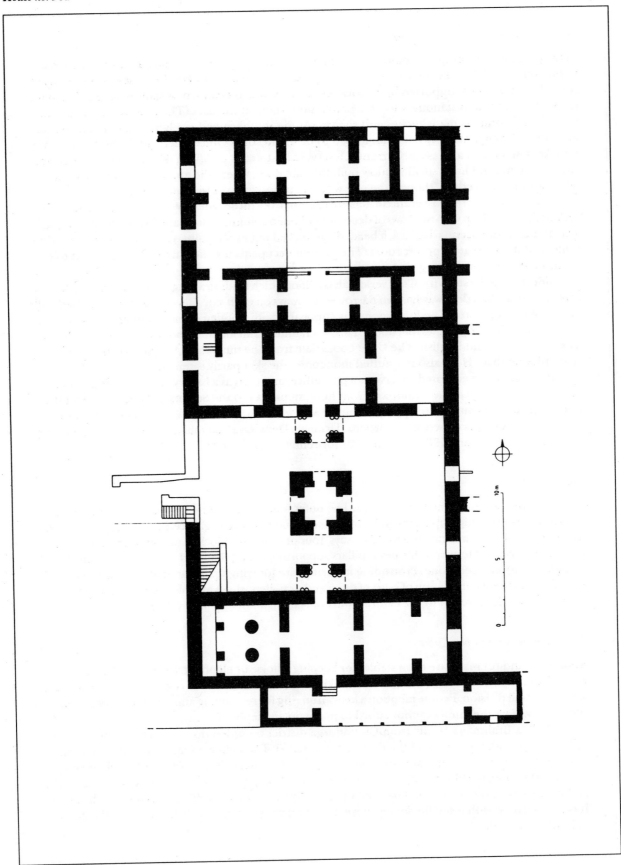

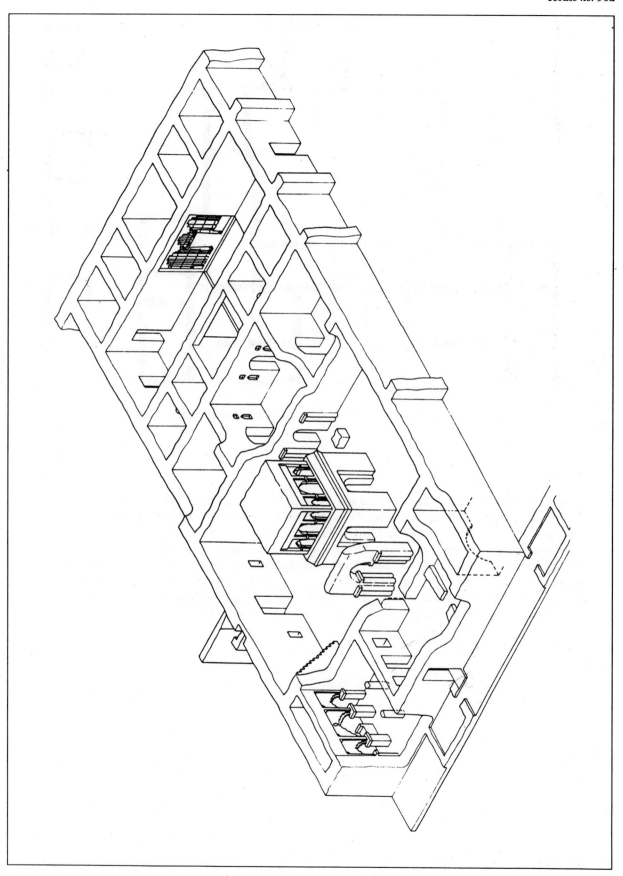

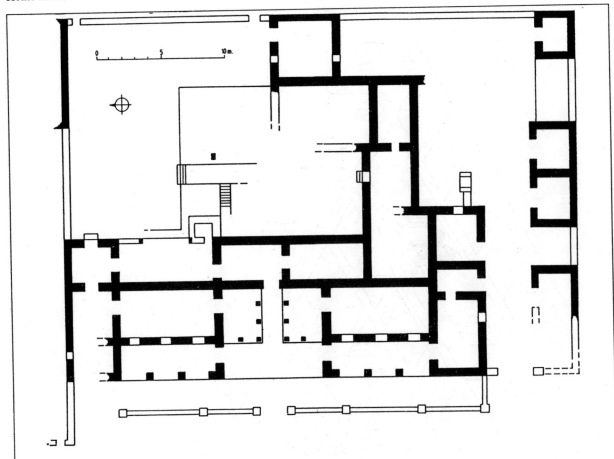

House no. 51

This large building behind House no. 50 once served as an administrative court, though it was also residential. Up until 1947 it was the residence of Hadi Hussein, the town judiciary, magistrate and local government officer who worked with the Anegondi raja. In 1949, these administrative offices were shifted to Gangavati. A dispensary took over the building, providing traditional Muslim medicines. When this moved to another part of Anegondi several years later, the building became dilapidated. In 1990 there was one old man squatting in a side room, while the remainder of the house was in a state of advanced decay. The building had wooden columns with finely carved lotus brackets.

In 1992, the house was completely razed, and brand new government offices were erected on the site.

House no. 51: Wooden columns

183

PART THREE

Appendices

APPENDIX 1

House Type, Religion, Caste and Occupation

House no.	Type	Religion	Caste	Occupation
1	A	Hindu	Vaddaru	house builder
2	A	Hindu	Vaddaru	
3	A	Hindu	Vaddaru	farm labourer
4	A	Muslim		farm labourer
5	A	Hindu	Bedaru	
6	B	Hindu	Vaishya	merchant
7	B	Hindu	Janata	government clerk
8	B	Hindu	Kambararu	blacksmith
9	B	Muslim		farm labourer
10	B	Hindu	Bedaru	
11	B	Hindu	Madagiru	farm labourer
12	B	Hindu	Bedaru	farm labourer
13	B	Muslim		farm labourer
14	C	Hindu	Banajigaru	domestic service
15	C	Hindu	Vaddaru	house builder
16	C	Hindu	Kshatriya	farmer
17	C	Hindu	Lingayat	electrician
18	C	Hindu	Brahmna	land owner
19	C	Hindu	Katguruh	butcher
20	C	Hindu	Kurabaru	shepherd, small trader
21	C	Hindu	Kshatriya	land owner
22	C	Hindu	Kshatriya	land owner
23	C	Hindu	Madagiru	
24	C	Hindu	Madagiru	farmer
25	D	Hindu	Banajigaru	electrician

House no.	Type	Religion	Caste	Occupation
26	D	Hindu	Lingayat	village level worker
27	D	Hindu	Lingayat	doctor
28	D	Hindu	Banajigaru	land owner
29	D	Hindu	Bedaru	local administrator
30	D	Hindu	Kshatriya	land owner
31	D	Hindu	Kshatriya	admin, tax collector
32	D	Hindu	Chetabanajigeru	land owner, politician
33	D	Hindu	Kshatriya	land owner
34	D	Hindu	Kshatriya	land owner
35	D	Hindu	Kshatriya	land owner
36	D	Hindu	Chetabanajigeru	land owner
37	D	Hindu	Madagiru	
38	D	Hindu	Kshatriya	boat contractor
39	D	Hindu	Chetabanajigeru	land owner
40	D	Hindu	Reddi	agriculturist
41	D	Hindu	Kshatriya	land owner
42	D	Hindu	Chetabanajigeru	land owner
43	D	Hindu	Chetabanajigeru	land owner
44	E	Hindu	Kshatriya	company director
45	E	Hindu	Kshatriya	land owner
46	E	Hindu	Kshatriya	land owner
47	E	Christian		pharmacist
48	E	Hindu	Chetabanajigeru	administrator
49	E	Hindu	Vaishya, Setty	trader
50	E	Hindu	Kshatriya	land owner, politician
51	E	Hindu		magistrate

APPENDIX 2

Household Kinship Diagrams

A series of kinship diagrams is presented on the following three pages. They indicate the relationships of the occupants in each dwelling. The number to the left of each diagram refers to the house number of the occupants. Here, the triangle indicates a man; the circle, a woman. When a symbol is filled with black, the individual is deceased. Marriage is designated by a line below the symbols which joins a triangle and a circle. A horizontal line with one or more pendant symbols links the children of the marriage; that is, a group of siblings. An 'm' indicates that a married individual lives elsewhere.

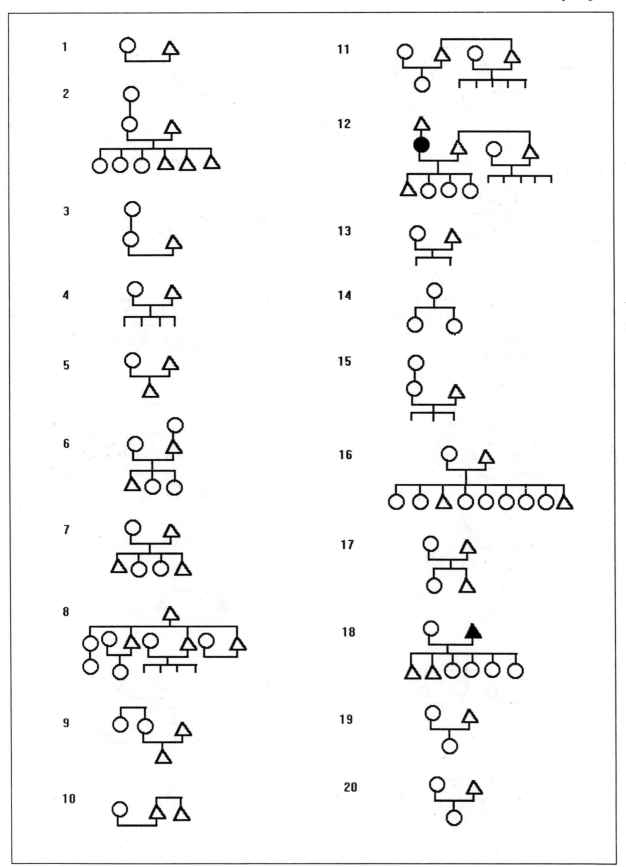

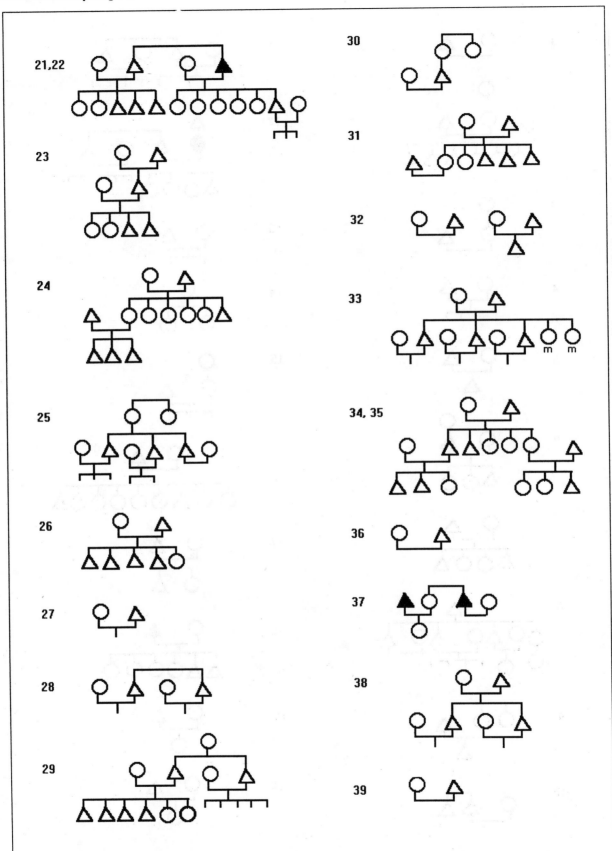

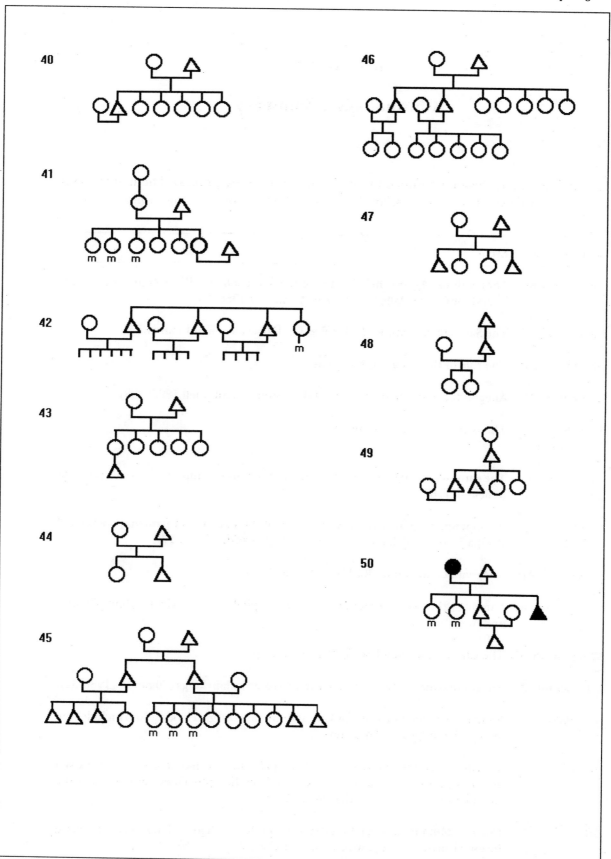

APPENDIX 3

Chronological Summary

Learning about the history of Anegondi has been a continuing process. The materials set out below have been collected from diverse sources. (See accompanying Bibliography for references.)

Century/Date	Event
3rd Century BC	Anegondi on the northern banks of the Tungabhadra River comes within the boundaries of the Ashokan empire (Sugandha 1986: 23)
2nd Century AD	The Satavahana empire which ruled for 450 years comes to an end.
4th Century AD	The rule of the Kadamba kings ends.
5th Century AD	Anegondi comes under the rule of the Yavanas (Campbell 1898: 438).
6th to 8th Centuries AD	The period of Chalukya rule.
7th Century AD	The earliest date suggested for the origin of the royal family of Anegondi (Firishta in Sewell, 1987: 6)
AD 689	A copper-plate grant notes the existence of the tank at Pampatirtha, now called Pampa Sarovar, 1.5 km west of Anegondi (Sugandha 1986: 27).
8th Century AD	Anegondi comes under Rashtrakuta rule.
10th Century AD	Kampili, 12 km east of Anegondi, serves as a capital. Kummata Durga, Kampili Kilya and Anegondi are fortress settlements.
12th Century AD	The Cholas and Chalukyas fight over the region.
13th Century AD	Anegondi is the seat of a small principality ruled by Jain kings (Sugandha 1986: 31).
AD 1308-14	Kampila Deva Raya succeeds as king at Kummata Durga. His kingdom includes the area of the outpost of Anegondi.
AD 1323	The Muslim army from Delhi sacks Warangal to the north-east of Anegondi, as well as Dorasamudra to the south (Sewell 1987: 4). Kampila Deva Raya occupies the fortress of Raichur (Sugandha 1986: 35).
AD 1324	Death of Mummadi Singa, founder of Kampili, who had fled to Anegondi, where he established a strong fortress (Stein 1989: 18).
AD 1327	Somadeva defeats the Delhi army at Anegondi. Death of Kampila Deva Raya. The sons of Sangama, a local chief, escape the invasion (Stein 1989: 18).

AD 1329   The territories around Kampili are annexed to the Hoysala kingdom of Ballala III after he drives out the viceroy of the Delhi army (Sugandha 1986: 46). The Muslims sack Kummata Durga on the third attempt. Sewell (1987: 17) notes that Kampila serves as the citadel of the predecessors of the kings of Vijayanagara. He suggests that the raja of Kampila fled to the citadel of Anegondi when attacked by the sultan of Delhi. Sugandha (1986: 38) mentions a fort called Hosamaladurga that Kampila fled to, and which she identifies with Anegondi. It is also referred to as Hosadurg (Shastri 1971: 230). However, Patil notes that this is erroneous, as Hosadurg is described as being to the south of the Virupaksha temple at Hampi (1991: 193). He notes that the pre-Vijayanagara forts existed at Kummata Durga, Kampila Durga and Sandur.

AD 1330   Anegondi has a citadel on the river banks before Vijayanagara is established, which Nuniz says is called Crynamata (Sewell 1987: 293). The fortified city of Anegondi is inhabited by a family of chiefs owning a small estate, and has 'a strong citadel having its base on the stream' (ibid: 6). Ibn Battuta (in Sewell) notes that the 'town and fortress of Anegondi' was captured by Muhammad Tughluq of Delhi. The ruler at Anegondi has 50,000 men, 5,000 of which go with him to the fortress (Nuniz in Sewell 1987: 294).

AD 1332   The sultan of Delhi appoints Malik Naib as governor of Anegondi (Sewell 1987: 18).

AD 1334   Anegondi is sacked, but just before the citadel is stormed the rulers and soldiers slaughter their own wives and children. Ibn Battuta (Sewell 1987: 17) suggests that 11 sons of the king remain; according to Nuniz (ibid.: 295), six ministers were left, one of whom (Deorao) was related to the king. From this time onwards, Anegondi becomes a burying place for kings. After living for two years in the citadel, Malik Naib is opposed by local chiefs and is himself besieged. Deorao (Deva Raya, the former chief minister of Anegondi) is appointed ruler.

AD 1336   Deva Raya moves from Anegondi to establish a new settlement on the south bank of the Tungabhadra, later named Vijayanagara (Sewell 1987: 19). Before leaving Anegondi 'he began work on his houses, and he enclosed the city round about; and that done he left Nagumdym and soon filled the new city with people' (Nuniz in Sewell 1987: 300).

AD 1340   Harihara I, the first king of Vijayanagara, mentions Anegondi in inscriptions as Pampa.

AD 1343   Death of Harihara. His brother Bukka I takes over the throne. The Vijayanagara kings adopt the boar as their crest. Longhurst (1988: 11) illustrates a stone carving of a boar, with dagger, sun and moon. (The same designs can be found on a later cloth flag in the possession of Achyuta Deva Raya; see Frontispiece.) Longhurst suggests that the early kings had their capital at Anegondi but as the empire grew it moved to the southern banks of the Tungabhadra.

AD 1344   The states of Anegondi, Warangal, and Dorasamudra combine to oppose the Muslim threat from the north (Sewell 1987: 5).

AD 1347   The Bahmani kingdom is founded at Gulbarga to the north of Anegondi. It challenges Vijayanagara control of the Deccan (Longhurst 1988).

AD 1354   Bukka succeeds to the throne, and begins work on the new capital Vijayanagara, City of Victory.

AD 1366	Muhammad Shah Bahmani attacks Vijayanagara but is repelled, even though Bukka has to buy peace (Verma 1985: 51).
AD 1368	First mention of Vijayanagara in the inscriptions (Sugandha 1986: 44).
AD 1378	Anegondi becomes an outpost of Vijayanagara. The Vijayanagara Empire extends from the Deccan to the southernmost tip of the peninsular (Longhurst 1988: 18).
AD 1399	Additions and improvements are made to the defences of Vijayanagara under Harihara II.
AD 1404	Death of Harihara II. Longhurst (1988:12) notes that three brothers of Harihara are governing the provinces; they include Mallappa Odeyar of Srirangapattana (near Mysore).
AD 1406	Firuz Shah the Bahmani king attacks Vijayanagara, but afterwards takes a princess from Vijayanagara as his wife (Shastri 1971: 247).
AD 1420	Nicolo Conti from Italy visits the area (Longhurst 1988: 14).
AD 1446	The Persian Ambassador, Abdur-Razzak visits Vijayanagara (Longhurst 1988: 18).
late 15th Century AD	The *polygars* (local chiefs) come into existence. One of the first is the chief of Anegondi (Stein 1989: 59).
AD 1510	Krishna Deva Raya is crowned.
AD 1513	Aliya Ramaraja imprisons the first of the Mysore Odeyars at Anegondi. Kempe Gowda I commences rule favoured by Krishna Deva Raya. However, he becomes disgraced, and is caste into prison in Anegondi where he is confined for five years (Stein 1989: 183).
AD 1520	Gulbarga is attacked by Krishna Deva Raya.
AD 1520-22	Domingo Paes from Portugal visits Anegondi 'which they call Sengumdym, and they say that of old it was the capital of the kingdom' (Sewell 1987: 259). He observes that it has good walls and two entrances. It has few inhabitants and is commanded by a captain of the king of Vijayanagara. At this time, Anegondi is considered as lying within the fortifications of Vijayanagara. Paes describes Anegondi thus: 'On the north side are rocky hills; a river runs between them, and the wall runs along the top of them, and on the further side is a city called Nagumdym; and it has only three gates, namely one by the river, which they cross in boats embarking just at this gate; one on the other side which is to the north, this is a stronger gate; and one on the north-west side, a little gate between two very high ridges; and it is such a bad road that only one horseman can pass out a time' (Sewell 1987: 290).
AD 1529	Krishna Deva Raya dies and his cremation ground is marked by the 64-columned *mandapa* on an island in the Tungabhadra to the east of Anegondi (Campbell 1898: 441).
AD 1535	Fernao Nuniz visits Vijayanagara.
AD 1554	According to Heras (1980: 22), Rama Raya is king and his brother Kondamma has a son called Konda who is governor of Anegondi.

AD 1565 Vijayanagara is destroyed by the combined armies of five sultans from the Deccan. It is never again reoccupied. Sewell suggests that the city of Vijayanagara has over 100,000 dwellings. Rama Raya's brother and Sadasiva take refuge at Penukonda until Tirumala usurps the crown to form the Aravidu dynasty. He dwindles in importance except as patron of the arts, and moves again in 1585 to Chandragiri. After the defeat of Vijayanagara and the departure of the nobility, the four sultans of the Deccan stop in Anegondi while their armies raid Vijayanagara. The four kings enter Vijayanagara by the bridge built by Rama Raya (Heras, 1980: 224). After sacking Vijayanagara, the Aravidu family stays united: different members settle in Penukonda, Chandragiri and Vellore, while some return to Anegondi (Imperial Gazetteer of India 1909: 100). The family possesses territory on both sides of the Tungabhadra, including the lands on which the city of Vijayanagara was established. This forms an independent state known as Anegondi for more than 200 years. While some relatives of the king of Vijayanagara remain in Anegondi from 1565, the direct descendants moved the seat of power from Penukonda to Chandragiri in southern Andhra Pradesh. The Vijayanagara royal family intermarries with the chiefs of Anegondi, presumably they were already close relatives or equal in royal status (see Figure 4).

AD 1566 The forces of Ali Adil Shah occupy Anegondi while trying to oust Tirumala and place Pedda Timma on the throne of Vijayanagara. Bijapur is attacked and Ali Adil Shah is forced to retreat from Anegondi.

mid 16th
Century AD Nominal rulers are left in possession of a small tract of land comprising Anegondi, and some districts adjoining it on both banks of the Tungabhadra. These form an independent state known as Anegondi, consisting of 121 villages and having an annual revenue of 1,78,725 gold *pagodas*.

AD 1568 Tirumala murders Sadasiva at Penukonda, and seizes the Vijayanagara throne for himself (Longhurst 1988: 25).

AD 1570 Penukonda is attacked by the Muslims and the royal families move their seat to Chandragiri (Longhurst 1988: 16).

AD 1575 Ranga II succeeds to the Vijayanagara throne.

AD 1579 A silver-plate grant in possession of Achyuta Deva Raya records a gift of nine *talukas* to Tirumala Raya.

AD 1586 Venkata I, son of Tirumala I, succeeds to the Vijayanagara throne.

AD 1600-90 Anegondi state comes under the authority of the Bijapur and Golconda kings.

AD 1604 The Vijayanagara king moves from Chandragiri to Vellore.

AD 1614 Venkata I dies.

AD 1639 Sri Ranga Raya VI grants the site of Fort St George at Madras to Francis Day (Chief Factor of the English) who is resident in Chandragiri. Relatives of the Vijayanagara kings move around this time to Chingleput and Srirangapattana. According to Longhurst (1988: 16), they intermarry with the chiefs of Anegondi.

AD 1653 Fort St George in Madras is raised to the rank of a Presidency.

AD 1657 Gulbarga falls to the Mughal emperor Aurangzeb.

195

AD 1689	Anegondi comes under the rule of Aurangzeb.
AD 1690-1750	Anegondi state comes under the emperors of Delhi and the Mughal governors of the Deccan. During this time the rulers of Anegondi are allowed to hold their land to the north and south of the Tungabhadra free of all rent or tribute.
AD 1707	Asaf Jah, the Mughal Viceroy at Hyderabad, annexes the land around Anegondi.
AD 1731	Two brothers, Vijaya Raj and Krishna Raya, go to Mysore to rule from there. Direct descent from the Vijayanagara kings ceases with the death of Dodda Krishna Raj.
AD 1749	The Anegondi territories are attacked by the Marathas (Sewell 1987: 234).
AD 1750	The Maratha chieftains come to Hampi, angry with the Anegondi ruler for neglecting to pay host to them. They impose a tax of 7,000 *pagodas*, depriving the Anegondi rulers of some settlements, leaving them with 78 villages and a revenue of 1,53,234 *pagodas*.
AD 1775	Anegondi is reduced by Haidar Ali of Mysore (Sewell 1987: 234), but continues to exist as a quasi-independent state. Haidar Ali raises the tax to 12,000 *pagodas*.
AD 1786	Haidar Ali's son, Tipu Sultan, annexes the state of Anegondi to his dominions: he destroys the temples of Anegondi and Hampi, expels the raja, burns the palace and all the records, occupies the territory, and deprives the family of its lands for 13 years until his death in 1799. Tipu's minister, Purniah, arranges that the Anegondi raja receives a monthly allowance of 2,000 rupees. The rulers of Anegondi move to Kamalapuram on the other side of the Tungabhadra after Tipu Sultan ousts them from their lands.
AD 1790	A treaty is signed between the British and the Nizam of Hyderabad by which the taxes are restored to the royal family at Anegondi. The raja becomes a Zamindar under the Nizam's government. Tipu Sultan relinquishes half his dominions when peace is restored (Imperial Gazetteer of India 1909: 16). A treaty is made with the Nizam and the United East India Company in 1790 against Tipu Sultan, to 'deprive him of the means of disturbing the general tranquillity'. At the time 'Annugoondy' is a *polygar* of Hyderabad.
AD 1792	An inscription stone found at Anegondi records the existence of the ruler Vira Venkata Maharayalu. Called Vira Kallu, it is a remembrance plaque for warriors who fought in 1792. The symbols on it include the sun and moon, and it is inscribed with the name Venkateshwara Raju. Such a stone is normally kept on a plinth or altar. Two other remembrance stones are dated 1801.
AD 1795	A map by William Faden shows 'ANAGOONDY Resid.ce of the Rayel'. It indicates areas on both sides of the Tungabhadra as belonging to Anegondi (see Figure 1).
AD 1798	During the last Mysore war, the territory of Anegondi reaches as far east as Adoni and Gooty, both fortress towns, and as far south as Penukonda.
AD 1799	Tipu Sultan is killed and his territory, including the state of Anegondi, is made over to the Nizam of Hyderabad; the lands to the south of the Tungabhadra are retained by the English Government (Sewell 1987: 234). The British recognise that these lands, which include the ruins of the capital city of Vijayanagara, once belonged to the rajas of Anegondi. Accordingly, they allocate a pension to the head of the

Anegondi family. The province of Anegondi is ceded by the Nizam to the British under Article Five of the Hyderabad Treaty of 1800. It is later divided between the British and the Nizam, the Tungabhadra serving as the boundary between the two dominions. One-third of the province remains under the Nizam, and two-thirds are allocated to the British as part of the Ceded Districts being absorbed into the Madras Presidency. Anegondi comes under a Muslim state with Urdu as the official language.

AD 1801   The British give a monthly pension of 1,377 rupees to the Anegondi raja. The Nizam's minister grants Anegondi tax-free revenue rights over five villages. New hamlets are built around the villages, and land cultivation is encouraged.

AD 1820   The seat of the kingdom of Anegondi is moved from Kamalapuram back to Anegondi village itself (Michell and Filliozat 1981).

AD 1824   Tirumala Deva Raja is the first Anegondi raja to be given a pension by the British in lieu of land taken south of the Tungabhadra. He is succeeded by his son Vira Venkatapati.

AD 1831   Vira Venkatapati dies unmarried and is succeeded by his father's grandson Tirumala Deva Rayalu.

AD 1859   Tirumala Deva Raya, the third British royal pensioner, calls Anegondi the Elephant Corner of Vijayanagara. He is granted some dependencies by the Nizam and some lands to the south of the river by the English, together with his pension. Colonel Meadows Taylor visits Vijayanagara.

AD 1862   In Mysore, a precedent is set for refusing to recognise an adopted heir as a raja. This ruling is to affect the Anegondi kingdom in years to come.

AD 1866   Tirumala Deva Raya is succeeded by his son Venkata Rama Rayalu.

AD 1871   Venkata Rama Rayalu dies and his brother Krishna Deva Raya succeeds him, but dies a year later.

AD 1872   Krishna Deva Raya dies. The kingdom deteriorates and heavy debts are incurred through the payment of high taxes. The Nizam's government give his two widows a small pension for ten years. His father's sister's son, Pedda Narasimha Raju, becomes the next Anegondi raja, the sixth to be given a pension by the British.

AD 1880   The gates of the temple near the Anegondi east side landing are removed to the Madras Government Museum (Campbell 1898).

AD 1883   Narasingamma becomes queen after the death of her husband Pedda Narasimha Raju.

AD 1884   The Madras Government declares the Anegondi royal family extinct (document in the possession of Achyuta Deva Raya).

AD 1889   Narasingamma dies and Rani Kuppamma, the remaining wife of Krishna Deva Raya becomes acting queen of the Anegondi kingdom. She adopts her youngest brother, Pampapati Raju (renamed Sri Ranga Deva Raya), and appoints him as raja of Anegondi. The Anegondi kingdom recovers, but Pampapati Raju is asked to pay taxes of 10,000 rupees a year, which impoverishes him. Sri Ranga Deva Raya has five offspring.

AD 1891   The Anegondi kingdom is handed over to Sri Ranga Deva Raya, but the tax is unchanged and he falls into arrears. The raja petitions the Madras Government for the remittance of the taxes.

AD 1898   The population of Anegondi is around 1,500. In a publication by Campbell (1898: 438-44) 'Anagundi' is taken to be synonymous with Vijayanagara: captions on p.439 read as 'The Raja's Palace, Vizianagar' and 'A Juggernath Car, Vizianagar'. Both illustrate scenes at Anegondi.

AD 1918   Sri Ranga Deva Raya dies. Rani Kuppamma again becomes acting queen and is given a pension the following year.

AD 1946   Durbar Raja Sri Krishna Deva Raya, son of Sri Ranga Deva Raya, succeeds as ruler of Anegondi.

AD 1947   The Anegondi principality is absorbed into the Indian Union.

AD 1948   The practice of taxes is stopped, though pensions continue to be paid by the Indian Government.

AD 1956   The state of Mysore is formed with Bangalore as its capital. A new system of village administration is introduced known as the Grama Panchayat.

AD 1966   Durbar Raja Sri Krishna Deva Raya dies without issue. His wife Rani Lal Kumari rules and is given a pension from 1970. She adopts as her son and heir Achyuta Deva Raya, the grandson of Sri Ranga Deva Raya.

AD 1973   Mysore state is re-named Karnataka, with Anegondi and Hampi coming under the Raichur and Bellary districts respectively.

AD 1984   Rani Lala Kumari dies and the government pension comes to an end.

AD 1987   Anegondi becomes the administrative headquarters for 29 villages in the area under the new Mandal Panchayat (group of villages administration).

AD 1998   Anegondi lies within the newly formed Koppal district.

Bibliographical References

Baker, S. (1990), *Caste. At Home in Hindu India*, Jonathan Cape, London.

Beals, A.R. (1974), *Village Life in South India*, Aldine Publishing Company, Chicago.

Campbell, A.C. (1898), *Glimpses of the Nizam's Dominions in Hyderabad State, Deccan India*, Bombay.

Chambard, J. (1980), *Atlas d'un Village Indien*, Laboratoire de Graphique de l'Ecole des Hautes Etudes en Science Sociales, France.

Dubois, Abbe J.A. (1990), *Hindu Manners, Customs and Ceremonies* (translated by H. Beauchamp), Asian Education Services, New Delhi (reprint 1897).

Fritz, J.M. and G. Michell (1991), *City of Victory. Vijayanagara, the Medieval Hindu Capital of South India*, Aperture Foundation Inc., New York.

Fritz, J., G. Michell and M.S. Nagaraja Rao (1984), *The Royal Centre at Vijayanagara. Preliminary Report*, Department of Architecture and Building, University of Melbourne, Melbourne.

Fuller, C.J. (1992), *The Camphor Flame. Popular Hinduism and Society in India*, Princeton University Press, Princeton.

Jackson, R. and D. Killingley, eds. (1988), *Approaches to Hinduism*, London.

Jagadisa Ayyar, P.V. (1985), *South Indian Customs*, Asian Educational Services, New Delhi.

——— (1989), *South Indian Festivities*, Asian Educational Services, New Delhi.

Heras, H. (reprint 1980), *South India under the Vijayanagara Empire, The Aravidu Dynasty*, 2 vols., Cosmo Publications, New Delhi.

Imperial Gazetter of India (1989), *Imperial Gazetteer of India Provincial Series. Hyderabad State*, Usha Publications, New Delhi.

Kramrisch, S. (1937), *A Survey of Painting in the Deccan*, The India Society, London.

Longhurst, A.H. (1917), *Hampi Ruins*, Asian Educational Services, New Delhi and Madras (reprint 1988).

Michell, G. and V. Filliozat, eds. (1981), *Splendours of the Vijayanagara Empire, Hampi*, Marg Publications, Bombay.

Michell, G. (1992), *The Vijayanagara Courtly Style*, Manohar, New Delhi.

Murthy, B.K. (n.d.), *Hampi Guide (Vijayanagara Ruins)*, R. Venkata Ramani Dass Publisher, Hampi.

Nagaraja Rao, M.S., ed. (1988), *Vijayanagara Through the eyes of Alexander J. Greenlaw 1856, John Gollings 1983*, Directorate of Archaeology & Museums, Mysore.

Nilakanta Shastri, K.A. (1966), *A History of South India*, Oxford University Press, Madras.

Patil, C.S. (1991), 'Mummadi Singa, Kampila and Kumara Rama', In *Vijayanagara, Progress of Research 1987-88* (eds. D.V. Devaraj and C.S. Patil), Directorate of Archaeology & Museums, Mysore, pp. 179-98.

Rajasekhara, S. (1985), *The Map Approach to Vijayanagara History*, Sujata Publications, Dharwad.

Sewell, R. (1900), *A Forgotten Empire. Vijayanagara*, Asian Educational Services, New Delhi (reprint 1987).

Stein, B. (1989), *The New Cambridge History of India. I.2 Vijayanagara*, Cambridge University Press, Cambridge.

Stacey, A. (1984), 'The Remains of a South Indian Empire', *Popular Archaeology*, vol. 5, no. 7, pp. 19-23.

Stutley, M. (1989), *Hinduism, the Eternal Law. An Introduction to the Literature, Cosmology and Cults of the Hindu Religion*, Aquarian Press (Crucible), Wellingborough.

Sugandha (1986), 'History and Archaeology of Anegondi', Ph.D. Thesis, University of Poona.

Verma, A. (1985), *Forts of India*, Government of India, New Delhi.

Vyas, S.N. (1988), *India in the Ramayana Age. A Study of the Social and Cultural Conditions in Ancient India as Described in Valmiki's Ramayana*, Atma Ram & Sons, Delhi and Lucknow.

Glossary

abhisheka, deity worship by anointing

acharya, craftsman

akkasaligaru, goldsmiths

anaya, elder brother

ane madugu, elephant pit

badagaru, carpenter

baghilu, gateway

Banajigaru, see Chetabanajigeru

bedaru, foot-soldier caste

betel, leaves used to decorate shrines

bhoi, see bedaru

bilvapatra, leaf of a tree used for Siva worship

bindi, red dot worn on forehead

bisakalu, rotary quern

brindavan, raised sacred garden; memorial

channa, rice

chaparu, cobbler

Chetabanajigeru, feudal lords from Andhra Pradesh, originally bangle traders

deva raya, suffix given to those of direct descent from the raja

devaru guwliy, god's stud bull

Diwali, festival of light

dhaniy, master

ediga, toddy tapper

ghat, flight of steps leading to a river

ghee, clarified butter

golaru, cow herders

gotra, eligible marriage partner

grama, single village

gundi, pit

gudisalu, small hut

guwliy hohriy, stud bull

harbowaiseh, vegetable sacrifice

harih, iron pestle

holi habba, spring time Hindu festival

homa, fire sacrifice

jaggari, brown sugar

jangama, spiritual leaders of the lingayat

kala, stone

kalasha, copper pot for holy water

khamba, pillar

karttika masa, lamp lighting month

katguruh, butchers

komataru, grocers and traders

korniwaise, animal sacrifice

kumbararu, blacksmiths

kumkuma, red or yellow powder

kurabaru, shepherds, farmers

lingam, phallic emblem of the god Siva

Lingayat, followers of the saint Basaveshvara

lowhas, entrance door

madagiru, fisherman caste, vegetable dyer

madigaru, sweeper, animal skinner

magota, upper fort

mandal, group of villages

mandapa, flat-roofed stone structure

marubhumi pradesha, dry lands

matha, residence for those visiting a sacred site

mihrab, prayer niche in mosque

munji, coming of age ceremony

murti puja, worship of images

nagara devara kallu, stone carving of snake deity

nayidu, high-caste people of the Chetabanajigeru group

naiyna, way of referring to a king without using his name

nekararu, weaver

niravari pradesha, wet lands

navadhanya, main entrance doorway

parishad, government controlling body

polygar, native chief or prince

phalapuja, prayer during the marriage of Siva and Parvati

Pongal, harvest festival, January

prasada, offering from the deity

purdah, hidden from view, to be in seclusion

rajaru, royalty

raju, royal,

rangoli, drawings in powdered chalk done on the ground

rubbughundu, stone pestle used to crush wet foodstuffs

samadhi, place of remembrance and meditation

samsthana, kingdom

Sankranti, harvest festival

sati sahagamana, self immolation of a wife after husband's death

setty, traders

shakti, energy of the goddess

shastras, texts or treatises

simpigaru, tailor

Sivaratri, commemoration of the night of Siva festival

supari, nut of the areca palm tree

tahsildar, revenue collection officer, magistrate

taluk, sub-division of a district

tapasya, life mission

thaiyata, house talisman with sacred text inside

trishula, three pronged weapon of Siva

tulsi, sacred basil plant

vaddaru, house builder caste

vaishnava, pertaining to Vishnu

vastu puja vigraha, protective amulet for dwellings

vastushilpi, traditional architect

vibhuti, sacred ash

wanakeh, wooden pestle, used to crush dry foodstuffs

waralu, stone mortar

yajna, fire sacrifice

yajnopavita, sacred thread worn by Brahmanas

yehtah, well

zilla, district

1.   Achyuta Deva Raya on the verandah of his residence
(House no. 44)

2. Coconut palms bordering rice fields outside Anegondi

3. Town centre from the granite hills above Ranganatha temple

4. Chintamani temple from the riverside

5. Gateway leading to the Tungabhadra river

6. South bastion on the riverside

7. Fortified riverside wall of the citadel

8.   Protected riverside steps

9.   Circular coracles ferrying people across the river

10.　Temple within the citadel walls

11.　Detail of temple within the citadel walls

12.   Magota Hill, fortress entrance gate

13.   Magota Hill, gateway to river inlet

14.   Magota Hill, royal family samadhi

15.   Cemetery, banajiga brindavan

16.   Samadhi, Nava Brindavan island

17.   House no. 41, garden brindavan

18.   Panchayat, former government offices and chariot

19.   Lotus Mahal, occupied by the Women's Institute

20.   Koranic school

21.   Entrance hall of the Ranganatha temple

22.   Market place, café

23.   Market place, grocery shop

24.   Water pump, main street

25.   Malemah shrine by sacred trees

26.   House no. 44, second storey

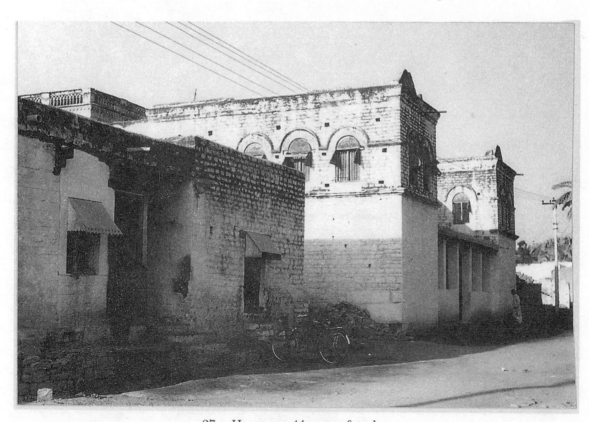

27.   House no. 44, street façade

28. House no. 44, roof-top view over skylights

29. House no. 47, street façade

217

30.   House no. 50, former secretariat, verandah

31. House no. 30, entrance verandah

32. House no. 46, inner verandah

33.   House no. 25, street façade

34.   House no. 45, entrance verandah

35.   House no. 28, street façade

36.   House no. 46, street façade

37.   House nos. 34 and 35, walled garden

38.   House no. 23, inner yard and cattle shed

39.   Doorway to passage linking House nos. 41 and 45

40.   House nos. 21 and 22, street façade

41.   House no. 15, street façade

42.   House no. 18, cattle tethered outside

43.   House no. 20, inner verandah and bathroom

44. House no. 13, with exterior cattle shelter

45. House no. 2, with exterior sleeping platforms

46. House no. 3, behind Panchayat

47. House no. 9, with exterior cattle shed

48.   House no. 50, path leading to back entrance

49.   House no. 50, front entrance

50. House no. 50, doorways through ruined palace (d)

51.   House no. 49, entrance door, with mango leaf garland

52.   House no. 11, doorway, images of deities, pair of cow heads

53.   House no. 45, doorway with pictures of ancestors and deities

54.   House no. 45, prayer room, stepped shrine

55.   House no. 40, prayer niche

56.   House no. 45, rotary quern

57.   House no. 44, kitchen hearth

58.   House no. 45, arched fire-place

59.   House no. 8, deep grindstone and pestles

60.   House no. 46, brindavan, snake-stones by well

61.   House no. 12, stacks of storage pottery

62.   House no. 44, royal mace

63.   House no. 44, betel nut box of Rani Lal Kumari

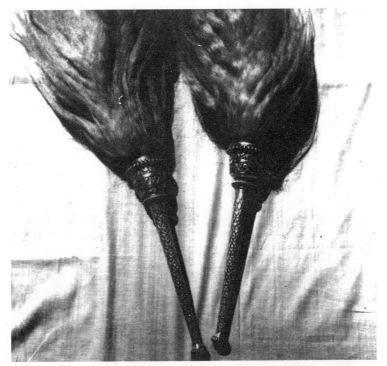

64.   House no. 44, silver-handled fly whisks

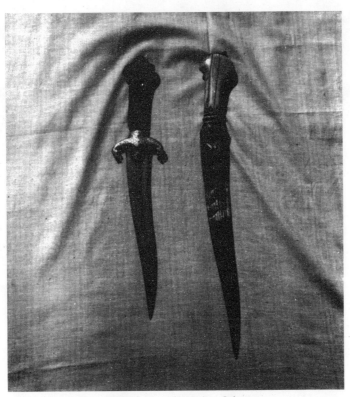

65.   House no. 44, pair of daggers

66.   House no. 44, embossed silver water pot and tray

Homage to Harihara Deva Raya young man of Anegondi
A song composed by B. Basuvaraj

I am going to tell you about a prince of Anegondi
Please listen to my story with full attention.

He was born to the Aravidu family, his father was King Narapathi.
He grew like the moon of the bright fortnight, his glory increased day by day.
He was ahead of all his childhood days, in sports and in studies.
As he grew older, our people knew him as Harihara Deva Raya.
We called him Anaiya, but he was not blessed with longevity.

He wanted our villages to have modern facilities, so we could be happy and content
Very popular, he was known as a leader: there will never be another like him.
He always ignored his own needs and helped others.
And he remained celibate until his death.

On 19th July 1987, on this terrible day, death was waiting at the village gate
And however much we tried, we could not save him. He left us all.
Like removing the most important stone from a fortress wall,
With his death, we all became orphans.

Though he paid his respects to all the deities
At the time of his death, none of them could help him.
He is no more, and though he has no physical body, his soul is eternal.
He remains in our minds and hearts, and no-one can forget him.
May the Almighty bless his soul with eternal peace.

We, the people of the village, our eyes filled with tears, all pray at his feet.
Let us take an oath, that we will not perform any act of injustice,
We will walk the path he paved for us, because his soul will be watching, day and night.
He grows like the moon of the bright fortnight, and his glory increases day by day
Harihara Deva Raya, born to the family of Aravidu.

Harihara Deva Raya was elected to political office in 1987. A popular young man, his death in tragic circumstances was mourned by all in Anegondi.